AF845853

REGULATING CROSS-BORDER DATA ACCESS FOR LAW ENFORCEMENT

This book explores the legal, political, and practical challenges that governments face when investigating local crimes involving digital evidence held by global cloud service providers.

Criminal investigations increasingly require access to data held across borders. This gives rise to unique jurisdictional competitions and conflicts of law, as even exclusively domestic criminal investigations necessitate international cooperation when the relevant user data is stored abroad.

Traditional systems of cross-border legal cooperation were designed for the pre-internet era and are ill-suited to address these challenges. This has led to extensive calls for reform and the proliferation of new policy initiatives at national, regional and international levels.

The book maps these emerging policy responses to cross-border data access problems and examines the extent to which they are fit for purpose. It then provides a framework to reconcile the practical necessities of law enforcement seeking digital evidence stored overseas with the territorial sovereignty of the countries hosting that data, the fundamental rights of individuals whose personal data is being sought, and the interests of technology companies whose cooperation is required.

It is an essential guide to understanding the different rules, safeguards and procedures that govern law enforcement access to data held by multinational technology companies, and key to future policy development and legal reform.

Hart Studies in Information Law and Regulation: Volume 6

Hart Studies in Information Law and Regulation

Series Editors
Tanya Aplin (General Editor)
Perry Keller (Advisory Editor)

This series concerns the transformative effects of the digital technology revolution on information law and regulation. Information law embraces multiple areas of law that affect the control and reuse of information, data and digital tools – intellectual property, data protection, privacy, freedom of information, state security, tort, contract and competition law. 'Regulation' is a similarly extensive concept in that it encompasses legal and non-legal modes of control, including technological design and codes of practice.

The series provides cross-cutting analysis and exploration of the complex and pressing issues that arise in a society where digital infrastructures are now pervasive and when massive volumes of digital information are shared globally. These issues include access to data; sharing, reuse, and governance of data; open source and public sector data; the legitimacy and transparency of training data; propertisation of data and digital tools; freedom of expression and information access rights; privacy rights and data protection regimes; and the role of the state and private entities in safeguarding the public interest in the uses of data.

In the spirit of representing the diverse nature of its topics, the series embraces various methodologies: doctrinal, comparative, empirical, theoretical, historical and socio-legal, and particularly welcomes monograph proposals.

The series is especially open to perspectives from jurisdictions or regions which have traditionally been underrepresented in the scholarly literature.

Recent titles in this series:

Constitutionalising Social Media
Edited by Edoardo Celeste, Amélie Heldt and Clara Iglesias Keller

Cybersecurity, Privacy and Data Protection in EU Law: A Law, Policy and Technology Analysis
Maria Grazia Porcedda

Critical Reflections on the EU's Data Protection Regime: GDPR in the Machine
Edited by Róisín Á Costello and Mark Leiser

Big Data for the Public Good: Regulating Access to Public Sector Big Data for Research and Innovation
Stergios Aidinlis

Conceptions of Data Protection and Privacy: Legal and Philosophical Perspectives
Edited by Elisa Orrù and Ralf Poscher

Regulating Cross-Border Data Access for Law Enforcement: Jurisdictional Games
Halefom H Abraha

Regulating Cross-Border Data Access for Law Enforcement

Jurisdictional Games

Halefom H Abraha

•HART•
OXFORD • LONDON • NEW YORK • NEW DELHI • SYDNEY

HART PUBLISHING

Bloomsbury Publishing Plc

Kemp House, Chawley Park, Cumnor Hill, Oxford, OX2 9PH, UK

1385 Broadway, New York, NY 10018, USA

Bloomsbury Publishing Ireland Limited, 29 Earlsfort Terrace, Dublin 2, D02 AY28, Ireland

HART PUBLISHING, the Hart/Stag logo, BLOOMSBURY and the Diana logo are trademarks of Bloomsbury Publishing Plc

First published in Great Britain 2026

Copyright © Halefom H Abraha, 2026

Halefom H Abraha has asserted his right under the Copyright, Designs and Patents Act 1988 to be identified as Author of this work.

All rights reserved. No part of this publication may be: i) reproduced or transmitted in any form, electronic or mechanical, including photocopying, recording or by means of any information storage or retrieval system without prior permission in writing from the publishers; or ii) used or reproduced in any way for the training, development or operation of artificial intelligence (AI) technologies, including generative AI technologies. The rights holders expressly reserve this publication from the text and data mining exception as per Article 4(3) of the Digital Single Market Directive (EU) 2019/790.

While every care has been taken to ensure the accuracy of this work, no responsibility for loss or damage occasioned to any person acting or refraining from action as a result of any statement in it can be accepted by the authors, editors or publishers.

All UK Government legislation and other public sector information used in the work is Crown Copyright ©. All House of Lords and House of Commons information used in the work is Parliamentary Copyright ©. This information is reused under the terms of the Open Government Licence v3.0 (http://www.nationalarchives.gov.uk/doc/open-government-licence/version/3) except where otherwise stated.

All Eur-lex material used in the work is © European Union, http://eur-lex.europa.eu/, 1998–2026.

A catalogue record for this book is available from the British Library.

A catalogue record for this book is available from the Library of Congress.

ISBN: HB: 978-1-50997-327-9
ePDF: 978-1-50997-329-3
ePub: 978-1-50997-326-2

Typeset by Compuscript Ltd, Shannon

For product safety related questions contact productsafety@bloomsbury.com

To find out more about our authors and books visit www.hartpublishing.co.uk. Here you will find extracts, author information, details of forthcoming events and the option to sign up for our newsletters.

ACKNOWLEDGEMENTS

This book grew out of my PhD research, completed at the University of Malta in 2023. I owe an immense debt of gratitude to Prof. Jeremias Adams-Prassl (University of Oxford), whose vision and guidance shaped the course of this work. It was Prof. Adams-Prassl who first encouraged me to transform my dissertation into a book, and who offered unwavering support and insightful suggestions throughout the process. This project would not have been possible without his mentorship and confidence in my work.

I am equally grateful to Dr Michael 'Six' Silberman (University of Oxford), Dr Richard Mackenzie-Gray Scott (University of Oxford), and Dr Elizabeth Coombs (University of Malta), for their constant encouragement. Their thoughtful feedback and enthusiasm sustained me through the many challenges of writing and revision. A special thanks to Six for conceiving the beautiful design of the book cover, which so perfectly captures the spirit of this work.

My heartfelt appreciation also goes to Dr Domenico Rosani (Utrecht University) and Sangh Rakshita (Tilburg University), whose friendship and creative energy helped me build an inspiring working environment. Domenico's support made the long hours of research and writing not only productive but truly enjoyable.

The publishing team at Bloomsbury also made the writing process enjoyable. I thank them for their support and patience.

HA

Utrecht, January 2026

CONTENTS

TABLE OF CASES AND BRIEFS

TABLE OF LEGAL INSTRUMENTS AND DOCUMENTS

Introduction

'This sounds like a mess', President Barack Obama drily noted after a group of experts had explained the predicament US technology companies face in response to foreign governments' demands for electronic data that US law prohibits them from disclosing, and vice versa.[1] The then president made this succinct remark during a meeting with a group of experts he had set up in 2015 to review the pressing privacy and surveillance issues of the time. Two high-profile disputes were central to the discussion.

The first case involved a conflict between Brazilian authorities and Microsoft, with the former demanding the disclosure of personal data of a Brazilian customer in connection with a domestic criminal investigation. The data in question happened to be stored in the US, where direct disclosure of content data (such as emails, files, and text messages) to foreign governments was illegal. Microsoft faced a dilemma: comply with the Brazilian legal order and risk violating US law or comply with US law and expose itself and its employees to criminal prosecution under Brazilian law.[2] The second dispute was between Microsoft and the US government. In what has come to be known as the *Microsoft Ireland* case (see chapter two), US law enforcement authorities served a search warrant on the company, ordering the disclosure of all emails and information associated with a particular email account, which happened to be stored in data centres in Dublin, Ireland, and were thus subject to EU data protection laws. Caught in the middle of reciprocally conflicting legal obligations (EU law prohibiting disclosure of personal data to foreign governments, and US law compelling disclosure), Microsoft went to court to challenge the warrant. President Barack Obama recognised the complex and evolving challenges for law enforcement's access to data held by global cloud service providers. He subsequently endorsed the development of a new framework to address these challenges.[3] This endorsement initiated a series of events and developments that culminated in the adoption of the Clarifying Lawful Overseas Use of Data Act (CLOUD Act) in 2018, during the first Trump presidency (see chapter four).

[1] B Obama, as cited in B Smith and CA Browne, *Tools and Weapons: The Promise and the Peril of the Digital Age* (Hodder & Stoughton, 2019) 53.

[2] International Conflicts of Law and Their Implications for Cross Border Data Requests by Law Enforcement: Hearing before the Committee on the Judiciary House of Representatives, 114th Cong Serial No 114–84 (2016) (Testimony of Brad Smith, president and chief legal officer, Microsoft Corporation).

[3] Smith and Browne, *Tools and Weapons* (n 1).

These disputes are not isolated incidents. They epitomised the increasing legal, political, and practical challenges governments around the world face when investigating local crimes involving digital evidence held by global cloud service providers. *Jurisdictional Games* is a comprehensive examination of the ways in which states' authorities are responding to these challenges. The book's key themes revolve around the tensions between the increasing importance of cross-border data access for law enforcement (state authority) and the corresponding interests of global cloud service providers (digital corporate power) and the protection of fundamental rights in the digital space.

In today's digital age, it is challenging to imagine a crime investigation that does not involve digital evidence. A 2018 study by the European Commission shows that digital evidence was relevant in around 85 per cent of total criminal investigations.[4] However, criminal evidence today is not only digital; it also defies traditional notions of geography and territorial jurisdictions, due to the ubiquity of cloud computing (see chapter one). Data that was once stored locally in end-user devices, and which was accessible under domestic legal procedures, is now often in the hands of global cloud service providers, and is frequently stored in foreign jurisdictions. Thus, criminal investigations are increasingly dependent on accessing user data held by private companies across borders. This leads to unique jurisdictional competitions and conflicts of law, as even exclusively domestic criminal investigations often require cross-border access to data held by multinational technology companies. It has increasingly become difficult – and at times, impossible – for law enforcement authorities around the world to effectively investigate and prosecute domestic crimes without the assistance of the foreign country where the data is stored and the service providers that control the sought-after data. The European Commission's 2018 study revealed that more than half of the criminal investigations in the EU involving digital evidence required cross-border access.[5] In the US, the Department of Justice reported that the number of requests by foreign governments for electronic evidence has increased by 1,000 per cent over the last few decades,[6] making cross-border access to electronic evidence by law enforcement authorities a norm rather than an exception.

With the continuous growth in Internet use and digitalisation, challenges in cross-border data access will intensify. As crime becomes more international and data increasingly falls under the control of global cloud service providers, domestic criminal investigation tools will become less effective. This trend highlights a fundamental mismatch between the global nature of cloud computing and the

[4] European Commission, 'Impact Assessment Accompanying the document Proposal for a Regulation of the European Parliament and of the Council on European Production and Preservation Orders for electronic evidence in criminal matters and Proposal for a Directive of the European Parliament and of the Council laying down harmonised rules on the appointment of legal representatives for the purpose of gathering evidence in criminal proceedings SWD(2018) 118 final'.

[5] ibid.

[6] See US Department of Justice Criminal Division, 'Performance Budget FY 2019 Congressional Submission', available at www.justice.gov/doj/fy-2019-congressional-budget-submission.

jurisdictional (territorial) scope of law enforcement powers. While data constantly flows across borders, traditional rules of international law dictate that a nation state's law enforcement activities, including evidence-gathering, should stop at its borders.

However, seeking evidence across borders is not new, nor is the jurisdictional limit on law enforcement powers. For many years, states have developed various channels of formal and informal co-operative arrangements to exchange evidence across borders while respecting each other's territorial sovereignty. Typically, mutual legal assistance treaties (MLATs) serve as formal government-to-government agreements that enable law enforcement authorities in one country to request mutual legal assistance (MLA) from another country, where the evidence relevant to an investigation is located (see chapter three). This system was developed to balance the jurisdictional limitations of law enforcement and the global nature of criminal investigations. However, the advent of the Internet, especially cloud computing, has significantly disrupted this system of cross-border legal co-operation. The MLAT framework, designed for a pre-Internet era, and for a different social and technological landscape, struggles to adapt to today's digital environment. The rapid, unpredictable flow of data across borders challenges the operational feasibility of MLAT assumptions and principles.

The situation is further complicated by the proliferation of conflicting domestic and regional laws. Many countries prohibit cloud service providers from directly disclosing data to foreign governments, while others use domestic procedures to compel service providers to disclose data under their control, regardless of where the data in question is stored. This leads to conflicting legal obligations where one country's laws mandate data disclosure while another's prohibit it. This jurisdictional puzzle and legal conflict precipitate dysfunction in the current international legal co-operation system.

The challenges of efficiently accessing data outside territorial boundaries have caused significant urgency and frustration among law enforcement authorities worldwide. This has driven numerous governments to take unilateral, often conflicting, actions influenced by their own jurisdictional advantages and regional considerations. Such disjointed and uncoordinated policy responses to the cross-border data-access problem risk creating a 'legal jungle', as the Council of Europe's Cybercrime Convention Committee described it.[7] Additionally, warnings from researchers at the Global Commission on Internet Governance and the Internet & Jurisdiction Policy Network about the 'legal arms race' in response to the Internet's increasing cross-border legal challenges suggest a dangerous path towards further legal fragmentation, jurisdictional conflict, and legal uncertainty.[8] The

[7] Cybercrime Convention Committee (T-CY), 'Transborder Access to Data and Jurisdiction: Options for Further Action' T-CY (2014) 16.

[8] B de La Chapelle and P Fehlinger, 'Jurisdiction on the Internet: From Legal Arms Race to Transnational Cooperation' (Global Commission on Internet Governance, Paper Series: No 28, April 2016) 16; DJB Svantesson, 'Internet & Jurisdiction Global Status Report' (Internet & Jurisdiction Policy Network, 27 November 2019), available at www.internetjurisdiction.net/news/release-of-worlds-first-internet-jurisdiction-global-status-report.

growing reliance on electronic data held by multinational service providers compels governments to adopt unilateral measures, a trend that risks rendering the rules governing cross-border data access increasingly incompatible and the problem more complex and intractable.

These concerns have sparked a global debate across academic and public policy circles. There is a widespread call for the overhaul or replacement of the current legal and institutional frameworks, aiming to align them with the current technological reality. In recent years, there has been a surge in initiatives to enhance law enforcement's ability to access electronic evidence across borders. A new wave of cross-border data-access agreements is gradually taking shape, underpinned by intensive negotiations at bilateral, regional, and international levels (see chapter three).

This intense debate and growing global push for reform in cross-border data access set the central themes of this book. A key challenge lies in striking a balance between the practical needs of law enforcement agencies to access digital evidence stored overseas and respecting the digital sovereignty of nations that house this data. Additionally, it involves safeguarding the fundamental rights of individuals whose personal data is being sought and recognising the interests of cloud service providers whose co-operation is required. However, prior to delving deeper into these aspects, it is crucial to first highlight some of the theoretical underpinnings that inform this discourse. Commencing the analysis with a discussion of the relevant theoretical foundations is indispensable, as the question of cross-border data access resides at the confluence of diverse and frequently competing legal and normative frameworks. Absent a clear conceptual map of the principles of sovereignty, jurisdiction, and the protection of fundamental rights, any subsequent examination risks being detached from the normative and doctrinal structures that both constrain and empower state action in the digital environment. Engaging with these conceptual underpinnings enables a critical interrogation of the values and interests at stake, ranging from state sovereignty and comity to privacy and procedural fairness, while exposing the assumptions that inform the articulation and interpretation of existing rules. In doing so, the section below situates the inquiry within its broader jurisprudential and doctrinal context, thereby providing an essential analytical lens through which to evaluate contested state practices and to interrogate potential reform trajectories in the governance of cross-border data access.

1. Theoretical Insights

Whose rules and values apply when law enforcement authorities seek access to data stored in the global cloud? Whether State A should be permitted under international law to access data stored in data centres in State B without the latter's consent and co-operation is a contentious question. Additionally, the treatment of the right to privacy and data protection within these contexts is complex. These questions, seemingly straightforward, lead to the intricate and unsettled issue of territorial public international law's application in the non-physical realm of cyberspace. The emergence of cloud computing has further complicated these issues, challenging traditional notions of jurisdiction and territoriality, and blurring the distinction between domestic and extraterritorial measures.

There is an ongoing theoretical debate regarding the regulation of law enforcement agencies' cross-border data access. Central to this debate is the complex relationship between data, territoriality, jurisdiction, and sovereignty. The principle of 'territoriality' has long shaped international law thinking.[9] According to a strict interpretation of international law, a state should not exercise its criminal investigation powers (enforcement jurisdiction) within another sovereign state's territory without consent.[10] The Permanent Court of International Justice established this principle in the famous *Lotus* case of 1927, stating that:

> the first and foremost restriction imposed by international law upon a State is that – failing the existence of a permissive rule to the contrary – it may not exercise its power in any form in the territory of another State. In this sense jurisdiction is certainly territorial; it cannot be exercised by a State outside its territory except by virtue of a permissive rule derived from international custom or from a convention.[11]

The Restatement (Third) of Foreign Relations Law in the US echoes this, acknowledging that it is 'universally recognised, as a corollary of state sovereignty, that officials in one state may not exercise their functions in the territory of another state without the latter's consent'.[12] Thus, unilateral attempts to access data stored outside a state's territorial jurisdiction could be considered as infringement upon the sovereignty of the state where the data is located. For example, China has a long-standing view that states 'should respect the sovereignty, jurisdiction and governance of data of other States, [and] avoid asking companies or individuals to provide data located in other States without the latter's permission'.[13]

While territoriality remains a key principle of international order,[14] its normative significance is increasingly challenged by the decentralised nature of the

[9] The principle of 'territoriality', which supports states' power to legislate, adjudicate, and enforce laws within their geographic region, was inspired by the Treaty of Westphalia in 1648.

[10] Consent can be given either on an ad hoc basis or via a treaty. See B-Jaap Koops and M Goodwin, *Cyberspace, the Cloud, and Cross-Border Criminal Investigation: The Limits and Possibilities of International Law* (Tilburg University, 2014) 12.

[11] PCIJ, *Case of the SS "Lotus" (France v Turkey)*, PCIJ Series A, No 10 (7 September 1927) 18–19.

[12] Restatement (Third) of the Foreign Relations Law of the United States, § 432. See also International Bar Association, 'Report of the Task Force on Extraterritorial Jurisdiction' (2009) 10.

[13] Ministry of Foreign Affairs of the People's Republic of China, 'China's Positions on Global Digital Governance', 25 May 2023, available at www.mfa.gov.cn/eng/wjb/zzjg_663340/jks_665232/kjlc_665236/qtwt_665250/202406/t20240606_11405184.html.

[14] M Kuijer and W Werner, 'The Paradoxical Place of Territory in International Law' in M Kuijer and W Werner (eds), *Netherlands Yearbook of International Law 2016: The Changing Nature of Territoriality in International Law* vol 47 (TMC Asser Press, 2017) 8.

Internet, the widespread use of cloud computing, and the ensuing cross-border movement of data. This has sparked legal academic debates about the physical location of data and its significance in asserting law enforcement jurisdiction. The debate centres on whether and how the concept of 'data location' should guide law enforcement jurisdiction. It addresses how and to what extent the advent of cloud computing challenges the conceptual understanding of territoriality and jurisdiction.

The scholarly debate on the normative relevance of data location generally falls into three strands: the 'exceptionalist', the 'territorialist', and the 'pragmatic' approaches. The first two constitute a continuation of the dichotomic debate of the 1990s regarding the legitimacy of governments to regulate the Internet.[15] The only difference between the early dichotomic debate and the recent ones is that the latter do not question the legitimacy of governments to regulate the Internet. Instead, the point of disagreement today is whether cloud-based data is different and necessitates a new regulatory approach other than the traditional territoriality-based rules.

The 'exceptionalist' view argues for the unique nature of data, challenging traditional territorial jurisdiction approaches. The leading voice in this camp, Jennifer Daskal, outlines the characteristics that distinguish data from tangible assets, highlighting how these features challenge the traditional views on the relationship between data's location and the associated legal rights and responsibilities.[16] A key feature is the 'ease, speed, and unpredictability' of cross-border data flows, unconstrained by territorial boundaries. Daskal notes that, while territoriality relies on defining specific 'here' and 'there' locations, data's ubiquitous nature questions the relevance of such distinctions.[17] Another distinctive aspect of cloud data is its divisibility: it can be duplicated and stored in multiple places at once. Moreover, cloud data can be segmented into various components and held in multiple locations. The physical separation between the location of data and the location of the user marks the third distinguishing characteristic, differentiating it from physical objects.[18] As will be discussed in next chapter, users often have little to no control over the storage and handling of their data in the cloud. The ease, speed, and unpredictability of data crossing borders, its divisibility into partitions, and the physical disconnect between data's location and its user's location lead to a phenomenon commonly known as 'loss of location'.[19] This term describes

[15] JP Barlow, 'A Declaration of the Independence of Cyberspace' (*Electronic Frontier Foundation*, 8 February 1996), available at www.eff.org/cyberspace-independence; DR Johnson and D Post, 'Law and Borders – The Rise of Law in Cyberspace' (1996) 48 *Stanford Law Review* 1367; *cf* JL Goldsmith, 'Against Cyberanarchy' (1998) 65 *The University of Chicago Law Review* 1199; JL Goldsmith and T Wu, *Who Controls the Internet? Illusions of a Borderless World* (Oxford University Press, 2006); L Lessig, *Code: Version 2.0* (Basic Books, 2006).

[16] J Daskal, 'The Un-Territoriality of Data' (2015) 125 *Yale Law Journal* 326.

[17] ibid 397; See also KE Eichensehr, 'Data Exterritoriality' (2017) 95 *Texas Law Review* 145, 145.

[18] Daskal, 'The Un-Territoriality of Data' (n 16) 373.

[19] JJ Schwerha, 'Law Enforcement Challenges in Transborder Acquisition of Electronic Evidence from Cloud Computing Providers' (Council of Europe discussion paper, 2010).

the practical difficulty, albeit not theoretical impossibility, of pinpointing data's precise location at any moment. Even if one could ascertain where data is stored, such a location would be arbitrary, random, unstable, and lacking intrinsic ties to any specific territory.[20] Consequently, exceptionalists argue against viewing data as something occupying an identifiable territory. Building on these unique data attributes, exceptionalists challenge the idea that the location of data dictates law enforcement jurisdiction, asserting that the 'un-territoriality' of data necessitates a re-evaluation, and sometimes rejection, of territorial-based distinctions in the context of digital data search and seizure.[21]

The 'territorialist' or 'unexceptionalist' school of thought contends that data is not inherently different from other intangible assets. Andrew Woods, a leading voice in this school, asserts that characteristics like intangibility, mobility, divisibility, and the spatial separation between the asset holder and the asset are not exclusive to data.[22] Using examples of other intangible assets, such as intellectual property, money, stock, and debts, Woods disputes the notion of data exceptionalism. Territorialists believe that the jurisdictional challenges posed by the global cloud are not sufficiently novel or unique to justify abandoning the principle of territoriality. They acknowledge the jurisdictional and legal conflicts associated with cloud data but argue that these challenges do not warrant discarding territorial principles. Some even assert that 'it remains impossible to think of international law without a territorial locus'.[23] Echoing this view, Woods suggests that jurisdiction over cloud-based data largely depends on territoriality.[24] After refuting the 'data is different' argument, territorialists maintain that traditional jurisdictional and conflict principles are applicable to cloud data.[25] This view is supported in the computer science community. In an amicus brief for the *Microsoft Ireland* case in the US Supreme Court, over 50 computer and data scientists agreed with the territorialist perspective regarding the location of data. They argued that cloud data always has a specific physical location, and that retrieving it from the cloud is 'no less physical or necessary than if the same data were protected in a bank-vault safe deposit box'.[26] They cautioned against confusing the accessibility of cloud data from anywhere with its actual location, clarifying that the ability to access cloud data from anywhere does not imply that the data physically follows its owner worldwide.

The third category of scholarship, which can be characterised as 'pragmatic', adopts a middle- ground approach. Paul M. Schwartz represents this perspective,

[20] J Daskal, 'Borders and Bits' (2018) 71 *Vanderbilt Law Review* 179.

[21] Daskal, 'The Un-Territoriality of Data' (n 16) 332.

[22] AK Woods, 'Against Data Exceptionalism: Jurisdictions in the Cloud' (2016) 68 *Sandford Law Review* 748.

[23] Kuijer and Werner, 'The Paradoxical Place of Territory' (n 14) 8.

[24] Woods, 'Against Data Exceptionalism' (n 22) 729.

[25] ibid 765; See also Kuijer and Werner, 'The Paradoxical Place of Territory' (n 14) 11.

[26] Brief for 51 Computer Scientists as Amici Curiae in Support of the Respondent, *United States v Microsoft* (2017) No 17-2 (2018).

offering a new approach to understanding legal analysis concerning law enforcement access to global cloud data. Critiquing the binary division between exceptionalist and unexceptionalist views, Schwartz posits that many current legal analyses are flawed due to lack of understanding of how different cloud models create distinct legal challenges.[27] The core of Schwartz's argument is that legal decisions regarding access to global clouds must be based on an understanding of how cloud models vary.[28] He identifies three cloud computing models – data shard, data localisation, and data trust clouds – each posing unique legal questions about the location of data and access. Schwartz suggests that whether the cloud raises new legal issues depends on the specific cloud model in question. This pragmatic view hinges on the notion that the relevance of the location of data in regulating government access depends on the cloud networks' technical architecture.[29] In the data-shard cloud model, a file is split and stored in multiple locations, defying national boundaries as data remains scattered and constantly in motion.[30] Conversely, data localisation (see chapter three) and data trust models limit data location to a specific country or region.[31] Schwartz argues that these models do not fundamentally challenge the principle of territoriality. His conclusion is that there is no one-size-fits-all approach when assessing the legal access to global cloud data.[32] Moreover, he attributes the difficulty in determining the location of data primarily to the service providers' policy and design choices rather than the inherent characteristics of data. The 'data shard' and 'data trust' models will be further explored in in chapter one.

While these perspectives have provided valuable conceptual frameworks, they are of limited practical use. Each of them tends to place disproportionate weight on the physical nature or geographic location of data, or alternatively on the architectural design of cloud service infrastructures. This narrow framing risks obscuring the more substantive interests at stake. Most notably, it disregards the position of individuals whose data is being accessed and the normative context of a criminal investigation for which such data is sought. From a legal and normative standpoint, if a criminal investigation pertains exclusively to a domestic matter and lacks any foreign dimension, it is difficult to see why the physical location of the data or the technological design of the data centre should carry decisive weight.

Although the territorial location of data continues to play a role in traditional MLA procedures, recent practice and emerging international frameworks in cross-border data access have highlighted a decisive shift in focus. Contemporary measures are less interested in where data is stored and instead prioritise two

[27] PM Schwartz, 'Legal Access to the Global Cloud' (2018) 118 *Columbia Law Review* 1681.
[28] ibid 1686.
[29] ibid 1758.
[30] ibid 1695.
[31] ibid 1696, 1697.
[32] ibid 1703.

factors: who ultimately controls access to the data, and whose data is involved. This distinction is crucial in an era of globalised cloud services, where the storage location of data is often fluid, distributed, or technically irrelevant to the substantive interests of law enforcement and rights protection. The emphasis should not be on technical storage architecture but on the individuals directly affected by law enforcement access measures.

In response to these shortcomings, the book advances a data-subject-centric framework. As developed in detail in chapter eight, the core of this approach lies in prioritising the nationality and residence of the data subject whose data is sought. This implies that the authority of State A to access data stored in data centres located in State B (or in any foreign jurisdiction) should primarily depend on the fact that the data belongs to its own nationals or residents. In such cases, the mere location of the data abroad constitutes the only element and should not, in itself, preclude access when no other normative connection to the foreign state exists. Such a perspective ensures that jurisdictional questions and conflict-of-law issues are linked to the rights and protections owed to the affected individual rather than to the arbitrary or shifting location of data storage facilities. By reorienting the debate in this way, the analysis recentres transnational data access on the protection of data subjects while ensuring effective access for law enforcement authorities.

Accordingly, the discussion of cross-border jurisdiction in the cloud environment should be reframed: the decisive elements are the location of the targeted individual, the nature and locus of the criminal conduct under investigation, and only subsidiarily the location of the service provider. This approach avoids the over-formalism of territorialist thinking and the narrowness of exceptionalist or pragmatic accounts while grounding cross-border data access in principles that acknowledge both the sovereignty of states and the primacy of fundamental rights. The added value of this data-subject-centric approach, together with its implications for doctrinal consistency and practical enforcement, will be further developed in chapter eight.

2. This Book's Approach and Contribution

The book undertakes a comprehensive doctrinal research approach, delving into the nuances of relevant legislation, case law, and emerging policy initiatives that govern law enforcement's access to data across borders. The focus is on dissecting the traditional mechanisms of cross-border legal co-operation and evaluating their efficacy in the context of cloud computing – a realm where data transcends geographical boundaries and poses unique legal challenges. A significant part of this research involves a thorough examination of the evolving legal landscape at national, regional, and international levels. It scrutinises new legislative measures being implemented to address the complexities of cross-border data access.

This includes an in-depth analysis of how these laws are shaped, their scope, and their effectiveness in addressing the increasing importance of law enforcement access to data across borders and the corresponding threats to digital sovereignty, fundamental human rights, and corporate interests. Central to this narrative are high-profile cases litigated in the US and the EU. These cases serve as critical reference points to frame and articulate the central themes of the book, including digital corporate power, state authority and sovereignty, and fundamental rights. They offer real-world insights into the practical challenges and legal implications of cross-border data access, shedding light on the evolving jurisprudence in this area. Through this multifaceted analysis, the book aims to provide a clear and comprehensive understanding of the current state of legal affairs in cross-border data access. It endeavours to highlight the gaps in existing frameworks and develops a possible pathway for future reforms, thereby contributing to the discourse in this rapidly evolving field.

The book also employs a comparative approach, analysing the similarities, differences, and trends in legislative and policy responses to the cross-border data-access problem in two major jurisdictions: the EU and the US. This method allows for the identification of regulatory approaches that best explain diverse reform initiatives and evaluates them against their stated objectives. In doing so, the analysis traces both divergence and convergence in cross-border data-access legislation adopted in the EU and the US. The choice of these two jurisdictions is deliberate. Both have introduced sweeping legislative initiatives that set the global agenda for cross-border data-access reform: the US through the CLOUD Act, and the EU through the e-Evidence Regulation.[33] Together, these measures are shaping a new model of cross-border co-operation whereby service providers are required to receive, assess, and respond directly to foreign law enforcement requests for data.[34] Building on these efforts, the US and EU are currently negotiating a cross-border data-access agreement under the CLOUD Act framework (see chapter six). Given their similar approaches and converging interests, there is a broad consensus that such agreement is necessary, and a series of negotiations are under way. At the same time, both jurisdictions exert significant influence globally. The US dominates the global technology and data market through control of the world's leading service providers, and by extension the vast reservoirs of data they manage. The EU, by contrast, leverages its substantial regulatory power to shape the behaviour of those same service providers.[35] Together, these forms of jurisdictional

[33] Regulation (EU) 2023/1543 of the European Parliament and of the Council on European Production Orders and European Preservation Orders for electronic evidence in criminal proceedings and for the execution of custodial sentences following criminal proceedings (e-Evidence Regulation) [2023] OJ L191/118.

[34] M Stefan and GG Fuster, 'Cross-Border Access to Electronic Data through Judicial Cooperation in Criminal Matters: State of the Art and Latest Developments in the EU and the US' (Centre for European Policy Studies, No 2018-07, November 2018).

[35] A Bradford, *The Brussels Effect: How the European Union Rules the World* (Oxford University Press, 2020).

leverage and regulatory powers enable the US and EU not only to advance their own policy agendas but also to set de facto international standards for cross-border data access. The rules adopted in the US and EU, consequently, carry an outsized impact on the rest of the world. The book thus explores not only the domestic and bilateral implications of the CLOUD Act and e-Evidence Regulation but also their global implications. The US and EU may dominate the field, yet they are not alone in attempting to shape these rules. International treaties, notably the Council of Europe's Convention on Cybercrime and the recent UN Convention on Cybercrime, also play a pivotal role. The book pays particular attention to how Global South countries, such as those on the African continent, might leverage these multilateral instruments in navigating the evolving legal order in cross-border data access.

Jurisdictional Games situates these developments within the broader landscape of cross-border data access. Conceptually, it expands the exiting literature by offering a comprehensive account of the jurisdictional tensions and conflicts of law that emerge in the global cloud environment. It articulates the legal and technological factors shaping the current debate on cross-border data access. The literature often attributes the cross-border data-access problem to the procedural and administrative hurdles of the MLAT system, implying that it can be resolved through comprehensive reform. However, drawing on cases litigated in the US and EU Member States, the book challenges this assumption. It demonstrates that the cross-border data-access problem extends beyond procedural and administrative difficulties, and identifies the legal and technical factors that should inform any legislative response. The book further explores and maps emerging regulatory responses. While the cross-border data-access problem has prompted policy-makers to introduce reform initiatives of various forms and types, a comprehensive and systematic analysis of these initiatives is lacking. This book fills this gap and makes an original contribution by developing a conceptual framework to understanding surging regulatory responses to the jurisdictional and conflicts-of-law challenges of the global cloud. This systemic approach is crucial for comprehending the various policy options employed by state authorities and their implications for digital sovereignty, fundamental human rights, and digital corporate power.

On a normative level, the book advocates for a pragmatic shift, proposing a data-subject-centric approach to cross-border data access. This perspective centres on the individual whose data is being sought. Challenging the current trend of pinning everything on service providers via domestic regulation, the book argues that refocusing the jurisdictional locus to the nationality and residence of the individual whose data is being sought could help balance the competing interests at stake, thus overcoming key challenges to cross-border data access in the digital age. At its core, the book argues that contemporary frameworks for cross-border access to electronic evidence are structurally misaligned with the realities of cloud computing, and with the normative commitments of human rights and public international law. A data-subject-centric framework that re-anchors jurisdictional claims and applicable standards in the concrete relationship between individuals and states offers a more normatively defensible and practically workable way of balancing the competing interests at stake and alleviating some of the systemic challenges of cross-border data access. Grounded in case law, legislative proposals, state practice, industry initiatives, and scholarly commentary, this framework seeks to ensure that states' protective and access authority follow their citizens and residents, subject to baseline human rights guarantees, while constraining unilateral access to the data of foreign nationals and residents. Properly designed, a data-subject-centric model can simultaneously improve the effectiveness and timeliness of access to electronic evidence, strengthen privacy and due process protections, reinforce sovereignty and comity, and provide greater legal certainty for service providers.

3. Outline of the Book

The remainder of the book unfolds in eight substantive chapters and a concluding chapter. Chapter one examines the technological and commercial underpinnings of cloud computing and the resulting challenges to the criminal justice system and data privacy. It presents a brief overview of how and where major cloud service providers keep their customers' data, as well as the legal and policy implications these choices entail. This is complemented by an illustrative overview of the cloud storage strategies adopted by Google and Microsoft. It shows how different cloud storage practices could result in different jurisdictional and conflicts-of-law questions. This chapter serves to highlight the unique features of various cloud data storage practices and their impact on long-standing legal conceptions of territorial-based jurisdiction, sovereignty, and related issues.

Chapter two frames and articulates the increasing jurisdictional and conflicts-of-law challenges in obtaining electronic evidence across borders – issues referred to broadly in this book as the 'cross-border data-access problem'. It does so in two ways. First, it explains the cross-border data-access problem through the analysis of four high-profile cases litigated in the US and the EU. Through these four cases, involving four service providers and two countries, the analysis illustrates the cross-border data-access problem triggered or exacerbated by the advent of cloud computing and exposes the cracks in the traditional system of international legal co-operation. Second, using the legal and factual questions revealed by these cases as an analytical framework, this chapter identifies five main drivers of the cross-border data-access problem – the unique role of service providers, the de-territorialisation of data, the globalisation of criminal evidence, the surge of conflicting norms, and the failure of the MLAT system – that have shaped the debate on cross-border data access and the legislative responses thereto.

There is a growing consensus that the traditional system of cross-border legal co-operation is unsustainable and needs to be reformed or replaced. That is where the consensus ends, however. Despite a shared understanding of the problem and repeated calls for reform or replacement of the traditional system, there is little agreement on what these reforms or alternative approaches should look like. Instead, there is a proliferation of uncoordinated initiatives that could lead to further jurisdictional conflict and legal uncertainty. Chapter three maps and examines these various initiatives based on the approaches they follow in addressing the challenges in obtaining electronic evidence across borders. It develops and distinguishes between four approaches – reformist, unilateralist, internationalist, and nuanced – that can best explain the current and emerging initiatives. It then examines the suitability and sustainability of these approaches against their stated objectives and some key principles that have enjoyed extensive support in policy and academic discussions.

The subsequent three chapters narrow the scope of the debate on cross-border data access and present an extensive analysis of recently adopted initiatives in the US and the EU. By introducing a new approach for international co-operation through the CLOUD Act, the US leads the global cross-border data-access reform agenda. The impact of the CLOUD Act in shaping international standards for law enforcement access to cloud data, and its influence on other impending cross-border data-access reform initiatives, warrants closer scrutiny. Chapter four presents a detailed analysis of the extraterritorial reach of the US government's law enforcement powers, and, conversely, the powers of foreign governments to obtain US-held communications content.

Chapter five considers the EU's regulatory response to the cross-border data-access challenge. Utilising its de facto 'regulatory power' to shape the behaviour of the major service providers, the EU has embarked on a three-pronged process to improve cross-border data access: reforming existing legal frameworks, negotiating new international agreements, and introducing a new pan-European framework (the e-Evidence Initiative). The e-Evidence Initiative grants EU law enforcement authorities the power to directly order the production of data held by cloud service providers irrespective of the location of the sought-after data, the location or nationality of the target, or the establishment of the service provider. This chapter examines the implications of this initiative for the sovereign interests of third countries, foreign service providers, and the fundamental rights of persons whose data is being sought.

Chapter six compares the US and EU's approaches to cross-border data access, presenting an overview of the approaches adopted by both sides and the areas of convergence and divergence. It argues that, even though both the EU and the US share a similar approach towards cross-border data access, they also face long-standing differences around privacy and security. This chapter illustrates how these differences give rise to reciprocal conflicts and jurisdictional competition. Lastly, the chapter draws some cautionary lessons from the US–UK CLOUD Act agreement, suggesting that it should not be taken as a blueprint for other executive agreements that may follow.

Chapter seven considers the broader implications of these initiatives for the Global South, where the cross-border data-access problem is particularly acute. Focusing on the African continent as a case study, this chapter examines the extent to which African countries could benefit from the emerging cross-border data-access reform initiatives in the US and internationally. It then outlines how African stakeholders should approach the Internet's increasing cross-border legal challenges.

Chapter eight draws key lessons from the analysis and charts the path forward. It makes the case for a data-subject-centric approach to cross-border data access, reorienting the debate on jurisdictional and conflicts-of-law issues of the cloud towards the targeted individual. Challenging the trend of ascribing liability exclusively to service providers through domestic regulation, the book argues for refocusing the jurisdictional locus to the nationality and location of the individual whose data is being sought. This approach offers a balanced solution to the competing interests at stake and alleviates some of the challenges inherent in cross-border data access today. The discussion then turns to the implications of the data-subject-centric approach for current initiatives in the US and EU, providing concrete reform proposals to the e-Evidence Regulation and the CLOUD Act. The last chapter concludes.

1

Cloud Computing

Billions of people around the world store and access their personal data (such as emails, files, text messages, and photographs) over the Internet. Users can access their data instantaneously from anywhere in the world. They can do so using any device connected to the Internet. The underlying infrastructure that enables this service is 'cloud computing'.[1] The legal decisions regarding law enforcement access to cloud data should be based on a comprehensive understanding of the underlying technology and its practical applications.[2] Therefore, prior to delving into the issue of criminal justice access to data in the cloud, it is crucial to highlight what cloud computing entails and how it works. This chapter provides an overview of the social and technological aspects of cloud computing and its implications for criminal justice and user privacy. The analysis includes an overview of two distinct cloud architectures adopted by Google and Microsoft, as well as the varying cross-border data-access scenarios that arise from these architectures. The diversity and variety among cloud services dictate that, in the context of law enforcement access, a one-size-fits-all legal approach may not be effective. As detailed below, these diverse cloud storage strategies may trigger varying legal and policy questions.

1.1. Welcome to the Cloud

The era of local data storage in personal computers, corporate networks, and portable storage devices has become obsolete. In the local storage and computing model, users purchase their hardware, software, and operating system and store their data locally on their home desktop, a portable storage device, or a server in the workplace. To access or retrieve their data, users must typically be in the same physical place as where their data is stored, and they are 'tied to specific computers

[1] 'Cloud computing' does not refer to a single technology or service; rather, it represents an ever-evolving concept that includes a wide range of services and deployment models, making it challenging to provide a single, fixed definition. For the purpose of this book, cloud computing can be defined as the storage, processing, and use of data on remotely located computers accessed over the Internet.

[2] Brief for 51 Computer Scientists as Amici Curiae in Support of the Respondent, *United States v Microsoft* (2017) No 17-2 (2018) 7.

and physical storage devices'.[3] The security of these computing resources and data is also the responsibility of the user or corporate network administrators. In the personal computing paradigm, users enjoy relative freedom and autonomy in customising their hardware, selecting software, coding as they see fit, and overseeing their privacy and security, among other things. Most importantly, users make critical decisions regarding where and how to store their personal data and who can access it. Therefore, maintaining control over one's data is one of the defining characteristics of the personal computing paradigm.[4] The advent of cloud computing has significantly changed the way users interact with their data and companies conduct business.

'Utility computing' has been the mantra behind the cloud computing revolution.[5] Just like other traditional utilities such as water, electricity, gas, and telephony, computing resources are delivered on demand and users pay service providers based on usage ('pay as you go'). Unlike local storage, cloud computing enables remote storage instantly accessible from anywhere, any time, via any device with an Internet connection. In order to store, retrieve, and manipulate their data, users do not need to know where and in which device the data is stored. For instance, if a user wants to write a document using Google Docs, there is no need to install the application software on the user's computer. Instead, the user can go to the Google Docs website using any device with Internet web-browsing capacity and do whatever they want. Furthermore, as data in the cloud is typically accessible anywhere via any device with an Internet browser software capability, cloud computing provides a new way of collaboration whereby two or more people residing in different parts of the world can work on a project, often simultaneously.The socioeconomic benefits of cloud computing are compelling. It offers unprecedented opportunities to businesses at all levels, individuals, the public sector, and society at large. Cloud computing transforms capital expenditures into operating expenditures, allowing small and large businesses to rent, rather than procure, resources from third parties at lower costs and with greater flexibility. This enables customers to easily access scalable computing power on demand without making significant capital investments. The advantages of cloud computing extend beyond individual or business cost-saving and convenience; they also contribute to larger socioeconomic objectives, such as sustainable development, and job creation. Companies worldwide migrate to the cloud, with most people relying on cloud services rather than personal computers. Governments around the world have long embraced the agenda of cloud computing as a major public policy objective.[6]

[3] ibid.

[4] C Soghoian, 'Caught in the Cloud: Privacy, Encryption, and Government Back Doors in the Web 2.0 Era' (2018) 8 *Journal on Telecomm & High Tech Law* 359.

[5] V Narayanan, 'Harnessing the Cloud: International Law Implications of Cloud-Computing' (2012) 12 *Chicago Journal of International Law* 783.

[6] European Commission Cloud Strategy (16 May 2019).

Cloud computing services vary based on the abstraction level and the type of resource they offer. They are commonly classified into three categories: 'software as a service' (SaaS), 'platform as a service' (PaaS), and 'infrastructure as a service' (IaaS).[7] These services form layers within the cloud ecosystem, with SaaS at the top, PaaS in the middle, and IaaS at the bottom layer.[8] In a layered cloud structure, a service – say SaaS – may be built on another cloud provider's PaaS or IaaS service. This layering is necessary because SaaS cannot exist independently of the other two layers. Distinct service providers may offer the services at each layer, and each layer provides different levels of customer flexibility, autonomy, and control over their data. IaaS, which includes computation, storage, and networking, offers low-level functionality and requires greater customer sophistication and expertise. Customers of IaaS enjoy more flexibility and control over operating systems and deployed applications, but not over the underlying cloud infrastructure, such as servers and networks.[9] In comparison, SaaS is known for its high-level functionality, requiring less customer technical expertise, and offering less customer control over data and flexibility. For instance, cloud services such as webmail, social networking services, web conferencing, and online music services do not demand sophisticated expertise from users, because the underlying resources (network, servers, operating systems, storage, application, security, and data) are primarily controlled and managed by the service provider.[10] PaaS provides customers with more control and flexibility than SaaS but less than IaaS. PaaS customers have control over the code they deploy but not the underlying cloud infrastructures.[11] Therefore, as customers move from SaaS to PaaS and then to the IaaS service models, they gain greater control over more resources and data. Reduced control in SaaS and PaaS also leads to greater privacy and data protection concerns compared with IaaS.

The involvement of different providers in a specific cloud service offering, each with varying degrees of control over the underlying technology and stored data, has legal and regulatory implications. For instance, this complicates the ability of law enforcement agencies to identify who is in control of the data when serving a disclosure order. Consequently, law enforcement orders may target service providers, such as infrastructure service providers, that do not have effective control or custody over the sought-after data.

[7] SaaS refers to the capability provided to customers to use the provider's software environment, such as email and word processing, running on a cloud infrastructure (eg Google Apps or Microsoft Office 365). PaaS provides a platform for customers to develop software applications (eg Google App Engine, Microsoft Windows Azure). On the other hand, IaaS provides to consumers raw computing resources, such as processing power, network, and storage (eg Amazon Web Services).

[8] WK Hon and C Millard, 'Cloud Technologies and Service' in C Millard (ed), *Cloud Computing Law* (Oxford University Press, 2014).

[9] ibid.

[10] SY Esayas, 'A Walk in to the Cloud and Cloudy It Remains: The Challenges and Prospects of "Processing" and "Transferring" Personal Data' (2012) 28 *Computer Law & Security Review* 662.

[11] Hon and Millard, 'Cloud Technologies and Service' (n 8).

1.1.1. Cloud Data Storage Strategies

Cloud computing offers myriad opportunities, with its four primary selling points being:

- *Speed of access* – ensuring data is accessible instantly, regardless of where the user is located or where the data is physically stored.
- *On-demand availability* – guaranteeing data availability when on demand, independent of storage location or access point, thus giving the impression that data follows the user.[12]
- *Efficiency* – the ability to handle millions of transactions simultaneously, facilitating instant access any time and anywhere.
- *Resilience* – robustness against any failure.

To fulfil these requirements, cloud service providers adopt various data storage strategies and cloud architectural designs. Primarily, they maintain data replication across multiple geographic locations for load balancing, redundancy, and resilience purposes. For example, Microsoft replicates all data held in Windows Azure storage a minimum of three times for fault tolerance.[13] Load balancing allows service providers to manage millions of transactions simultaneously by dynamically allocating resources in cases when a computer service is overwhelmed by user requests or experiences a failure.[14] Dillon Reisman points out that, 'if one region sees more user activity and has trouble meeting demand, the network might instead route some user activity to a service's replica in a different region'.[15] Service providers maintain clusters of interconnected servers dispersed worldwide for this purpose. These clusters are designed to provide redundancy and resiliency, ensuring continuous availability. Each cluster contains a replica of the same data and collaborates in providing data access, processing, and storage. Secondly, some service providers store user data in data centres physically closer to the user, to achieve, among other objectives, 'low latency'.[16] It is assumed that the greater the geographical distance between a user and the data centre where the user's data is stored, the slower the service will be.[17] Thirdly, service providers may fragment data into smaller components, known as 'data shards', distributing them across multiple global data centres. Automated algorithms determine

[12] Brief for 51 Computer Scientists (n 2).

[13] 'Azure Storage Redundancy' (*Microsoft Ignite*, 22 September 2023), available at https://learn.microsoft.com/en-us/azure/storage/common/storage-redundancy.

[14] Brief for 51 Computer Scientists (n 2).

[15] D Reisman, 'Where Is Your Data, Really? The Technical Case Against Data Localization' (*Lawfare*, 22 May 2017), available at www.lawfareblog.com/where-your-data-really-technical-case-against-data-localization.

[16] Microsoft explains network latency as 'the principle of network architecture that the greater the geographical distance between a user and the data centre where the user's data is stored, the slower the service'. See Writ of Certiorari at 14–18, *United States v Microsoft*, No 17-2-01.

[17] Brief for 51 Computer Scientists (n 2).

storage locations based on performance metrics. Sharding or partitioning is the process of dividing a large database across several computers. It enhances the efficiency of cloud computing resources in responding to queries and commands.[18] This technique has several benefits, including the ability to scale the system by adding further shards running on additional storage nodes and improving performance by balancing the workload across shards. The varying architectural designs of service providers' cloud networks often dictate where and how service providers store their customers' data. These decisions lead to diverse legal questions, as illustrated by the distinct architectural models of Microsoft and Google, which are discussed below.

1.1.2. Illustrations: Service Providers are not a Monolith

Microsoft and Google have distinct cloud infrastructure designs and data storage practices, as well as different policies regarding where they store their customers' data and how they respond to government requests. Microsoft follows a policy of storing user data in data centres physically closer to the residency of the user. This means that users do not have the option to choose a region or data centre to store their personal data. Microsoft determines the user's physical location based on the 'information provided during account registration process'.[19] This strategy, driven by legal constraints, user expectations, and business incentives, aims to meet compliance requirements like data residency while achieving low latency, high performance, and resiliency.[20] Microsoft may store backup data in data centres in other regions and replicate them at least three times, maintaining several copies for redundancy.[21] Content and non-content data might also be separated and kept in different countries. The *Microsoft Ireland* case (see chapter two) revealed that, while the content information (such as email content, attachments, and text messages) sought by the US government was stored in Ireland, the corresponding non-content information was stored on servers located in the US.[22] In determining the identity and physical location of the user, Microsoft relies on the information provided in the sign-up process. Therefore, Microsoft does not verify user identity or location before making the decision on where to store data.[23] In fact, the location of data at any given time may have no relationship to the location of the user who created the data, and the user could remain anonymous or provide a false identity and location, potentially leading to arbitrary decisions by

[18] ibid. See also S Bagu and LT Nguyen, 'Database Sharding: To Provide Fault Tolerance and Scalability of Big Data on the Cloud' (2015) 5 *International Journal of Cloud Applications and Computing* 36–52.
[19] Writ of Certiorari at 14–18 (n 16).
[20] ibid.
[21] ibid.
[22] ibid.
[23] TF Brier, 'Defining the Limits of Governmental Access to Personal Data Stored in the Cloud: An Analysis and Critique of Microsoft Ireland' (2017) 7 *Journal of Information Policy* 327.

the service provider.[24] Storing user data in multiple locations other than the country where the user resides could create complex legal and jurisdictional issues, as will be discussed in the subsequent chapters.

Microsoft has also introduced a unique cloud storage model, called the 'Data Trust Model', which places customer data beyond the jurisdictional reach of the US government by partnering with foreign companies. In 2015, for instance, Microsoft entrusted Deutsche Telekom with its German data centres.[25] Under this strategy, T-Systems (a subsidiary of Deutsche Telekom) operated and managed these data centres independently of Microsoft, with customers contracting directly with T-Systems rather than Microsoft.[26] As a result, personal data belonging to a US person and required for domestic crime investigations could be neither located in the US nor under the effective control of a US company.

Unlike Microsoft, Google does not rely on the self-identified location of the user to decide where to store data. Instead, Google's cloud architecture is designed to automatically select the storage location of user data, not based on the user's location but on performance measurements. The Google cloud system allows the company to automatically select 'the best datacentre location to serve a particular user from, based on real-time performance measurements'.[27] Furthermore, Google has adopted a distinct cloud storage policy, which Paul M. Schwartz described as a 'data shard cloud'.[28] In this model, Google divides user data into digital pieces, also known as 'shards' or 'chunks', for different purposes. Each piece of data is a designated random filename, making it untraceable to a specific user, and is replicated in near real-time across multiple servers and data centres, to prevent single point of failure. Consequently, different parts of a single file may be stored in different countries, the location of each piece continually changes, and each piece of data is meaningless until Google compiles and reassembles it. A magistrate judge in the District Court in Pennsylvania, ordering Google to disclose user data to the FBI, noted that Google operates a state-of-the-art intelligent network which automatically moves data within its network as needed to optimise for performance, reliability, and other efficiencies, causing the location of specific user data or components to change frequently.[29] The location of each piece of data, determined by algorithms and kept in constant motion, means that national

[24] J Daskal, 'The Un-Territoriality of Data' (2015) 125 *Yale Law Journal* 326.

[25] P Judge, 'Microsoft Puts Deutsche Telekom in Charge of German Data' (*Datacenter Dynamics*, 12 November 2015), available at www.datacenterdynamics.com/en/news/microsoft-puts-deutsche-telekom-in-charge-of-german-data/.

[26] M Ahmed and R Waters, 'Microsoft Unveils German Data Plan to Tackle US Internet Spying' (*Financial Times*, 11 November 2015), available at www.ft.com/content/540a296e-87ff-11e5-9f8c-a8d619fa707c.

[27] A Vahdat and B Koley, 'Espresso Makes Google Cloud Faster, More Available and Cost Effective by Extending SDN to the Public Internet' (*Google*, 4 April 2017), available at https://cloud.google.com/blog/topics/inside-google-cloud/making-google-cloud-faster-more-available-and-cost-effective-extending-sdn-public-internet-espresso.

[28] PM Schwartz, 'Legal Access to the Global Cloud' (2018) 118 *Columbia Law Review* 1681.

[29] *In re Search Warrant No 16-1061-M to Google* 2017 WL 3535037 (ED Pa 2017).

boundaries are largely irrelevant, and that even Google itself may not be able to ascertain the exact location of that data at any given time. As Google explained in several litigations with the US government, the company 'does not have the capability' to determine the location of user data. For example, in response to a search warrant issued on 19 December 2016 by the District Court of New Jersey, Google produced only part of the required data (such as emails, header information, and subscriber information) that it confirmed was stored in the US, and refused to produce other parts of the sought-after data, including attachments, because the company could not confirm whether those attachments were stored in the US or in other countries.[30] One critical normative question regarding this cloud storage practice is whether the technical impossibility created by Google itself can be used as a valid justification for not complying with government requests.

Based on their cloud architectural designs, Microsoft and Google also adopt distinct policies on how they co-operate with and respond to law enforcement authorities' requests for user data. Microsoft's response to law enforcement requests varies depending on whether it is enterprise customer data or individual user data. If the requested data pertains to enterprise customers, Microsoft may either redirect the request to the customer or notify the customer about the request. These policies could be prohibited by law, in which case Microsoft itself is to respond to the government request and keep the request confidential. In 2013, Microsoft challenged the secrecy imposed by the US government that prevented the company from redirecting government requests to its customers or notifying them about the requests.[31] Microsoft's policy regarding government requests for individual user data is different: it does not have a clear policy of notifying its individual users about government requests for their data, even though the company has been advocating for a 'universal right to notice' as part of its contribution to updating international agreements governing law enforcement access to user data.[32]

Regarding the legal requirements governing law enforcement requests, Microsoft distinguishes between content and non-content data. While a subpoena or its local equivalent is sufficient to disclose non-content data, a court order or warrant, or its local equivalent, is required for content data.[33] Microsoft has a team named Global Criminal Compliance (GCC), dedicated to handling law enforcement data requests.[34] GCC is tasked with reviewing and responding globally to law enforcement requests under the laws of different countries and in accordance with

[30] ibid.

[31] B Smith and CA Browne, *Tools and Weapons: The Promise and the Peril of the Digital Age* (Hodder & Stoughton, 2019) 53.

[32] B Smith, 'A Call for Principle-Based International Agreements to Govern Law Enforcement Access to Data' (*Microsoft on the Issues*, 11 September 2018).

[33] Microsoft, 'Law Enforcement Requests Report', available at www.microsoft.com/en-us/corporate-responsibility/law-enforcement-requests-report.

[34] Writ of Certiorari at 14–18 (n 16).

the company's internal policies.[35] This team operates from seven locations in six countries on three continents.[36] In responding to valid law enforcement requests, the first procedure the GCC team follows is to determine the physical location of the data sought. The team uses a special 'database management program' that determines, upon entering the identifying information about the user, where the requested data is stored.[37]

Similarly to Microsoft, Google has a team, the Legal Investigation Support Team, dedicated to responding to government requests for user data. Unlike Microsoft, however, Google's team operates exclusively from the US. This means that data can only be accessed directly from the Google offices in the US regardless of where in the world the data is stored, and not from anywhere else. The implication of such an access policy for the MLAT system is discussed in the next chapter. Another critical difference is that, unlike Microsoft's GCC team, which can determine the exact location of user data, Google's Legal Investigation Support Team cannot easily identify where in the world a specific piece of data is stored.

The cloud storage strategies adopted by Microsoft and Google reveal that a single undifferentiated view of the 'cloud' is overly simplistic and misleading. It is important to note that different service providers design their cloud architecture differently, which can affect their ability to determine the exact location of certain data. The distinct cloud approaches followed by Microsoft and Google have 'distinct implications for how the law should govern access to international cloud data'.[38] Furthermore, regardless of the type of cloud storage strategy, it is effectively impossible for users to know where their data is stored; service providers regularly and automatically move user data across multiple locations for a host of reasons, without the user's knowledge. An additional complication is that the instant accessibility and retrieval of user data, regardless of its storage location, may give users – especially average users – the illusion that data is stored locally in their computer's hard drive.

1.2. A Blurred Distinction between Local and Remote Storage

Given the ubiquity of cloud services, local and remote data storage have become almost indistinguishable, a phenomenon often described as 'technological development of blurring'.[39] After examining some cloud-based services and their desktop counterparts, R. Bruce Wells concluded that users might reasonably believe that

[35] Smith and Browne, *Tools and Weapons* (n 31).
[36] ibid.
[37] Writ of Certiorari at 14–18 (n 16).
[38] Schwartz, 'Legal Access to the Global Cloud' (n 28) 1694.
[39] RB Wells, 'The Fog of Cloud Computing: Fourth Amendment Issues Raised by The Blurring of Online and Offline Content' (2009) 12 *Journal of Constitutional Law* 223.

their data is stored on their computer, when, in fact, it is stored remotely in the cloud.[40] The author states that,

> while people using email must realise that their message travels over the Internet …, it is likely that many people using an online calendar or online documents do not realise that their information is on a remote server rather than on their computer.[41]

The former UN Special Rapporteur on the Right to Privacy (UN SRP) also noted, in his amicus brief submitted in the *Microsoft Ireland* case, that 'even the savviest of users may not know whether their information is stored on their device or in the cloud'.[42]

In terms of privacy, less experienced users may reasonably believe that their data is stored on their personal computer. This belief, in turn, may give users a false impression that they are in control of their data while, in fact, the essence of cloud data storage requires users to relinquish control of their data to the service providers. The illusion of control could prompt users to disclose sensitive personal data and inhibit them from having a realistic sense of privacy threats. More importantly, users could reasonably expect that their data is protected, for instance, in the same way it is stored in their computer, while in reality their data is often disclosed to law enforcement agencies without the user's knowledge. The blurring between local and remote data storage also makes it difficult to distinguish between territorial and extraterritorial activity, with a resulting significant implication for law enforcement access to data, and the rights and obligations that apply. As will be discussed in chapter two, the compelling of service providers to disclose overseas data could be considered a domestic procedure by some countries and an extraterritorial activity by others.

Before the advent of cloud computing, data storage and processing were primarily local, giving users substantial control over their data. However, cloud computing shifts physical control of user data to third parties. This change disconnects users from their personal data, with significant implications for law enforcement and privacy. In the cloud, service providers, not users, make key decisions about data storage, access, and security.[43] Users might remain unaware whether their data was sought by and disclosed to law enforcement agencies unless the service provider chooses to notify them. In some jurisdictions, service providers could be prohibited by law from notifying their users prior to disclosing data to law enforcement authorities.[44] Consequently, users lose the opportunity to challenge the legality

[40] ibid.

[41] ibid.

[42] Brief Amicus Curiae of UN Special Rapporteur on the Right to Privacy Joseph Cannataci in Support of Neither Party, *United States v Microsoft* (2017) No 17-2 (2017).

[43] Smith and Browne, *Tools and Weapons* (n 31) 11. See also Daskal, 'The Un-Territoriality of Data' (n 24).

[44] For detailed comparative analysis of laws, see W Maxwell and C Wolf, 'A Global Reality: Governmental Access to Data in the Cloud' (A Hogan Lovells White Paper, 2012); on the consequences of secret orders, see N Richards, 'Secret Government Searches and Digital Civil Liberties' (National Constitution Center, A Twenty-First Century Framework for Digital Privacy White Paper series, 2018).

of government data requests, a right that they retain with locally stored data.[45] Another aspect in which data stored in the cloud may be subject to weaker legal protections than the data stored in personal computers involves the long-standing US precedent known as 'third-party doctrine'.[46] This doctrine stipulates that data exposed to third parties is not protected by Fourth Amendment rights, specifically the reasonable expectation of privacy.[47] Therefore, at least in the US, data in the cloud is not afforded the same protection and procedural safeguards as data stored in personal computers. US law enforcement can access cloud data under less stringent standards than those for obtaining that same data stored in a personal computer.[48] This practice contradicts global initiatives advocating for uniform data protection regardless of where and how the data is stored.[49] The concept of 'user control over data', central to data protection law, has become more rhetorical and increasingly less practical in the age of cloud computing.

[45] Smith and Browne, *Tools and Weapons* (n 31) 23; CISPE, 'Response to the Public Consultation on Improving Cross-Border Access to Electronic Evidence in Criminal Matters' (CISPE Cloud, 2017).

[46] LR Kattan, 'Cloudy Privacy Protections: Why the Stored Communications Act Fails to Protect the Privacy of Communications Stored in the Cloud' (2011) 13 *Vanderbilt Journal of Entertainment and Technology Law* 617.

[47] The doctrine originates from two 1970s Supreme Court opinions: *Smith v Maryland* and *United States v Miller*. See also Daskal, 'The Un-Territoriality of Data' (n 24) 377; IS Rubinstein, GT Nojeim, and RD Lee, 'Systematic Government Access to Private-Sector Data: A Comparative Analysis' in FH Cate and JX Dempsey (eds), *Bulk Collection: Systematic Government Access to Private-Sector Data* (Oxford University Press, 2017) 29.

[48] Rubinstein et al, 'Systematic Government Access' (n 47) 38.

[49] For instance, data protection authorities in Europe have emphasised that the challenges raised by the use of cloud computing services should not lead to a lowering of data protection standards compared with those applicable to conventional data processing operations. See EDPS, 'Opinion of the European Data Protection Supervisor on the Commission's Communication on "Unleashing the Potential of Cloud Computing in Europe"' (2012); J Zittrain, 'Lost in the Cloud' (*New York Times*, 20 July 2009), available at www.nytimes.com/2009/07/20/opinion/20zittrain.html.

2

The Cross-Border Data-Access Problem: A Framework for Analysis

Criminal investigations today increasingly require access to data held overseas by cloud service providers.[1] This chapter frames and articulates the increasing jurisdictional and conflicts-of-law challenges in obtaining electronic evidence across borders. It does so in two ways. First, it explains the cross-border data-access problem through the analysis of four high-profile cases litigated in the US and Belgium. Through these cases, the analysis illustrates the cross-border data-access problem triggered or exacerbated by the advent of cloud computing, revealing the weaknesses in the traditional system of international legal co-operation. Second, using the legal and factual questions exposed by these cases as an analytical framework, this chapter identifies five main factors that make the issue of cross-border data access more challenging than ever.

2.1. Litigating Cross-Border Data Access

Several courts around the world have been called upon to resolve complex jurisdictional and conflicts-of-law issues involving cross-border data access.[2] Nothing illustrates the challenges of cross-border data access and exposes the problems with the traditional system of international legal co-operation better than the high-profile cases litigated in the US and Europe. This section briefly discusses four cases, involving four service providers and two countries, in which the respective courts ultimately arrived at similar conclusions but used slightly different reasoning.

These legal battles are particularly relevant for several reasons. First, the legal arguments used in courts and the outcomes of these cases have profoundly influenced the academic and policy debates about the rules that should govern law

[1] European Commission, 'Impact Assessment Accompanying the document Proposal for a Regulation of the European Parliament and of the Council on European Production and Preservation Orders for electronic evidence in criminal matters and Proposal for a Directive of the European Parliament and of the Council laying down harmonised rules on the appointment of legal representatives for the purpose of gathering evidence in criminal proceedings SWD(2018) 118 Final'.

[2] AK Woods, 'Litigating Data Sovereignty' (2018) 128 *Yale Law Journal* 328.

enforcement's access to data held by cloud service providers.[3] Second, they have provided the discursive and normative background for new legal initiatives introduced on both sides of the Atlantic. As *Microsoft Ireland* prompted the adoption of the CLOUD Act in the US, the Belgian cases inspired the enactment of the Internet Investigatory Powers Act, codifying *Yahoo! Belgium* and *Skype Belgium*.[4] The case law in Belgium has also informed the content and approach adopted in the e-Evidence Regulation at the EU level.[5] Lastly, although these specific cases were resolved some years ago, the key legal questions remain. While they occurred at different times, in different countries, involving different technology companies and different factual and legislative details, they all attempted to answer one overarching question: can domestic legal procedures be legitimately used to unilaterally compel the production of data stored on foreign soil? In other words, should State A be allowed to get access to data stored in State B without the prior consent of the latter?

These disputes illustrate the ongoing efforts by nation states worldwide to legitimise domestic production orders for obtaining extraterritorial data. The cases themselves provide empirical examples that are central to the focus of this book, which explores how these rules reconcile the practical needs of law enforcement authorities with the corresponding challenges to the digital sovereignty of other countries, the fundamental rights of individuals whose personal data is sought, and the interests of service providers whose co-operation is necessary.

2.1.1. *Microsoft Ireland*

On 4 December 2013, a magistrate judge in the US District Court for the Southern District of New York issued a warrant under the 1986 Stored Communications Act (SCA) requiring Microsoft to disclose the contents of a particular email account. The required data happened to be stored in Microsoft's data centre in Dublin, Ireland. Microsoft found itself in a dilemma: whether to comply with the court warrant and risk violating EU law, which prohibits service providers from transferring personal data to third countries outside an international agreement, or to comply with EU law and violate US law. Microsoft disclosed the user's non-content information (metadata) stored in the US but refused to hand over the actual content of the email. The company argued that the data was stored in Ireland and that the SCA does not have extraterritorial reach.[6] The government agreed that the

[3] AK Woods, 'Against Data Exceptionalism: Jurisdictions in the Cloud' (2016) 68 *Sandford Law Review* 748; J Daskal, 'Borders and Bits' (2018) 71 *Vanderbilt Law Review* 179; M McKenna, 'Up in the Cloud: Finding Common Ground in Providing for Law Enforcement Access to Data Held by Cloud Computing Service Providers' (2016) 49 *Vanderbilt Journal of Transnational Law* 1417.

[4] V Franssen, 'The Belgian Internet Investigatory Powers Act – A Model to Pursue at European Level?' (2017) 3 *European Data Protection Law Review* 534.

[5] European Commission, 'Impact Assessment' (n 1).

[6] Brief for Respondent, No 17-2 *United States v Microsoft Corp* (11 January 2018).

SCA does not have extraterritorial reach but argued that the warrant was domestic because Microsoft could comply by 'undertaking acts entirely within the United States'.[7] The magistrate judge and the district court agreed with the government's position and held that the production of the data 'does not require the presence of government personnel or provider employees abroad, and places obligations only on the service provider to act within the United States'.[8] This approach suggested that the jurisdictional basis should be the location of the service provider, not the location of the sought-after data. In other words, the legal and material control over the data, regardless of where it was stored, was enough for Microsoft to comply with the warrant.

Upon appeal, US Court of Appeals for the Second Circuit reversed this decision, in 2016, ruling that enforcing the warrant for data stored abroad would constitute an impermissible extraterritorial application of the SCA, suggesting that the determining factor for jurisdiction is the location of data.[9] As the case made its way up to the Supreme Court, it posed a serious dilemma, aptly summarised by Jennifer Daskal:

> A win for Microsoft would impose a set of territorial-based rules onto un-territorial data. This outcome fails to reflect the unique features of data and would likely fuel data localization movements, which in turn undercut the overall efficiency of the Internet. Conversely, a win for the government would establish a dangerous precedent under which nations can unilaterally – without agreed-upon substantive or procedural standards – compel the production of data located anywhere in the world simply by asserting jurisdiction over the company controlling the data.[10]

At this stage, the US Congress intervened by passing the CLOUD Act, bringing *Microsoft Ireland* to an end after a joint request by the two parties.[11]

2.1.2. *Google Pennsylvania*

In August 2016, a magistrate judge issued two search warrants requiring Google to disclose to the FBI 'electronic communications and other records and information associated with four Google accounts belonging to United States citizens connected with two domestic wire fraud investigations'.[12] Relying on the Second Circuit regarding *Microsoft Ireland*, Google refused to produce communications content that the company could not confirm as being stored in the US.[13] The Eastern District of Pennsylvania affirmed the warrant, arguing that compelling

[7] Reply Brief for the United States, No 17-2 *United States v Microsoft Corp* (12 February 2018).
[8] *In re Microsoft Corp* 15 F Supp 3d 466 (SDNY 2014).
[9] *Microsoft v United States*, No 14-2985 (2d Cir 2016).
[10] J Daskal, 'The Un-Territoriality of Data' (2015) 125 *Yale Law Journal* 326, 397.
[11] *Per Curiam* No 17–2 *United States v Microsoft Corp* (584 US, 17 April 2018).
[12] *In re Search Warrant No 16-1061-M to Google* 2017 WL 3535037 (ED Pa 2017).
[13] ibid.

Google to disclose information was not an extraterritorial application of the SCA because the disclosure occurred in the US, where Google is located, regardless of where Google has chosen to store the data. Contrary to the Second Circuit decision in *Microsoft Ireland*, the Eastern District of Pennsylvania found that the location of the service provider should be the determining factor.[14]

2.1.3. *Yahoo! Belgium*

In November 2007, Belgian authorities requested Yahoo!, under article 46*bis* of the Belgian Code of Criminal Procedure (BCCP), to disclose certain personal data (IP address, email address, and any other personal information) in connection with computer fraud investigations.[15] Yahoo! refused to comply with the request, on the grounds that: (i) Yahoo!, being headquartered in the US, was not subject to Belgian jurisdiction; and (ii) the request would extend Belgian jurisdiction extraterritorially, thereby infringing the territorial sovereignty of the US.[16] This case was indicative of the complex issues involved: it took almost six years to be determined, and made its way to the Supreme Court three times (2011, 2012, and 2015). The Court of Cassation ultimately held that Yahoo! had an obligation to co-operate with law enforcement agencies and upheld the lower court's decision to fine the service provider for not obeying the production order.[17] The court found that: (i) even if Yahoo! did not have a physical presence in Belgium, it was virtually and economically present by offering its service to Belgian customers; (ii) Yahoo! was a provider of electronic communication services that fell within the BCCP; (iii) the sought-after data was in connection with a criminal offence investigation conducted from Belgian territory; and (iv) the measure did not require the presence abroad of Belgian police officers or magistrates or any persons acting on their behalf.

2.1.4. *Skype Belgium*

In September 2012, Belgian authorities ordered Skype to disclose data relating to a criminal investigation and provide technical assistance to intercept a suspect's communication, according to sections 88*bis* (2) and 90*quater* (2) BCCP. Skye

[14] ibid.

[15] Court of Appeal of Antwerp, 12th chamber for criminal cases, 2012/CO/1054 *Yahoo! Inc* (20 Nov 2013): Unofficial translation (2014) 11 *Digital Evidence and Electronic Signature Law Review* 137–43.

[16] Hof van Cassatie van België (Court of Cassation of Belgium), Nr P132082N (1 Dec 2015): Unofficial translation (2016) 13 *Digital Evidence and Electronic Signature Law Review* 156–58.

[17] ibid; See also P de Hert, C Parlar, and J Thumfart, 'Legal Arguments Used in Courts Regarding Territoriality and Cross-Border Production Orders: From Yahoo Belgium to Microsoft Ireland' (2018) 9 *New Journal of European Criminal Law* 326.

refused to comply with the order on two main grounds: (i) that all communications content was encrypted, and Skype did not store such data; and (ii) that Skype was established in Luxembourg, and requests for communications content should be made through MLA processes with Luxembourg. Skype lost in both the lower court in Mechelen and the Court of Appeals in Antwerp.[18] The courts applied similar reasoning to that used in the *Yahoo!* case.[19]

2.1.5. Initial Lessons

One crucial difference between the cases in the US and Belgium was the location of the service providers involved. In the two Belgian cases, the service providers in control of the sought-after data had no physical presence in Belgium. The only connecting factor was that the service providers offered their services in Belgium, creating a 'virtual presence'. These cases exemplify a scenario where the investigating authorities and the service providers concerned are located in different territorial jurisdictions. In the two US cases, in contrast, Microsoft and Google are headquartered on US soil, meaning that the requesting authorities and the service providers concerned are located in the investigating country, even though the sought-after data was stored abroad. Despite this difference, four common initial lessons can be drawn from these legal battles.

First, the cases demonstrated that service providers play an unavoidable role in today's criminal justice system. As local data storage in end-user equipment gives way to remote storage, electronic evidence required for criminal investigations often resides in the custody of cloud computing providers. As a result, the ability of law enforcement authorities to access electronic evidence relies on the (voluntary or compulsory) assistance of the service provider controlling the data. Cloud computing has bestowed upon service providers a new role, new responsibilities, and unique power in mediating cross-border data access.

Second, and relatedly, the cases epitomised the untenable position of service providers with respect to conflicting obligations. All the service providers refused to comply with disclosure orders because doing so would violate the laws of other countries. As the demand for cross-border data access increases, service providers will continue to be at the forefront of jurisdictional battlegrounds.

Third, the cases revealed how the ubiquity of cloud computing could globalise an otherwise exclusively domestic criminal investigation. At first glance, all the cases appeared to be entirely domestic matters, dealing with local crime, local victims, and local suspects. The competent authorities issued the production orders or warrants based on the relevant substantive and procedural requirements

[18] *Procureur-Général v Skype*, Correctionele Rechtbanken [Corr] [Criminal Tribunal] Antwerp, Division Mechelen, Oct 27, 2016, No ME2041 105151-12, 12–15 (Belg); See also Daskal, 'Borders and Bits' (n 3).

[19] de Hert, Parlar, and Thumfart, 'Legal Arguments' (n 17).

in their respective national laws. For instance, the two Belgian cases were related to investigations of criminal offences committed on Belgian soil by suspects who were Belgian residents, or at least presumably present in Belgium at the time of the offence.[20] Nonetheless, the jurisdictional conflicts arose from the mere fact that the required data happened to be stored on foreign servers because of the business decision of the service provider or the online activities of the user.

Lastly, these cases demonstrated how cloud computing blurs the line where the territorial reach of law enforcement power ends and extraterritorial activity begins. For instance, one striking similarity between the arguments advanced by the governments in all the cases was that they did not consider their laws and practices (compelling the disclosure of data stored overseas) as extraterritorial. They argued that their acts did not imply any intervention outside their respective territorial boundaries. Their justifications were simple: the production orders did not require any person to physically enter the foreign jurisdiction where the data was stored ('there is no physical presence abroad argument').[21] They used different ways to legitimise their use of domestic tools and access methods to obtain extraterritorial data. For instance, while the US authorities cited the physical establishment of the service providers concerned, the Belgian authorities employed virtual presence as a necessary and sufficient condition to unilaterally order the production of data stored in a foreign territory.

2.2. Factors Driving Cross-Border Data Access Frameworks

While the challenges exemplified in the cases mentioned are numerous, they can be categorised into five distinct yet interrelated legal and technological 'drivers' arising from the growth of cloud computing. These drivers, whether considered individually or in combination, have played a pivotal role in shaping the ongoing academic and policy discussions surrounding cross-border data access. Below is a summary of the factors that have reshaped the cross-border data-access debate, and their implications for privacy, the rule of law, and territorial sovereignty.

2.2.1. The Unique Role of Cloud Service Providers

The service providers that control the vast majority of data in the world today occupy a unique position concerning the protection of fundamental rights and the ability of law enforcement agencies to gather electronic data across borders.

[20] Franssen, 'The Belgian Internet Investigatory Powers Act' (n 4).

[21] For detailed analysis of different arguments used in these courts, see de Hert, Parlar, and Thumfart, 'Legal Arguments' (n 17).

On the one hand, the detection, investigation, and prosecution of criminal offences that involve digital evidence rely on the co-operation of these service providers. When data is migrated to the cloud, it is the service provider, not the user, that governments call upon to produce that data when needed for criminal evidence.[22] As digitalisation continues to grow, it has become difficult, and sometimes impossible, for governments to effectively investigate and prosecute domestic crimes without the assistance of these service providers. Consequently, cloud computing has witnessed a dramatic increase in the number of government requests for data held by service providers. It is now an undeniable responsibility of service providers to assist law enforcement authorities involved in criminal investigations.[23]

At the same time, these service providers bear the responsibility of safeguarding their users' data from government overreach. Typically, it is these service providers who act as the last line of defence between governments and the user's personal data. This distinctive position grants service providers an extraordinary power, coupled with the corresponding responsibility to mediate a multitude of often conflicting interests. They possess 'significant discretion in deciding when to cooperate with government requests for their users' personal data, and when to resist such requests'.[24] As service providers become increasingly vital to the law enforcement apparatus, they assume the role of critical gatekeepers capable of pushing back against unlawful demands for personal data by governments.[25] When responding to government requests for data, service providers hold the power to determine the amount of data accessible to governments and the level of privacy rights granted to their users.

The discretion of service providers in determining the government's ability to access user data and the rights and protections applied comes with significant responsibilities. As Albert Gimsai noted, service providers find themselves in a position where the privacy community, users, and governments all look to them as the solution to privacy and security issues.[26] Notably, the power wielded by service providers 'is not the product of purposeful design'.[27] This role is one that service providers stumbled into 'by virtue of their omnipresence in our day-to-day lives'.[28]

[22] Daskal, 'The Un-Territoriality of Data' (n 10) 377.

[23] C Soghoian, 'The Spies We Trust: Third Party Service Providers and Law Enforcement Surveillance' (PhD, Indiana University 2012); AZ Rozenshtein, 'Surveillance Intermediaries' (2018) 70 *Stanford Law Review* 99.

[24] 'Developments in the Law – More Data, More Problems' (2018) 131 *Harvard Law Review* 1714, 1717.

[25] Soghoian, 'The Spies We Trust' (n 23); 'Developments in the Law' (n 24); Rozenshtein, 'Surveillance Intermediaries' (n 23).

[26] A Gimsai, Jr, 'Companies Caught in the Middle' (2007) 41 *University of San Francisco Law Review* 535.

[27] 'Developments in the Law' (n 24) 1723.

[28] ibid.

The extraordinary power held by service providers and its implications for the right to privacy, the ability of law enforcement authorities to gather electronic data across borders, and the resulting effects on the territorial sovereignty of other states have garnered significant attention in recent years. There is a global trend whereby the location of data storage as a determining factor for asserting jurisdiction is increasingly disregarded, and greater emphasis is placed on service providers. New legal frameworks have been introduced or are under consideration, granting service providers new responsibilities to directly receive, assess, and respond to law enforcement requests.

Three schools of thought emerge regarding the evolving role of service providers in mediating cross-border data access. The first of these schools of thought characterises service providers as facilitators of law enforcement access to personal data. This perspective draws on historical events, such as the Snowden revelations of mass digital surveillance of the US and its allies, and the growing tendency of major service providers to comply with data localisation laws worldwide. The central idea here is that technology companies often co-operate with government access to personal data, whether through legal processes or informal voluntary arrangements, and are sometimes viewed as potential accomplices in government surveillance.

The second view conceives service providers as crucial constraints on law enforcement access to user data, serving as a 'greater check on government surveillance'.[29] In his *Stanford Law Review* article titled 'Surveillance Intermediaries', Alan Rozenshtein provides a comprehensive analysis of how technology companies can limit, rather than enable, the surveillance powers of law enforcement agencies in the US. Rozenshtein's insights, although US-centric, are applicable to other jurisdictions. He argues that understanding how surveillance intermediaries constrain government surveillance would advance debates in privacy and security, including issues like end-to-end encryption and offshore data storage.[30] For Rozenshtein, technology companies that store and process our data are best positioned to resist government surveillance, and they have the incentives and the means to do so. He presents examples of successful litigations initiated by technology companies, such as *Microsoft Ireland*. The means that service providers possess to constrain illegitimate government data requests include litigation; requiring governments to use formal legal processes; rejecting overly broad orders; making technological changes to their systems and products, such as end-to-end encryption; and engaging in policy mobilisation through lobbying and transparency reports.[31]

The third perspective rejects the dichotomous debate that service providers either exclusively assist or resist government requests for data, advocating for a nuanced approach that recognises that service providers can 'do both'. The central

[29] Rozenshtein, 'Surveillance Intermediaries' (n 23) 131.
[30] ibid 106.
[31] 'Developments in the Law' (n 24) 1722.

argument of this view is that not all service providers are the same: 'each company is likely to assist and resist law enforcement agencies to different degrees and in different ways, depending on factors like current events, the technical structure of their product, their business models, and customer concerns'.[32] In other words, we cannot expect a single service provider to have a fixed commitment that remains unchanged over time, nor can we anticipate all service providers responding in the same way to any specific situation.

The analysis above is particularly relevant to the voluntary co-operation between service providers and law enforcement authorities. Since there is no standard 'yes' or 'no' approach to voluntary co-operation, most service providers establish their own policies and practices for receiving, assessing, and responding to law enforcement requests. Consequently, service providers often face criticisms for being arbitrary, unfair, and discriminatory in their decision-making when it comes to resisting or co-operating with government requests. For instance, African stakeholders criticised US-based service providers for what they considered unfair treatment in responding to data requests for legitimate criminal investigations (see chapter seven).[33]

2.2.2. The 'Location' Problem

Traditionally, investigators first inquire about the location of the sought-after data. Procedures, such as obtaining a court warrant and conducting search and seizure, follow the determination of the location of the required evidence. Cloud computing complicates this process, at times making it practically impossible. As discussed in chapter one, cloud data is stored and processed in data centres distributed around the world, including in jurisdictions the user has never physically entered.

Service providers often move data, by automated algorithms, across jurisdictions for various reasons, including but not limited to storage efficiency, addressing performance issues, minimising storage costs, and meeting security requirements. To use the words of the Article 29 Data Protection Working Party, data in the cloud environment 'can be in one datacentre at 2pm and on the other side of the world at 4pm'.[34] The ease, speed, and unpredictability with which data flows across borders gives rise to a problem commonly known as 'loss of location'[35] – a situation

[32] ibid 1730–36.

[33] M Fidler, 'Africans Want Cross-Border Data Access Reform, But They Might Get Left Out' (*Council on Foreign Relations*, 26 October 2016), available at www.cfr.org/blog/africans-want-cross-border-data-access-reform-they-might-get-left-out.

[34] Article 29 Data Protection Working Party, 'Opinion 05/2012 on Cloud Computing' (2012) (WP196).

[35] JJ Schwerha, 'Law Enforcement Challenges in Transborder Acquisition of Electronic Evidence from Cloud Computing Providers' (Council of Europe Discussion Paper, 2010).

in which it is practically challenging, though not theoretically impossible, to determine the exact location of data at a given moment.

The automated movement of data across borders raises complex legal questions, including whether users enjoy the same level of protection as their data moves across borders. How can the principle of territoriality be operationalised in the cloud environment? The uncertainty of where in the world data is stored at a given moment in time, and the increasingly diminishing normative significance of the physical location of data, create uncertainty as to who has jurisdiction over that data and whose legal framework should govern law enforcement access. These uncertainties challenge the underlying assumptions of traditional law enforcement jurisdictions and privacy laws.

2.2.3. Criminal Evidence Goes Global

The growing demand for cross-border data by law enforcement agencies challenges traditional notions of geography and territorial jurisdiction.[36] Traditionally, criminal evidence was generally available within the investigating country's territorial jurisdiction.[37] The advent of the Internet, and particularly cloud computing, has dramatically changed this situation. Criminal evidence once stored locally and accessible under domestic legal procedures is increasingly located in jurisdictions outside the investigating country. As Andrew Woods pointed out, 'evidence of crimes is now often digital, often stored in the cloud, and often managed by a service provider located in another jurisdiction'.[38] For instance, a 2018 study by the European Commission revealed that more than half of the criminal investigations in the EU involving digital evidence required cross-border access.[39] In the US, the Department of Justice reported that the number of requests by foreign governments for electronic evidence has increased by 1,000 per cent over the last two decades.[40] Therefore, extraterritorial access to electronic evidence by law enforcement authorities is not the exception but the norm. The more criminal evidence becomes globalised, the more traditional methods and procedures of evidence-gathering become ineffective. The problem with the globalisation of evidence is particularly acute when evidence required for entirely domestic criminal investigations is routinely stored in foreign servers, or is held by foreign service providers.

[36] J Daskal, P Swire, and T Christakis, 'The Globalization of Criminal Evidence' (*International Association of Privacy Professionals*, 16 October 2018), available at www.iapp.org/news/a/the-globalization-of-criminal-evidence.

[37] ibid.

[38] Woods, 'Litigating Data Sovereignty' (n 2) 330.

[39] European Commission, 'Impact Assessment' (n 1).

[40] See Department of Justice Criminal Division, 'Performance Budget FY 2019 Congressional Submission', available at www.justice.gov/doj/fy-2019-congressional-budget-submission.

2.2.4. MLAT System Outlived its Usefulness

Gathering evidence across borders is not a novel issue, nor are the territorial constraints on law enforcement authority. Historically, governments have forged a mix of formal and informal methods, such as letters rogatory and mutual legal assistance treaties (MLATs), to share evidence across national borders. However, these systems, specifically the MLAT system, which is the commonly used framework, have been struggling to adapt to the digital environment, making the acquisition of evidence from the global cloud increasingly ineffective. The MLAT system has structural problems, some of which are worth highlighting.

2.2.4.1. Procedural and Administrative Difficulties

The first and commonly understood problem with the MLAT system can be framed as procedural and administrative. Due to the ease and speed with which data can be moved, changed, or deleted, law enforcement authorities want to act swiftly to secure access to critical evidence across borders. As Jonah Force Hill and Matthew Noyes aptly pointed out, the MLAT system simply does not allow, and indeed may not be structurally designed to allow, for the kind of rapid international co-operation that is required in today's globalised digital environment.[41] The procedural and administrative problems of the MLAT system largely stem from the significant number of formal approvals and involvement of multiple actors in the requesting and receiving countries.

Consider how a typical MLA process for electronic evidence works in the US. When a foreign country that has an MLA agreement with the US seeks access to data held by a US-based service provider, its investigative body prepares and submits the request to the national central authority designated in the MLA agreement to process such requests. The central authority then sends the request to the corresponding central authority in the US, which is the Office of International Affairs within the Department of Justice. The Office of International Affairs reviews each MLA request to ensure compliance with US constitutional and statutory requirements. In addition to the requirements of the domestic procedural and substantive laws of the requesting country, the specific conditions of the MLA instrument and US law have to be met; translations need to be obtained.[42] In the event that the request is incomplete, overly broad, or lacks consistency with prescribed formats, the Office of International Affairs will work with the requesting body to remedy it. The Office of International Affairs then works with the US Attorney's Office, which will take the request to a local magistrate judge for review.

[41] JF Hill and M Noyes, 'Thinking Data, Geography, and Jurisdiction: Towards A Common Framework for Harmonizing Global Data Flow Controls' (New America and Cybersecurity Initiative, 2018).

[42] European Commission, 'Impact Assessment' (n 1) 24.

Before approving the MLA request, the US court must establish that the request is consistent with the relevant requirements of US law, including the Fourth Amendment's probable cause standard and the text of the relevant MLAT. Once the reviewing court has issued a warrant, the warrant will be served on the service provider controlling the sought-after data. The service provider will then assess whether the warrant complies with relevant US laws and with its internal policies. Most service providers have teams that are dedicated to receiving, processing, and responding to law enforcement requests.[43] Once the service provider has submitted the required data, the Office of International Affairs reviews the evidence to ensure that it meets data minimisation and human rights standards. The data will be transferred back through the same chain to the central authority in the requesting country, and then to the investigating body. An ex post review may also take place after the data has been transferred to the relevant bodies in the requesting state.

This multi-layer, multi-step, and rigorous procedure of the MLAT system was designed with good intentions: to 'ensure that the right authorities are involved and that appropriate … safeguards are taken into account'.[44] However, the process also renders the MLAT system dysfunctional in the current digital age. It is not structurally designed to allow for the kind of rapid international co-operation needed in the digital environment.[45] In a best-case scenario, the entire process of an MLA request may take up to ten months, and in some cases up to two years.[46] For this reason, the MLAT system is often described as slow, cumbersome, bureaucratic, and ineffective.

The MLAT system did not contemplate that cross-border data access would become a routine law enforcement activity. It was designed to handle rare transnational cases. Now, the system is struggling to keep pace with the increasing demand for cross-border data. A combination of procedural and administrative factors resulted in delays and a substantial backlog of pending cases, in terms of response time for foreign MLA requests. On the other hand, there has been a dramatic increase in the number of requests for data from governments worldwide.

These procedural and administrative challenges have far-reaching consequences for both the US and its foreign counterparts. During the lengthy process, the statute of limitation may expire, making the evidence inadmissible in courts. Furthermore, the data could be changed, deleted, or moved across jurisdictions between the time a production order is sought and the time it is served on the service provider. The inability to obtain cross-border data in a timely manner jeopardises law enforcement's ability to identify and prosecute perpetrators of serious

[43] B Smith and CA Browne, *Tools and Weapons: The Promise and the Peril of the Digital Age* (Hodder & Stoughton, 2019) 25.

[44] S Carrera, M Stefan, and V Mitsilegas, 'Cross-Border Data Access in Criminal Proceedings and the Future of Digital Justice Navigating the Current Legal Framework, and Exploring Ways Forward within the EU and across the Atlantic' (Report of CEPS and QMUL Task Force, October 2020).

[45] Hill and Noyes, 'Thinking Data, Geography, and Jurisdiction' (n 41).

[46] Assessment Report on Mutual Legal Assistance (Cybercrime Convention Committee, 2017) 17.

crimes. This, in turn, undermines the rule of law in democratic societies. These frustrations could force more and more governments to pursue alternatives, and potentially threaten reciprocal co-operation when the US seeks evidence from other countries. The US Department of Justice has acknowledged that delays in responding to requests for electronic evidence in the custody or control of US-based providers prompt calls by foreign governments for data localisation, trigger foreign demands that US providers produce information directly in response to foreign orders or face criminal penalties, and encourage foreign proposals that US providers be subject to foreign or global data protection regimes.[47]

2.2.4.2. *Practical Impossibility*

The MLAT system is designed based on the categorical presumption that the investigating authorities always know where the required data is located and to which foreign authorities the MLA request is to be made. This presumption is difficult, if not impossible, to operationalise in the digital environment, where data constantly moves across borders. It is even difficult to determine whether the investigative measure involves a cross-border component. It is this 'unterritorial' nature of data that has made the MLAT system not only procedurally cumbersome and slow but also of no practical relevance.

Compare, for example, the cases of *Microsoft Ireland* and *Google Pennsylvania*. Microsoft has a regionalised cloud system and it stores data in data centres closer to the user, for efficiency purposes, among other reasons. As highlighted in the previous chapter, this architectural design enables Microsoft's GCC team to determine where in the world a specific piece of data is stored. Based on this architectural design, the company argued that *Microsoft Ireland* constituted an impermissible extraterritorial application of the SCA, as the required data was stored in Ireland. In such circumstances, it makes sense to argue that the government must go through the MLAT process, despite its procedural and administrative problems, to compel the production of the required data. *Google Pennsylvania* is a different story based on a different design and policy choice. Google's cloud architecture is designed to automatically select where to store user data based on performance measurements, not the location of the user. Furthermore, Google confirmed that 'user files may also be broken into component parts' (shards) to the extent that each piece of data is 'unintelligible … until Google reassembles the relevant shards [so] that they form an intelligible and useable piece of information, such as an e-mail or an attachment to an e-mail'.[48] As a result, Google claimed that it was unable to tell where in the world a piece of data was located at a given moment.

Google's argument that it cannot ascertain where the data is located is a futile argument for several reasons. First, the 'location' problem is created by Google's

[47] 'Performance Budget FY 2019 Congressional Submission' (n 40).
[48] *In re Search Warrant to Google, Inc.*, Mag. No. 16-4116 (D.N.J. Jul. 10, 2017).

design and policy choice, and it should not be used as an excuse for not complying with a lawful government request. Second, the claim that it was technically impossible for Google to determine the location data was rebutted by computer and data scientists, who argued that 'cloud data always has a specific physical location', and that retrieving data from the cloud is 'no less physical or necessary than if the same data were protected in a bank-vault safe deposit box'.[49] Third, Google's argument that the data requests must go through the MLA process does not make any sense. Even if one accepts the claim that it was technically impossible for Google to determine the location of the sought-after data, it will also mean that there would be no foreign country to which MLA requests can be addressed. This would effectively leave the law enforcement authorities with no options. Furthermore, unlike Microsoft, which has a compliance team that operates from different jurisdictions,[50] Google's Legal Investigation Support Team operates only from California. The District Court of Pennsylvania found that 'support team members are the only Google personnel authorized to access the content of user communications in order to produce such materials in response to legal process, and all support team members are located in the United States'.[51] This means that, even if the location of data was known, foreign governments would not have jurisdiction over US-based employees to issue production orders.[52] In cloud systems such as that of Google, the 'extraterritoriality' argument would result in what Alan Rozenshtein called 'a warrant black hole'[53] – a situation where the government can pursue neither a unilateral production order nor the MLAT system.

2.2.4.3. Jurisdictional Asymmetry

The third challenge with the MLAT system is what de La Chapelle and Fehlinger call the 'asymmetry' problem.[54] The MLA system dictates that the laws of the country where the sought-after data is located should govern law enforcement access. Accordingly, MLA requests should be executed in accordance with the domestic laws of the recipient country, including the requirement that the offence be punishable under that country's laws (the principle of double criminality), and the execution of the request must comply with the constitutional requirements and criminal procedure standards applicable to domestic matters in the recipient state. Essentially, the MLAT system de facto imposes the law of the recipient country over the law of the requesting one, even if neither the investigation nor

[49] Brief for 51 Computer Scientists as Amici Curiae in Support of the Respondent, *United States v Microsoft* (2017) No 17-2 (2018).

[50] Smith and Browne, *Tools and Weapons* (n 43) 24.

[51] *In re Search Warrant No 16-1061-M to Google* (n 12).

[52] Rozenshtein, 'Surveillance Intermediaries' (n 23).

[53] ibid.

[54] B de La Chapelle and P Fehlinger, 'Jurisdiction on the Internet: From Legal Arms Race to Transnational Cooperation' (Global Commission on Internet Governance, Paper Series: No 28, April 2016) 6.

the required data has anything to do with the recipient state.[55] As more and more electronic data required for criminal investigations enters the custody of service providers, it creates a 'power imbalance' between countries or regions that enjoy jurisdiction over major service providers and those which do not.[56] The countries in the former category have disproportionate power and leverage to enforce their laws globally while depriving others of similar jurisdictional leverage, 'even in cases where the laws in question are identical, or near-identical'.[57] Those countries that have cloud servers in their territorial jurisdiction can have relatively straightforward access to the data stored in those servers under domestic procedures.

As the large majority of today's service providers are headquartered in the US, the US is the largest recipient of MLA requests from around the world, and the US law is 'the gatekeeper for all requests for data' from these service providers.[58] The US receives more than twice as many MLA requests as it makes.[59] While this situation generates additional workload and administrative costs for US authorities, it also gives disproportionate power to the US. The global trend to focus on service providers could produce an imbalance whereby providers based in one country apply the law of that country at the international level. This power imbalance frustrates an increasing number of governments and forces them to pursue alternative means, such as data localisation.

2.2.4.4. Normative Problem

There is a clear global trend in disregarding the location of data as a determining factor in asserting law enforcement jurisdiction. The more the location of data becomes irrelevant, the more the MLAT system is disregarded and the more its normative significance is undermined. The normative problem also arises from the fact that the investigation and prosecution of an entirely domestic crime are often determined by the laws and authorities of a foreign country (typically the US). There is little normative justification for the US to impose its domestic requirements, such as probable cause, on matters that do not involve US interests in any way.[60] This does not mean that any government should have access to data on its citizens held by US-based service providers at will; a threshold of

[55] ibid.

[56] DJB Svantesson, 'Internet & Jurisdiction Global Status Report' (Internet & Jurisdiction Policy Network, 27 November 2019), available at www.internetjurisdiction.net/news/release-of-worlds-first-internet-jurisdiction-global-status-report.

[57] ibid 65.

[58] K Westmoreland and G Kent, 'International Law Enforcement Access to User Data: A Survival Guide and Call for Action' (2015) 13 *Canadian Journal of Law and Technology* 226.

[59] A Rizer and A Hobson, 'Cross-Border Data Requests: Evaluating Reforms to Improve Law Enforcement Access' (R Street Policy Study No 120, Nov 2017).

[60] Center for Strategic & International Studies (CSIS), 'Cybercrime Symposium International Electronic Evidence Gathering 2025' (21 June 2016).

privacy and due process requirements is necessary. Nonetheless, there is no clear normative justification to subject a purely domestic matter to international negotiation. This arbitrary approach would create more problems than it solves.

As the European Commission has stated, a number of countries are questioning the appropriateness and usefulness of MLA procedures in circumstances where the only connecting factor to the foreign country on whose territory an investigative/enforcement action needs to be performed is that the sought-after data happens to be stored there.[61] The increasing trend in governments bypassing MLAT could render the system functionally redundant, and hence normatively less desirable.

2.2.5. Mutually Exclusive Legal Regimes

The failure of the MLAT system has resulted in an increasing shift from formal international co-operation mechanisms towards a model of direct public–private cross-border co-operation. This shift is demonstrated by the proliferation of unilateral laws compelling the production of data stored in foreign servers when required for criminal investigation (see chapter three). Parallel to this global trend of extraterritoriality is the corresponding surge of (domestic or regional) laws that prohibit or restrict service providers from disclosing user data to foreign governments outside a formal international agreement. Studies show that a total of 162 countries around the world have data protection laws in place, as of 2023.[62] These laws regulate the use, international transfer, and disclosure of personal data. One of the common elements of data protection laws is that they 'tend to focus on data not leaving a country or region'.[63] As a result, data protection and privacy laws put some sort of restriction on cross-border data flow, including in response to foreign law-enforcement demands. In addition to data protection and privacy laws, other legal frameworks may also prohibit disclosure of data to foreign authorities for different reasons, including protecting trade secrets and national security.[64] A 2016 report by the European Commission revealed that the 'majority of national legislations (in the EU) either do not cover or explicitly prohibit that service providers established in the Member State respond to direct requests from law enforcement authorities from another EU Member State or non-EU country'.[65] Commonly known as 'blocking statutes', these laws are intentionally

[61] European Commission, 'Impact Assessment' (n 1) 22.

[62] G Greenleaf, 'Global Data Privacy Laws 2023: 162 National Laws and 20 Bills' [2023] *SSRN Electronic Journal*, available at www.ssrn.com/abstract=4426146.

[63] DR Desai, 'Beyond Location: Data Security in the 21st Century' (2013) 56 *Communications of the ACM*.

[64] See, for instance, Bank Secrecy Law of China; the UK's Protection of Trading Interests Act 1980; French blocking statute, Law n° 68-678 of July 26, 1968, 1*bis*; Swiss Penal Code, art 271.

[65] European Commission, 'Non-paper: Progress Report following the Conclusions of the Council of the European Union on Improving Criminal Justice in Cyberspace' (2 December 2016).

designed to prevent foreign governments from directly engaging with service providers established in the imposing country.[66] Some blocking statutes may entail criminal penalties.[67]

The consequence of such mutually exclusive laws is clear: a government request or production order in one country may constitute a violation of domestic law in another country, and service providers are caught in the middle. As David Kris put it, we are witnessing the proliferation of 'mutually exclusive legal requirements prohibiting and compelling production of information'.[68] In such a situation, a service provider would face a difficult dilemma: to choose between the laws of a nation that seeks production of data and the laws of another nation that prohibits such production.[69] The more incompatible these laws are, the harder the problem will become. Concrete examples and detailed analysis of such reciprocal conflicts of norms (disclosure obligations and disclosure prohibitions) are provided in chapter six, in the context of the US and the EU.

2.3. An Inflection Point

The traditional international system of cross-border data access is broken. While law enforcement's access to data held by cloud service providers has become a practical necessity, an effective framework to manage the growing significance of such cross-border data access is currently lacking. Governments are increasingly frustrated, and are pursuing alternative mechanisms to get timely access to data across borders. Paddy McGuinness, the UK deputy national security adviser in 2017, once testified before the US Congress in the lead up to the adoption of the CLOUD Act: 'The current legal situation is bad for public safety, bad for companies and bad for privacy'.[70] The inability to get timely access to electronic evidence held by foreign service providers for a legitimate law enforcement purpose means that perpetrators of serious crimes may go free. The European Commission found that 'almost two-thirds of crimes involving cross-border access to e-evidence cannot be effectively investigated or prosecuted' in the EU.[71] Law enforcement authorities

[66] Woods, 'Against Data Exceptionalism' (n 3) 779.

[67] For instance, according to art 1*bis* of the French blocking statute, 'any person is prohibited from requesting, researching or communicating, in writing, orally or in any other form, documents or information of an economic, commercial nature, industrial, financial or technical tending to the constitution of evidence for or within the framework of foreign legal or administrative proceedings'. Violation of this prohibition is punishable with up to six months of imprisonment (art 3). See Law n° 68-678 of July 26, 1968.

[68] D Kris, 'Preliminary Thoughts on Cross-Border Data Requests' (*Lawfare*, 28 September 2015), available at www.lawfareblog.com/preliminary-thoughts-cross-border-data-requests.

[69] J Daskal, 'Law Enforcement Access to Data Across Borders: The Evolving Security and Rights Issues' (2016) 8 *Journal of National Security Law & Policy* 473.

[70] Written Testimony of Mr Paddy McGuinness, United Kingdom Deputy National Security Adviser, Before the Judiciary Sub-Committee on Crime and Terrorism, United States Senate (10 May 2017).

[71] European Commission, 'Impact Assessment' (n 1) 17.

could be deprived of their power and responsibility to investigate and prosecute exclusively domestic crimes. Some have analogised this challenge to the 'going dark' problem in the context of end-to-end encryption,[72] in the sense that law enforcement authorities are unable to access user data stored in foreign jurisdictions even when they have a legitimate interest and lawful authority to do so.[73] The current situation also threatens individual privacy and other fundamental rights, as governments pursue unilateral and privacy-intrusive alternatives, including mandated data localisation, covert surveillance, and the unilateral assertion of extraterritorial jurisdiction over foreign-held data. The increasing disregard for the existing system of international legal co-operation and the increasing trend in unilateral cross-border data-access powers also affect the territorial and digital sovereignty of other countries.

A 2019 global status report by the Internet & Jurisdiction Policy Network reveals an alarming prospect for the future of cross-border legal co-operation. Of the 150 respondents, 95 per cent believed that cross-border legal challenges on the Internet would become increasingly acute in the next three years.[74] Consequently, the system of cross-border legal co-operation in criminal matters is at a critical juncture. Jennifer Daskal pointed out that:

> There is, on the one hand, the risk of governments demanding access to all information anywhere and everywhere, in ways that will almost certainly result in reduced cybersecurity, privacy, and civil liberties for all. But, on the other hand, there is a unique opportunity for governments, technology companies, and civil society to respond to these cross-border challenges by collectively setting baseline standards and clear jurisdictional rules and thereby facilitating law enforcement access while also protecting, and ideally elevating, speech, privacy, and other rights protections in the process.[75]

Allowing the status quo to continue would lead to the proliferation of incompatible norms around the world. The respondents of the survey mentioned above sought urgent new initiatives that would either reform, complement, or replace the traditional mechanism of cross-border legal co-operation.

2.4. Conclusion

Courts around the world have grappled with intricate jurisdictional and conflicts-of-law challenges related to cross-border data access. This chapter examined the cross-border data-access conundrum through the lens of four landmark cases litigated in the US and the EU. The outcomes of these disputes have had a profound

[72] For details on this debate, see B Schneier and others, 'Don't Panic: Making Progress on the "Going Dark" Debate' (Berkman Center for Internet & Society, Research Publication, 1 February 2016).

[73] PM Schwartz, 'Legal Access to the Global Cloud' (2018) 118 *Columbia Law Review* 1681.

[74] Svantesson, 'Internet & Jurisdiction Global Status Report' (n 56).

[75] J Daskal, 'Privacy and Security Across Borders' (2019) 128 *The Yale Law Journal Forum* 1031.

impact on academic and policy discussions regarding the regulation of cross-border data access. Additionally, they have laid down the groundwork for new legal initiatives introduced or under consideration on both sides of the Atlantic. Drawing on the legal disputes, this chapter identified five factors reshaping the policy initiatives regarding cross-border data access: the distinctive role of service providers, the de-territorialisation of data, the globalisation of criminal evidence, the proliferation of conflicting norms, and the failure of the MLAT system to address these evolving challenges. The overarching conclusion is that any initiative aiming to address the complexities of cross-border data access should carefully consider these key factors.

3

Mapping Policy Approaches and Emerging Initiatives

A growing consensus among stakeholders – governments, technology companies, civil society organisations, and academia – acknowledges that the traditional cross-border legal co-operation system based on MLATs is increasingly seen as unsustainable in the context of current technological realities. There is a widespread agreement that it requires reform or replacement to better align with these realities. However, consensus dissolves beyond this point. Despite the shared recognition of the problem, there is considerable disagreement on the specifics of what these reforms or alternative approaches should entail. While there are some promising initiatives, the proliferation of uncoordinated policy responses could lead to further jurisdictional conflicts and legal uncertainties.

The purpose of this chapter is to map and examine these various initiatives based on the approaches they follow in addressing the challenges of obtaining electronic evidence across borders. It addresses two key questions: what approaches can best elucidate the proliferation of initiatives aimed at improving law enforcement access to electronic evidence across borders? And to what extent are these frameworks appropriate for addressing the cross-border data-access problem? After critically reviewing different initiatives proposed or implemented by a wide range of actors, this chapter develops and distinguishes between four approaches – reformist, unilateralist, internationalist, and nuanced – that best explain the current and emerging legal frameworks. It then assesses the suitability and sustainability of these approaches against their stated objectives and some key principles that have garnered extensive support in policy and academic discussions.

3.1. An International Moment for Cross-Border Data-Access Reform

In recent years, there has been a surge in initiatives aimed at improving law enforcement's access to electronic evidence across borders, commonly known as 'cross-border data-access reforms'. These efforts included organising numerous conferences and commissioning projects to tackle the jurisdictional challenges and conflicts of law intensified by cloud computing.[1] New platforms, forums, and research centres focusing on these issues have emerged.[2] A variety of stakeholders, including regional and international organisations, academics, civil society groups, service providers, and public policy think tanks, have been investigating alternative solutions that could replace or complement the MLA system.[3] Negotiations are currently in progress at bilateral, regional, and international levels to establish new legal frameworks for cross-border data access.[4] Numerous countries have introduced or are considering legislation granting their law enforcement agencies unilateral authority to access digital evidence stored in foreign jurisdictions. Additionally, more governments are taking action locally, influenced by their own bargaining power and local sensitivities. Various courts have also been called upon to resolve complex jurisdictional and conflicts-of-law issues involving cross-border data access.[5] The widespread response to the cross-border data-access challenges raises two essential questions. Firstly, what approaches can best explain these diverse responses and emerging initiatives? Secondly, how effective and fit-for-purpose are they?

[1] For instance, The Information Society Project, 'Extraterritorial Enforcement: Developing Norms for the Information Society' (Workshop White Paper, 2018); D Keller (ed), 'Law, Borders, and Speech: Proceedings and Materials' (Center for Internet and Society, Stanford 2017); Global Network Initiative, 'New World Borders: How Governments Assert Authority Across Borders in the Internet Age' (18 September 2018); EVIDENCE2e-CODEX Project, 'Digital Cross-Border Cooperation in Criminal Justice Conference' (21 January 2020); MAPPING Project, 'Managing Alternatives for Privacy, Property and Internet Governance (2019); 'Cross-Border Requests for Data Project' (*Georgia Tech, Institute for Information Security & Privacy*), available at www.peterswire.net/cross-border-requests-data-project/. This chapter builds on a previous article by the author: see H Abraha, 'Law enforcement access to electronic evidence across borders: mapping policy approaches and emerging reform initiatives' (2021) 29 *International Journal of Law and Information Technology* 118.

[2] For instance, 'Cross-Border Data Forum', available at www.crossborderdataforum.org/; 'Internet & Jurisdiction Policy Network', available at www.internetjurisdiction.net.

[3] For instance, P Swire and JD Hemmings, 'Mutual Legal Assistance in an Era of Globalized Communications: The Analogy to the Visa Waiver Program' (2017) 71 *NYU Annual Survey of American Law* 687; J Daskal and AK Woods, 'Cross-Border Data Requests: A Proposed Framework' (*Lawfare*, 24 November 2015), available at www.lawfareblog.com/cross-border-data-requests-proposed-framework; G Kent, 'Sharing Investigation Specific Data with Law Enforcement – An International Approach' (2014) Stanford Public Law Working Paper; B Smith, 'Time for an International Convention on Government Access to Data' (*Microsoft on the Issues*, 20 January 2014), available at https://blogs.microsoft.com/on-the-issues/2014/01/20/time-for-an-international-convention-on-government-access-to-data/.

[4] See, for instance, United States and Canada Negotiations of a CLOUD Act Agreement and United States and European Commission Negotiations of a CLOUD Act Agreement, available at www.justice.gov/criminal/cloud-act-resources. See also UN Cybercrime negotiations, available at www.unodc.org/unodc/en/cybercrime/ad_hoc_committee/home; OECD Declaration on Government Access to Personal Data Held by Private Sector Entities, available at https://legalinstruments.oecd.org/en/instruments/OECD-LEGAL-0487.

[5] *In re Microsoft Corp* 15 F Supp 3d 466 (SDNY 2014); *In re Search Warrant No 16-960-M-1 to Google*; *In re Search Warrant No 16-1061-M to Google* 2017 WL 3535037 (ED Pa 2017); *Procureur-Général v Yahoo! Inc, Hof van Cassatie [Cass]* [Court of Cassation], Jan 18, 2011, Nr P101347N (Belg); *Procureur-Général v Skype, Correctionele Rechtbanken [Corr]* [Criminal Tribunal] Antwerp, Division Mechelen, Oct 27, 2016, No ME2041 105151-12, 12–15 (Belg).

While these developments are frequently discussed in the literature, comprehensive and systematic analyses are relatively scarce and in need of improvement.[6] This chapter aims to bridge this gap by systematically mapping recent and emerging policy efforts and evaluating their effectiveness in addressing the cross-border data-access problem. These initiatives are heterogeneous and can be analysed from various perspectives. For instance, Westmoreland and Kent have documented some initiatives based on the stakeholders involved, including governments, intergovernmental organisations, private companies, and civil society groups.[7] This chapter, however, adopts a slightly different perspective. Instead of focusing on the actor or combination of actors who put forward the policy initiative, it maps and examines the *approaches* followed to address the cross-border data-access problem. Each approach has specific assumptions about rules that should govern law enforcement access to cloud data, and the connecting factors that should determine enforcement jurisdiction.

Some caveats are in order. First, capturing every policy development in this dynamic field is not possible. While making comparative references to other regions, this chapter focuses on cross-border data-access reform initiatives in Europe, in the US, and at the international level. Second, the initiatives discussed are not mutually exclusive: a single actor may propose multiple approaches, or multiple actors may propose reform initiatives that overlap or complement each other. Third, the objective of this chapter is not to take sides in those approaches, nor to offer an alternative one. Instead, it examines the extent to which each approach reconciles the mutually legitimate but sometimes competing interests, such as sovereignty, security, and privacy. There is no 'one-size-fits-all' solution to the complex jurisdictional and conflicts-of-law challenges in cross-border data access. Each approach has its strengths and weaknesses, depending on specific situations.

3.2. Responses to the Cross-Border Data-Access Problem

Four policy response types can be identified in addressing the challenges of cross-border data access: reformist, unilateralist, internationalist, and nuanced. Reformist responses typically focus on adapting and updating existing legal and regulatory frameworks. Unilateralist strategies involve individual countries imposing their own data-access and transfer regulations, often prioritising national sovereignty

[6] The most comprehensive study thus far is the Global Status Report of the Internet & Jurisdiction, which tries to map Internet jurisdiction-related policy trends, actors, and initiatives. See D Svantesson, 'Internet & Jurisdiction Global Status Report 2019', *Internet & Jurisdiction Policy Network*, available at www.internetjurisdiction.net.

[7] K Westmoreland and G Kent, 'International Law Enforcement Access to User Data: A Survival Guide and Call for Action' (2015) 13 *Canadian Journal of Law and Technology* 226.

and control over data flows. Internationalist approaches emphasise multilateral co-operation through international treaties, agreements, and protocols, aiming to create harmonised global standards and mechanisms for secure and lawful data-sharing across borders. Lastly, nuanced policies provide context-specific solutions that are negotiated among like-minded countries and tailored to respect domestic norms and legal frameworks of each participating country, subject to minimal overarching conditions. The following discussion will explore these four response types in detail, examining their characteristics, advantages, limitations, and implications for the future of cross-border data-access governance.

3.2.1. Reformist Approach

This approach encompasses a range of efforts that focus on improving the effectiveness of *existing* cross-border data-access tools. The reformist perspective posits that the first step in improving cross-border data access in criminal matters while safeguarding fundamental human rights and respecting other countries' sovereignty is to modernise existing co-operation regimes. Most reformist efforts focus on what Woods called 'changes in degree' – enhancing the speed and reliability of law enforcement's cross-jurisdictional data access using current investigative tools.[8] However, this does not exclude the possibility of reformists endorsing new or complementary forms of co-operation ('change-in-kind'). Many initiatives to overhaul the existing cross-border data-access system may coincide with novel alternative approaches. The reformist approach has two aspects: (a) fixing the problem with the MLAT system; and (b) reforming the ad hoc and voluntary regime of direct co-operation between law enforcement authorities and service providers.

3.2.1.1. MLAT Reform

The MLAT system, slow, cumbersome, bureaucratic, and ineffective as it is, remains the primary channel for cross-border legal co-operation in criminal matters, including cybercrime. According to the United Nations Office on Drugs and Crime (UNODC), for instance, more than 70 per cent of the 69 UN Member States who participated in its survey reported that they use MLA requests for cybercrime cases.[9] Consequently, discussions about cross-border data access invariably emphasise the need to resolve the MLAT system's shortcomings. A closer examination of various initiatives reveals that MLAT reforms are taking two forms: practical and legislative. The practical reform aims to make the existing

[8] AK Woods, 'Why Does Microsoft Want a Global Convention on Government Access to Data?' (*Just Security*, 19 February 2014), available at www.justsecurity.org/7246/microsoft-global-convention-government-access-data/.

[9] UNODC, 'Comprehensive Study on Cybercrime' (2013) xxv.

process faster, more efficient, and cost-effective without legislative changes. These short-term solutions can buy time for developing long-term alternatives.

An early notable effort to address the MLAT system's practical issues came from President Obama's 2013 Review Group on Intelligence and Communication Technologies. Established in response to the public outcry following the Snowden revelations, the Review Group suggested streamlining the MLAT process for legitimate international requests.[10] Recognising the reciprocal nature of the MLAT problem, the Review Group noted that if the US fails to provide adequate support to foreign governments seeking electronic data held by US service providers, the US government could probably face similar problems when trying to access data stored outside its territorial jurisdiction. The Review Group then proposed four practical measures of reform: (i) increasing resources for the office that handles MLA requests; (ii) creating an online submission form for MLA requests; (iii) simplifying the process steps; and (iv) streamlining the provision of the records back to the foreign countries.[11] Subsequent efforts by different actors, including by international organisations, have echoed the Review Group's recommendations.[12]

In response, the US government implemented some practical reforms in the Office of International Affairs (OIA), the Department of Justice's central authority for handling MLA requests. A significant step was establishing a new 'Cyber Unit' dedicated to reviewing, analysing, and filing foreign requests for electronic evidence.[13]

Internationally, the UNODC and Interpol have initiated practical reforms. The UNODC, in collaboration with its partners, has launched a *Practical Guide for Requesting Electronic Evidence Across Borders* for investigators and prosecutors around the world.[14] This guide aims to streamline MLA practices and includes country-specific information, service providers' procedures, and guidelines for formal and informal mutual legal assistance co-operation. Interpol have developed an e-MLA system, a technical platform for voluntary use by their 192 member countries when carrying out MLA exchanges.[15] The e-MLA system is a crucial step

[10] RA Clarke and others, 'Liberty and Security in a Changing World: Report and Recommendations of The President's Review Group on Intelligence and Communications Technologies' (2013) 226–29.

[11] ibid.

[12] AK Woods, 'Data Beyond Borders: Mutual Legal Assistance in the Internet Era' (Global Network Initiative, 2015); Kent, 'Sharing Investigation Specific Data' (n 3); 'Reform Government Surveillance (RGS) Coalition', available at www.reformgovernmentsurveillance.com/; G Nojeim, 'MLAT Reform: A Straw Man Proposal' (3 September 2015), available at https://cdt.org/insights/mlat-reform-a-straw-man-proposal/; D Mitnick, 'The Urgent Need for MLAT Reform' (*Access Now*, 12 September 2014), available at www.accessnow.org/the-urgent-needs-for-mlat-reform/.

[13] US Department of Justice Criminal Division, 'Performance Budget FY 2019 Congressional Submission', available at www.justice.gov/doj/fy-2019-congressional-budget-submission.

[14] 'UNODC and Partners Release Practical Guide for Requesting Electronic Evidence Across Borders' (*UNODC*, 1 February 2019), available at www.unodc.org/unodc/en/frontpage/2019/January/unodc-and-partners-release-practical-guide-for-requesting-electronic-evidence-across-boarders.html.

[15] 'INTERPOL E-MLA Initiative', available at www.interpol.int/en/News-and-Events/News/2018/INTERPOL-s-e-MLA-initiative-focus-of-EU-expert-meeting.

to overcome the lack of international and secure networks to exchange requests for data across borders. Similarly, the European Commission has introduced several practical measures to improve MLA processes within the EU and beyond (see chapter five).

The legislative aspect of MLAT reform involves amending existing treaties or introducing new MLA frameworks adapted to the digital environment. The EU has, notably, undertaken perhaps the most successful reform of the MLAT system with a legislative intervention by adopting the European Investigation Order (EIO) Directive, which replaces the traditional frameworks of MLA proceedings between the Member States.[16] Premised on the principle of 'mutual recognition', the EIO Directive requires the judicial authorities of a Member State to recognise and execute investigative measures issued by the judicial authorities of another Member State without the need to check any further formalities, and in the same way, and under the same modalities as if the investigative measure concerned had been ordered by an authority of the executing state.[17]

3.2.1.2. *Reforming Direct Co-operation with Foreign Service Providers*

While national laws in many countries restrict data disclosure to foreign authorities, some countries (like the US and Ireland) permit service providers to co-operate directly with foreign law enforcement authorities for non-content data (eg subscriber information). Consequently, a practice of direct co-operation between law enforcement authorities around the world and US-based service providers, who control a significant amount of the world's data, has become the primary channel for law enforcement authorities to obtain non-content data.[18]

However, this informal and voluntary co-operation is often inefficient and poses significant concerns. The European Commission identified eight shortcomings in the direct co-operation between European authorities and service providers headquartered in third countries. Those shortcomings were: transparency of the process; reliability of stakeholders; accountability of stakeholders; admissibility of evidence; unequal treatment of Member States; reimbursement of service providers' costs; lack of harmonised procedures to indentify and contact the relevant service provider; and lack of harmonised standards to assess authenticity and legitimacy of requests.[19] To address these issues, the Commission outlined three

[16] Directive 2014/41/EU of the European Parliament and of the Council regarding the European Investigation Order in criminal matters (EIO Directive) [2014] OJ L13/1.

[17] ibid, art 9.

[18] European Commission, 'Impact Assessment Accompanying the document Proposal for a Regulation of the European Parliament and of the Council on European Production and Preservation Orders for electronic evidence in criminal matters and Proposal for a Directive of the European Parliament and of the Council laying down harmonised rules on the appointment of legal representatives for the purpose of gathering evidence in criminal proceedings SWD(2018) 118 Final'.

[19] ibid 27.

possible practical reforms: establishing single points of contact within Member States and on the service providers side, and streamlining service providers' policies to reduce the heterogeneity of approaches.[20]

Service providers have also been at the forefront of improving this informal and voluntary process of co-operation. Some of the critical roles that providers play include setting their own requirements for law enforcement requests;[21] establishing teams dedicated to handling global law enforcement requests;[22] streamlining request processes, and publishing periodic transparency reports on government requests;[23] and engaging in, and advocating for, international cross-border data-access reform initiatives.[24]

3.2.2. Unilateralist Approach

The term 'unilateralist approach' refers to the measures governments take to address the challenges of cross-border data access independently, often bypassing existing bilateral, multilateral, or international legal frameworks.[25] It encompasses policies where countries opt to make their own decisions on how to handle foreign-stored data.[26] Despite varying in their methods and substantive details, all unilateral policies aim to ensure law enforcement access to cloud data via domestic procedures.

This approach stems from the difficulties in accessing data stored outside national borders efficiently and effectively, amplified by the growing need for digital evidence. Faced with increasing numbers of criminal investigations requiring electronic evidence, many governments 'feel compelled to act on their own',[27] reflecting their respective jurisdictional leverages and local norms. As the number of criminal investigations that require access to electronic evidence are increasing at an alarming rate, judicial authorities cannot afford to wait for a new

[20] ibid 46–47.

[21] Many service providers have publicly available guidelines for law enforcement authorities, including information about which data sets can be requested, and to which legal entity the data requests should be addressed.

[22] For instance, Microsoft and Google have dedicated teams: Global Criminal Compliance (GCC) and Legal Investigation Support (LIS), respectively.

[23] Pioneered by Google in 2010, it has become a common practice for service providers to issue periodic reports concerning the requests they receive from public authorities and the percentage of requests fulfilled.

[24] B Smith, 'Time for an International Convention' (n 3); Brief for Technology Companies as Amici Curiae in Support of Respondent, *United States v Microsoft* (2017) No 17-2 (2017).

[25] M Tahraoui, 'Unilateralism Ahead? Human Rights, Digital Surveillance and the "Extraterritorial Question" in International Law' (*International Law Blog*, 12 December 2016), available at www.voelkerrechtsblog.org/unilateralism-ahead/.

[26] Brief of Former Law Enforcement, National Security, and Intelligence Officials as Amici Curiae in Support of Neither Party, *United States v Microsoft* (2017) No 17-2 (2017) 8.

[27] B de La Chapelle and P Fehlinger, 'Jurisdiction on the Internet: From Legal Arms Race to Transnational Cooperation' (Global Commission on Internet Governance, Paper Series: No 28, April 2016) 4.

international law to solve the problem,[28] hence the proliferation of unilateralism. Brad Smith, Microsoft's president, observed that, with the ease of cloud computing and data availability, 'the temptation for governments to act unilaterally to seek data in other countries proved irresistible'.[29] Unilateral measures can include forcing technology companies to enable access in encrypted cases, arresting non-compliant service providers' employees, imposing significant fines, seizing assets, or blocking services.[30] Two intuitively appealing legal trends have become particularly pervasive: extraterritorial production orders, and data localisation. While these legal trends differ in scope and design, their ultimate purpose is essentially the same: to ensure that data migrated to the cloud remains under the purview of national enforcement jurisdictions.

3.2.2.1. Extraterritorial Production Orders

The most prevalent unilateral approach to cross-border data access involves compelling the disclosure of user data stored overseas or managed by service providers in foreign jurisdictions. Commonly known as an extraterritorial production order, this method allows governments to unilaterally acquire data held abroad, deviating from traditional mechanism such as the MLAT system. This approach is a direct response to the internationalisation of criminal evidence and the concept of 'loss of location', whereby the physical location of data becomes irrelevant in the digital realm.

This global trend is evidenced by an increasing number of governments adopting or considering unilateral laws that grant law enforcement authorities the power to demand data from service providers located outside their national borders. A comprehensive survey by Hogan Lovells found that nearly all of the 10 countries studied had legal provisions enabling their respective law enforcement authorities to request service providers within their jurisdiction to disclose customer data stored overseas.[31] Furthermore, a study by the UNODC indicated that 50 per cent of European countries have laws that permit unilateral cross-border data access for investigating cybercrime and other criminal activities.[32]

Recent legislative initiatives illustrating this approach include the US CLOUD Act and EU's e-Evidence Regulation, which is applicable to foreign service

[28] Keller, 'Law, Borders, and Speech' (n 1) 27.

[29] B Smith and CA Browne, *Tools and Weapons: The Promise and the Peril of the Digital Age* (Hodder & Stoughton, 2019) 48.

[30] P Swire, 'From Real-Time Intercepts to Stored Records: Why Encryption Drives the Government to Seek Access to the Cloud' (2012) 2 *International Data Privacy Law* 200; Australian Assistance and Access Act 2018; In Brazil, there is a history of court orders demanding that service providers block user access to their applications, and the arrest of local executives of these companies for failing to comply with orders requiring the disclosure of personal data.

[31] W Maxwell and C Wolf, 'A Global Reality: Governmental Access to Data in the Cloud' (A Hogan Lovells White Paper, 2012).

[32] UNODC, 'Comprehensive Study' (n 9) 219; Cybercrime Convention Committee (T-CY), 'Transborder Access to Data and Jurisdiction: Options for Further Action' T-CY (2014) 16.

providers and extends to individuals or data located in third countries.[33] The e-Evidence Regulation empowers law enforcement authorities in any EU Member State to directly order service providers operating within the EU, or those established or represented in another Member State, to produce data regardless of the actual location of the data. Similarly, the CLOUD Act grants American authorities extraterritorial power to compel service providers under US jurisdiction to disclose data stored abroad. These initiatives reflect a growing recognition of the need for a legal framework that accommodates the realities of data storage and access in an increasingly digital and interconnected world. Both instruments are further examined in detail in chapters four and five.

3.2.2.2. Data Localisation

At the other extreme is the global trend to reassert territorial control by erecting borders for data, commonly known as 'data localisation': a policy that mandates that data about a nation's citizens or residents be collected, processed, and stored inside the country. The proliferation of data localisation policies is evident globally, with the tally of nations implementing such mandates escalating from 35 in 2017 to 62 by 2021, nearly a twofold increase.[34]

Data localisation policies come in different forms and shapes, with a wide range of policy objectives, both declared and undeclared. For instance, Cory and Dascoli identified three main forms of data localisation: restrictions by some countries on the transfer of specific types of data, like personal data and financial information; limitations by others on ambiguous categories of data deemed sensitive or critical to national security; and indirect enforcement by several nations through imposing complex and costly data transfer procedures that compel companies to store data locally.[35] The motivations driving data localisation policies also vary. While it is beyond the purview of this book to catalogue all types and policy objectives of data localisation, the primary justifications include preventing foreign surveillance, protecting the privacy of citizens, promoting domestic economic development, asserting digital sovereignty, and facilitating domestic law enforcement access to data for the purpose of criminal investigations.[36]

[33] Regulation (EU) 2023/1543 of the European Parliament and of the Council on European Production Orders and European Preservation Orders for electronic evidence in criminal proceedings and for the execution of custodial sentences following criminal proceedings (e-Evidence Regulation) [2023] OJ L191/118; Clarifying Lawful Overseas Use of Data Act (CLOUD Act) 2018.

[34] N Cory and L Dascoli, 'How Barriers to Cross-Border Data Flows Are Spreading Globally, What They Cost, and How to Address Them' (ITIF, 19 July 2021).

[35] ibid.

[36] For a detailed review of data localisation policies around the world, the different forms of data localisation, and their motivations, see A Chander and UP Lê, 'Data Nationalism' (2015) 64 *Emory Law Journal* 677; JF Hill, 'The Growth of Data Localization Post-Snowden: Analysis and Recommendations for U.S. Policymakers and Industry Leaders' (2014) 2 Lawfare Research Paper Series; J Selby, 'Data Localization Laws: Trade Barriers or Legitimate Responses to Cybersecurity Risks, or Both?' (2017)

Data localisation policies are often attributed to less democratic regimes, such as Russia and China. This is a mischaracterisation. As highlighted above, a growing number of countries – large and small, democratic and authoritarian, developed and developing – have introduced or are considering the introduction of a wide variety of forms of data localisation policies for different purposes.[37] The EU is a good case in point. Some characterise the GDPR as 'the world's greatest de facto localization framework'[38] because of its adequacy scheme that imposes a stringent data transfer requirement, making it difficult for service providers to transfer data outside the Union. Additionally, factors such as the *Schrems II* judgment of the Court of Justice of the European Union (CJEU), which invalidated the EU–US Privacy Shield Framework, the introduction of the CLOUD Act allowing the US government to compel technology companies to disclose data stored overseas, and the EU's desire to assert digital sovereignty have reinforced the increasing calls for data localisation policies in the EU.

From the perspective of law enforcement access, data localisation policies are perceived to serve a dual purpose: *facilitative* and *preventive*. Countries may conceive of data localisation as a facilitative tool, in the sense that it would allow law enforcement authorities to use domestic judicial processes within the imposing country to compel local and foreign service providers to comply with data-access requests. Storing data within a country's borders diminishes the likelihood of foreign service providers denying law enforcement access to that data. For instance, 'boosting law enforcement access to data' was one of the main reasons behind India's 2019 Data Protection Bill, though the strict data localisation requirements have not made it to the final data protection law, adopted in 2023.[39]

The imposing country could also view data localisation as a preventive tool, particularly as a response to extraterritorial foreign law enforcement and surveillance laws. To the extent that data localisation policies could enable the law enforcement authorities within the imposing country to access data using domestic procedures, they could also prevent foreign governments from having such straightforward access. In other words, when data is stored within a country's borders, it is less likely that foreign governments would access that data without the consent of the country where the data is stored.

25 *International Journal of Law and Information Technology* 213; Cory and Dascoli, 'How Barriers to Cross-Border Data Flows Are Spreading Globally' (n 34).

[37] For instance, the European Centre for International Political Economy developed a digital platform restrictiveness index for 64 countries and identified eight categories of restriction: E van der Marel and MF Ferracane, 'Patterns of Trade Restrictiveness in Online Platforms: A First Look' (2019) European Centre for International Political Economy, DTE Working Paper 03.

[38] N Cory, E Dick, and D Castro, 'The Role and Value of Standard Contractual Clauses in the EU-U.S. Digital Trade' (ITIF, 17 December 2020).

[39] Committee of Experts under the Chairmanship of Justice BN Srikrishna, 'A Free and Fair Digital Economy Protecting Privacy, Empowering Indians' (July 2018).

In this regard, the dual purpose of data localisation policies may not be explicit. For instance, while protecting the privacy of citizens is the declared policy objective of data transfer restriction in the EU (preventive), it also enables European law enforcement authorities to get access to data under EU and Member States' laws, and thereby avoid the lengthy process of the MLA system and other inefficient channels.

As opposed to extraterritorial assertion of jurisdiction, data localisation policies are premised on the assumption that the physical location of data determines who should have jurisdiction over that data. These policies could be particularly appealing for governments unable to get swift and easy access to critical evidence needed for entirely domestic criminal investigations. Such situations reinforce the increasing desire of governments to have control over, and access to, data generated by their citizens.[40]

3.2.3. Internationalist Approach

The increasing challenges in cross-border data access have also prompted the emergence of various internationalist initiatives. While internationalist initiatives come in different forms and from different actors, they share at least one commonality: they all suggest that the best avenue to address the cross-border data-access problem is for countries to seek some sort of global framework. In this book, any initiative that advocates for any form of global legal instrument, procedure, or institution (be it anchored in soft law, multilateral treaty, or independent body) to address the cross-border data-access problem is characterised as an internationalist approach. Considering the legal and institutional shortcomings of the current model of international co-operation in criminal matters, internationalist initiatives focus on developing and negotiating international rules or exploring the establishment of new institutional designs that could be tasked with handling cross-border data-access requests globally.

Several legal scholars have suggested that the complex jurisdictional and conflicts-of-law challenges in cross-border data access can only be addressed through new multilateral treaties.[41] However, the most specific and ambitious internationalist initiative comes from technology companies. Mindful of the global outcry in the wake of the Snowden revelations, and worried about the increasing tendency towards unilateral actions to obtain user data across borders, Microsoft has long advocated for an 'international convention on government access to data'

[40] J Hicks, 'Digital Colonialism: Why Some Countries Want to Take Control of Their People's Data from Big Tech' (*The Conversation*, 26 September 2019), available at https://theconversation.com/digital-colonialism-why-some-countries-want-to-take-control-of-their-peoples-data-from-big-tech-123048.

[41] See, for instance, KE Eichensehr, 'Data Exterritoriality' (2017) 95 *Texas Law Review* 145; S Bilgic, 'Something Old, Something New, And Something Moot: The Privacy Crisis Under the CLOUD Act' (2018) 32 *Harvard Journal of Law & Technology* 321; I Brown and others, 'Towards Multilateral Standards for Surveillance Reform' (Oxford Internet Institute Discussion Paper, January 2015).

that would replace or supplement the existing MLA rules.[42] Microsoft's proposal for an international convention focuses on establishing uniform global standards for government access to data. This initiative reflects a private sector perspective, emphasising the need for a balanced approach that reflects both privacy and security.

In a separate call, Microsoft set out six principles to guide global rules on law enforcement access to data: the universal right to notice (with exception); prior independent judicial authorisation requiring a meaningful legal and factual showing; clear legal processes and avenues to challenge demands; mechanisms to resolve conflicts with third-country laws; a modernising of rules for enterprise data control; and transparency for public awareness on government data access.[43] These principles aim to ensure that government data requests respect digital privacy, due process, and international legal boundaries. This is not the first instance of Microsoft leading advocacy for global solutions to Internet policy challenges: the company has also pushed for an international convention on cyber norms in the realm of cybersecurity.[44]

Echoing Microsoft's internationalist vision, the US-based public policy think tank Information Technology and Innovation Foundation (ITIF) have also called for a 'Geneva Convention on the Status of Data'[45] akin to international treaties governing warfare and humanitarian issues. This ambitious initiative aims to resolve jurisdictional issues; establish uniform terminology, safeguards, and corrective measures; enhance accountability and transparency; offer independent oversight; and foster collaboration and understanding among national security agencies, data protection agencies, and the general public.[46] The European Centre for International Political Economy (ECIPE) also advocates for a new international framework along these lines.[47] ECIPE's 'Multilateral Legal Assistance Protocol' envisions an international framework that would, among other aspects, prohibit regulations intended to enforce or result in data localisation.

[42] B Smith, 'Time for an International Convention' (n 3).

[43] B Smith, 'A Call for Principle-Based International Agreements to Govern Law Enforcement Access to Data' (*Microsoft on the Issues*, 11 September 2018), available at https://blogs.microsoft.com/on-the-issues/2018/09/11/a-call-for-principle-based-international-agreements-to-govern-law-enforcement-access-to-data/.

[44] 'The need for a Digital Geneva Convention' (*Microsoft*, 14 February 2017), available at blogs.microsoft.com/on-the-issues/2017/02/14/need-digital-geneva-convention/; For detailed analysis of how Internet companies are taking the lead in international norm-creation in cyberspace, see I Kilovaty, 'Privatized Cybersecurity Law' (2020) 10 *UC Irvine Law Review* 1181.

[45] A McQuinn and D Castro, 'How Law Enforcement Should Access Data Across Borders' (ITIF, 2017).

[46] ibid; The former UN special rapporteur on the right to privacy, Joseph Cannataci, was also quoted suggesting that the world needs a 'Geneva convention-style law' on cross-border data access. See The Information Society Project, 'Extraterritorial Enforcement' (n 1) 17; M Milanovic, 'Human Rights Treaties and Foreign Surveillance: Privacy in the Digital Age' (2015) 56 *Harvard International Law Journal* 81.

[47] H Lee-Makiyama, 'A Multilateral Legal Assistance Protocol: Preventing Fragmentation and Re-Territorialisation of the Internet' (ECIPE Policy Briefs No 09/2013).

At a multilateral level, three significant initiatives stand out: the Council of Europe's Convention on Cybercrime (also known as the Budapest Convention); the OECD Declaration on cross-border data access; and the UN Cybercrime Treaty.

3.2.3.1. The Budapest Convention

The Budapest Convention and its Second Additional Protocol constitute the cornerstone of the international legal framework for addressing cross-border data access in criminal justice proceedings. These instruments shape states' co-operation in combatting cybercrime, regulate transnational access to electronic evidence, and balance digital privacy safeguards with law enforcement needs. Entering into force in 2004, the Budapest Convention was the first binding international treaty on cybercrime. It was designed to standardise substantive and procedural criminal law in relation to cybercrime, and to foster international co-operation. Substantively, the Convention requires signatories to criminalise specific offences and to establish institutional and procedural powers to secure and collect electronic evidence.

The procedural chapters outline measures to be implemented domestically for investigating offences covered by the Convention, as well as other crimes committed using computer systems. Beyond adapting traditional investigative tools such as search and seizure to the digital environment, the Budapest Convention introduces novel measures like expedited data preservation, ensuring that evidence-collection methods remain effective in the digital context.

Cross-border data access – particularly situations where a State Party could unilaterally access data stored in the territory of another State Party – was one of the most controversial issues during the negotiation of the Budapest Convention. The sensitive and contentious nature of the measure is clearly reflected in the Convention's Explanatory Report:

> The issue of when a Party is permitted to unilaterally access computer data stored in another Party without seeking mutual assistance was a question that the drafters of the Convention discussed at length. There was detailed consideration of instances in which it may be acceptable for States to act unilaterally and those in which it may not. The drafters ultimately determined that it was not yet possible to prepare a comprehensive, legally binding regime regulating this area. In part, this was due to a lack of concrete experience with such situations to date; and, in part, this was due to an understanding that the proper solution often turned on the precise circumstances of the individual case, thereby making it difficult to formulate general rules. Ultimately, the drafters decided to only set forth in Article 32 of the Convention situations in which all agreed that unilateral action is permissible. They agreed not to regulate other situations until such time as further experience has been gathered and further discussions may be held in light thereof. In this regard, Article 39, paragraph 3 provides that other situations are neither authorised, nor precluded.[48]

[48] Explanatory Report to the Convention on Cybercrime, para 293.

Article 32 represents an exception to the principle of territoriality, delineating scenarios under which a State Party may unilaterally access computer data stored in another party's territory without resorting to mutual legal assistance. It permits unilateral transborder access under limited circumstances. This provision allows law enforcement authorities in one State Party to access stored computer data located in another State Party without mutual legal assistance, provided that data is publicly accessible or the person with lawful authority over the data consents to provide access. It attempts to reconcile cross-border data access in criminal investigations with respect for sovereignty. However, although Article 32 applies to all data types, its practical utility is limited and its scope debated. Article 32(a) permits access to publicly available data irrespective of its geographic location – such as accessing content data on a public website hosted overseas – without requiring foreign authorisation. This provision offers limited operational utility, as critical evidence is seldom publicly accessible. The cross-border data-access problem arises only when data is not openly available.

Article 32(b) governs this situation, and allows law enforcement authorities to access data located abroad if the person with lawful authority voluntarily consents to such access. Yet, this is similarly constrained and contested. The specific identity of the party whose consent is required and 'lawfully authorised' remains unclear.[49] The Explanatory Report provides that Article 32(b) applies both to a physical individual person and a service provider. The Cybercrime Convention Committee's *Guidance Note on Transborder Access* (Guidance Note 3) also cites typical instances where Article 32(b) may apply, such as when an individual user voluntarily shares email stored overseas with authorities or consents to accessing data on a seized device.[50] However, such scenarios are rare in practice: for example, it is unlikely that a suspect would willingly give consent to law enforcement access.

Whether service providers qualify as having 'lawful authority' within the meaning of Article 32(b) to consent to data disclosure also remains controversial. Guidance Note 3 highlights that user acceptance of terms of service typically does not constitute explicit consent for sharing data with law enforcement authorities. Specifically, Guidance Note 3 states that 'service providers are unlikely to be able to consent validly and voluntarily to disclosure of their users' data under Article 32(b)' because they typically only hold the data rather than controlling or owning it.[51] Furthermore, domestic data protection laws and other blocking statutes often prohibit or restrict service providers from directly disclosing data to foreign authorities. Consequently, data disclosures by service providers may be unlawful under Article 32(b).

[49] C Ryngaert, 'Extraterritorial Enforcement Jurisdiction in Cyberspace: Normative Shifts' (2023) 24 *German Law Journal* 537.

[50] Cybercrime Convention Committee (T-CY) Guidance Note # 3 'Transborder access to data (Article 32)', 3 December 2014.

[51] ibid.

Moreover, this provision applies only if the location of data is known and is 'located in another State Party' – a requirement that has become increasingly unrealistic in the cloud era, where data locations are often unknown or fluid.[52] Article 32(b) does not apply when the data is outside the territory of another State Party (such as in jurisdictions not party to the Budapest Convention) or when the location of data is uncertain. Notably, the provision is silent on the location of the service provider, although scenarios involving service providers located either in another party or in a non-signatory country are common. Therefore, the practical effectiveness of Article 32(b) in addressing the cross-border data-access problem is severely limited due to these jurisdictional and technical constraints.

Article 18 is another key provision that establishes two domestic investigative measures with extraterritorial effects. Specifically, Article 18(1) obliges each party to adopt legislative and other measures empowering its competent authorities to order:

a. a person in its territory to submit specified computer data in that person's possession or control, which is stored in a computer system or a computer-data storage medium; and
b. a service provider offering its services in the territory of the Party to submit subscriber information relating to such services in that service provider's possession or control.

According to the Cybercrime Convention Committee's 2017 *Guidance Note on Production Orders* (Guidance Note 10), the addressee ('person') in paragraph 1(a) covers both a natural persons and service providers. Three key cumulative requirements must be met for this paragraph to apply. First, the individual person or the service provider must be physically present in the territory of the party issuing the production order. This means that the addressee subject to the order must either reside or be located or established within the issuing state's jurisdiction. Second, the production order may cover all types of computer data, including content data, traffic data, and subscriber information. Third, the addressee must have possession or control over the data. The phrase 'possession or control' in both paragraphs 1(a) and 1(b) includes not only physical custody but also data stored remotely yet accessible under legitimate control.[53] The Explanatory Report clarifies that paragraph 1(a) extends to cases where data is outside the person's physical possession but can be freely controlled and produced from within the ordering party's territory. A typical example is an individual who receives a production order requiring them to produce information stored in their account via a remote online storage service, even though the data is not physically in their possession but can be accessed and controlled remotely from within the ordering party's territory.

[52] ibid.
[53] Explanatory Report (n 48), para 173.

Article 18(1)(b) addresses service providers that may not have a physical presence within the territory of the ordering party but are offering their services there. This paragraph differs from Article 18(1)(a) in three key aspects. First, it exclusively applies to service providers. Second, it establishes the legal basis for jurisdiction over service providers offering services within the party's territory, regardless of where the data is stored. This mandate enables a direct co-operation mechanism with service providers that bypass traditional MLA procedures, addressing the challenges posed by cross-border data movement and uncertain data locations. Guidance Note 10 clarifies that the service provider subject to a production order need not be physically present in, but must offer services in, the issuing party's territory. This situation often arises when a service provider headquartered in one jurisdiction stores data in another. Parties may thus apply this provision even if the service provider is neither legally nor physically present in the issuing party. Third, the scope of Article 18(1)(b) is limited to subscriber information: a category of data that is less intrusive than content or traffic data but is nevertheless the most frequently sought data in cybercrime investigations.

Nevertheless, Article 18(1)(b) remains closely linked to the concept of territoriality. Even if a service provider is established outside the jurisdiction of the issuing party and the requested data is stored abroad, the service provider must still be present in that jurisdiction by virtue of offering its services there. As analysed in chapter two, in relation to *Yahoo! Belgium*, a service provider need not have a physical presence in the issuing country, but must maintain an economic presence by making its services available to residents of that country. The underlying principle is that, by accessing the market and deriving benefits from the issuing country, the service provider is subject to that country's laws, regardless of its physical location or the location where subscriber data is stored. Without this territorial connection (ie offering a service within the territory), Article 18(1)(b) does not apply, and thus does not create a legal basis for competent authorities in one State Party to issue production orders to service providers that are not active in that State Party's jurisdiction.

Beyond the measures to be taken at the national level, the Budapest Convention also establishes a comprehensive framework for international co-operation (Articles 23 to 31), aimed at enabling assistance where no bilateral or multilateral treaties exist. Chapter III of the Convention provides legal and practical tools to overcome jurisdictional and procedural hurdles commonly faced in cross-border data access. Article 27 explicitly prescribes reliance on the Convention itself as an autonomous legal basis for mutual assistance requests, circumventing dependency on traditional MLA treaties.

Despite this robust framework, the Budapest Convention alone cannot meet the evolving demands for cross-border data access. Its reliance on MLA-based procedures clashes with the realities of cloud computing, where digital evidence is often fragmented, shifting, and stored across borders – or even in unknown jurisdictions. Article 32 is severely limited due to these jurisdictional and technical constraints. While Article 18 provides foundational authority for direct engagement with foreign service providers, significant legal uncertainties and territorial limitations persist, particularly concerning providers without territorial service offerings. These challenges underscored the need for enhanced mechanisms, prompting the Cybercrime Convention Committee (T-CY) to initiate negotiations of a Second Additional Protocol, in 2017.[54] After over four years of deliberation, the Protocol was adopted in May 2022.[55]

The Additional Protocol's primary objective is to establish a legal foundation for direct co-operation between law enforcement authorities and service providers in other jurisdictions. It highlights the necessity for improved co-operation between states and the private sector, and emphasises enhanced clarity and legal certainty for service providers responding directly to foreign criminal justice requests. The Additional Protocol introduces several new measures that clarify and expand international co-operation on cross-border data access. Its key legal innovations are summarised in the following paragraphs.

Article 6 of the Protocol obliges States Parties to introduce legislative and other measures empowering their competent authorities to request information from domain name registrars in other signatory countries, to identify or contact domain name registrants. Under Article 7, competent authorities may directly order service providers in other Parties to disclose specific subscriber information necessary for criminal proceedings, bypassing traditional MLA processes. The production order applies only to subscriber information (rather than content or traffic data), ensuring that the measure remains proportionate and less intrusive. Article 7 represents a significant expansion of Article 18(1)(b) of the Budapest Convention. Unlike the Convention, which restricts a production order of subscriber information to service providers present in the territory of the issuing party by virtue of offering services there, Article 7 is not tied to such a territorial requirement.

While Article 18(1)(b) of the Convention is often interpreted to apply to foreign service providers, so long as they offer their services in the issuing party, the Convention fails to address the potential conflicting legal obligations in such scenarios. The Protocol resolves this uncertainty by requiring each State Party to introduce legislative measures allowing service providers in its territory to directly respond to production orders issued by competent authorities in another party. This reciprocal responsibility would require a State Party to remove any blocking statutes, clarifying that the duty to disclose subscriber information rests on a clear legislative basis within the provider's host state, thereby resolving any potential conflicts of law and ensuring that service providers are not left in legal ambiguity when responding to foreign production orders. Article 7 also provides detailed safeguards and transparency requirements. For example, a party may declare that

[54] The Convention was already supplemented by the Additional Protocol concerning the criminalisation of acts of a racist and xenophobic nature committed through computer systems (ETS No 189).

[55] Second Additional Protocol to the Convention on Cybercrime on enhanced cooperation and disclosure of electronic evidence (Second Additional Protocol), CETS No 224.

production orders for subscriber information must be issued or supervised by an independent body, ensuring proper oversight in the issuing party.

Furthermore, the Protocol specifies that every production order must contain certain mandatory elements to ensure transparency and legal certainty. These elements include identification of the issuing authority and the date the order was issued, establishing the legitimate origin and timing of the request. It must also state the legal basis for the order, confirming that the request complies with applicable laws. The specific service provider to be served must be named, along with its address. The order must describe the offences under investigation, clarifying the relevance of the data request. Moreover, it must include a detailed description of the exact subscriber information sought, preventing overly broad or vague demands.[56] In addition to these core details, the order must be accompanied by supplemental information to facilitate proper execution. This includes citing the domestic legal grounds that empower the issuing authority and referencing the legal provisions and penalties relevant to the offence. Contact details must be provided, so that the service provider knows where data is to be returned to or further instructions requested from. At the time of signature of the Protocol, Parties can require simultaneous notification when an order targets service providers within their territory, allowing them to intervene if disclosures might prejudice ongoing proceedings or violate grounds for refusal under the Convention.

If a service provider does not comply in time with a production order under Article 7, the Protocol establishes an enforcement mechanism by requiring authorities in the provider's jurisdiction to issue an enforcement order to compel disclosure. Article 9 establishes a framework for the expedited disclosure of stored computer data, including content data, in emergency situations, without the need for a formal MLA request. It requires each party to have a 24/7 network point of contact capable of quickly transmitting and receiving requests for immediate assistance from its counterparts in other Parties. The objective is to obtain specific stored data swiftly, particularly when there is an emergency involving a significant and imminent risk to a person's life or safety. The emergency framework balances the need for urgent access to critical data with procedural safeguards and security measures.

Article 13 reiterates that law enforcement powers and procedures under the Protocol are subject to the conditions and safeguards provided under domestic law to guarantee adequate protection of human rights and liberties. However, the Additional Protocol and the Convention leave substantial discretion to the Parties on what constitutes 'adequate' protection, risking fragmented standards and potential loopholes, depending largely on national legislation. This is particularly concerning because both instruments are open to accession by any country, which risks allowing states with inadequate human rights protections, lacking judicial independence and meaningful oversight mechanisms, to join.

[56] ibid, art 7.

Article 14 of the Protocol establishes detailed and comprehensive data protection rules, absent in the Convention itself. It enshrines key data protection principles, such as lawfulness, fairness, transparency, purpose limitation, data minimisation, accuracy, storage limitation, and integrity and confidentiality. Importantly, it requires that personal data obtained under the Protocol be processed only for specified criminal justice purposes, prohibiting incompatible or excessive use. The Article also imposes restrictions on the processing of sensitive data, automated decision-making, and retention periods. It mandates judicial or independent oversight and provides rights to judicial and administrative remedies for data subjects. However, despite its comprehensive scope, the safeguards and protections are vulnerable to circumvention through bilateral agreements and exceptions where Parties are bound by international data protection frameworks or informal agreements that may allow data transfers without equivalent safeguards. Additionally, the Protocol relies heavily on mutual trust and voluntary supervision to ensure compliance, lacking strong enforcement mechanisms. Oversight and remedies depend greatly on domestic legislation, which varies widely across Parties.

3.2.3.2. *The UN Convention on Cybercrime*

The adoption of the UN Convention on Cybercrime (UNCC) in December 2024, and its signing by more than 60 states in October 2025 in Hanoi, represents another milestone in the quest for global cybercrime governance.[57] International co-operation on cybercrime has long been recognised as essential, given the inherently cross-border nature of cyber offences. However, the pathway to the Convention's adoption was hindered by profound geopolitical divisions, reflecting discord over Internet governance, state sovereignty in cyberspace, and human rights.[58] The negotiation process began with the Russian Federation presenting a draft for a UN-based cybercrime treaty in 2017.[59] This initiative gained traction with the submission of a corresponding resolution in 2019 by Russia and allied states, leading to the establishment of an ad hoc committee, open to all Member States and non-Member State observers, to steer the process and draft the Convention. The resolution was institutionalised by the UN General Assembly despite vigorous opposition from Western countries, particularly the US and EU.[60]

[57] United Nations Convention against Cybercrime; Strengthening International Cooperation for Combating Certain Crimes Committed by Means of Information and Communications Technology Systems and for the Sharing of Evidence in Electronic Form of Serious Crimes 2024; V Mishra, 'Sixty-five nations sign first UN treaty to fight cybercrime, in milestone for digital cooperation' (*UN News*, 25 October 2025), available at news.un.org/en/story/2025/10/1166182.

[58] L Novo, 'The UN finally advances a convention on cybercrime … and no one is happy about it' (*Atlantic Council*, 14 August 2024), available at www.atlanticcouncil.org/blogs/new-atlanticist/the-un-finally-adopts-a-convention-on-cybercrime-and-no-one-is-happy/.

[59] Letter dated 11 October 2017 from the Permanent Representative of the Russian Federation to the United Nations addressed to the Secretary-General, A/C.3/72/12.

[60] Resolution adopted by the General Assembly on 27 December 2019, A/RES/74/247.

These contested discussions unfolded against the backdrop of a polarised international environment, evidenced by the failure of the 2016–17 UN Group of Governmental Experts (GGE) to produce a consensus on state norms of responsible behaviour in cyberspace.[61] The subsequent creation of parallel forums, such as the Open-ended Working Group (OEWG), underscored persistent divergence and fragmented multilateralism on cyber issues.[62] This context shaped the contentious and protracted negotiation process that culminated in the UNCC's adoption in late 2024. It will take 40 ratifications to bring the Convention into effect.

The negotiation crystallised two distinct camps competing over foundational visions of the Internet's future, the balance between state control and individual rights, and the role of multilateral institutions. Western liberal countries, including the EU and US and their allies, adhered to the Budapest Convention as the global standard for cybercrime regulation and cross-border data access. They viewed the Budapest Convention as embodying principles of an open, global Internet governed by rule of law and human rights protections. Instead of negotiating a new treaty under the UN auspices, these nations advocated for the universal adoption of the Budapest Convention. For example, the European Parliament, in a 2017 resolution, urged its Member States to promote the Budapest Convention in the appropriate international forums.[63] Similarly, the European Commission had long expressed a preference for the Budapest Convention over a new UN treaty.[64] They also challenged the normative and political premises underpinning the UNCC initiative. They perceived the initiative as an effort by Russia to establish a competing treaty that reflects authoritarian conceptions of 'cyber sovereignty' aimed at state control over digital spaces and suppression of dissent. Western opposition was grounded in concerns that the UN process was being instrumentalised as a geopolitical battleground rather than a genuine effort towards effective cybercrime governance.[65]

In counterpoint, Russia, China, and over 40 supporting states, including several African countries and India, sought a UN-based treaty as a means to create a more inclusive and representative global legal architecture. They criticised the Budapest Convention for Western-centrism, limited membership, and perceived disregard

[61] M Markoff, 'Explanation of Position at the Conclusion of the 2016–2017 UN Group of Governmental Experts (GGE) on Developments in the Field of Information and Telecommunications in the Context of International Security' (*United States Mission to the United Nations*, 23June2017),availableathttps://2017-2021.state.gov/explanation-of-position-at-the-conclusion-of-the-2016-2017-un-group-of-governmental-experts-gge-on-developments-in-the-field-of-information-and-telecommunications-in-the-context-of-international-sec/.

[62] GIP Digital Watch Observatory for Internet Governance and Digital Policy, 'At a Glance: UN GGE and OEWG', available at www.dig.watch/processes/un-gge.

[63] European Parliament Resolution of 3 October 2017 on the Fight Against Cybercrime (2017/2068(INI)), available at www.europarl.europa.eu/doceo/document/TA-8-2017-0366_EN.pdf.

[64] European Commission, 'Impact Assessment' (n 18) 239.

[65] K Bannelier, 'The U.N. Cybercrime Convention Should Not Become a Tool for Political Control or the Watering Down of Human Rights' (*Lawfare*, 31 January 2023), available at www.lawfaremedia.org/article/the-u.n.-cybercrime-convention-should-not-become-a-tool-for-political-control-or-the-watering-down-of-human-rights.

for the sovereignty and developmental priorities of Global South countries.[66] Their vision emphasised a sovereign-controlled Internet model, rejecting foreign interference under the principle of non-intervention and advocating broader criminalisation scopes addressing diverse cyber-enabled offences.

Despite the complex and polarised negotiation process, the UNCC was adopted by consensus and hailed as a 'landmark treaty' for cybercrime governance. It establishes a binding global criminal justice policy to protect society against cybercrime by fostering international co-operation. The Convention articulates four broad objectives: (a) criminalisation and establishing jurisdiction of certain cyber offences; (b) establishing procedural measures; (c) promoting, facilitating, and strengthening of international co-operation; and (d) providing technical assistance and capacity-building for developing countries (Article 1). To this end, the Convention encompasses substantive cybercrime offences, procedural tools, and international co-operation modalities including the sharing of digital evidence, designed to address the complex challenges of cybercrime.

The most consequential and controversial areas of the Convention concern jurisdiction, sovereignty, procedural measures and law enforcement co-operation, and human rights safeguards. The Convention acknowledges state sovereignty as a core principle, enshrined explicitly in Article 5, which requires States Parties to implement obligations under the Convention consistent with sovereign equality, territorial integrity, and non-intervention. It prohibits states from exercising jurisdiction or performing functions reserved for another state's authorities within that other state's territory without consent. Building on this principle, the Convention outlines flexible but territorially grounded rules that enable states to assert jurisdiction over offences committed domestically, against nationals abroad, or targeting the state itself.

Importantly, the Convention establishes procedural powers and law enforcement measures adapted for the digital environment. These measures mirror those in the Budapest Convention and include expedited preservation of data, production orders, and search and seizure of electronic evidence. Article 27, mirroring Article 18 of the Budapest Convention, empowers domestic authorities to order service providers offering services within the state's territory to produce *subscriber information* relating to such services when required for criminal investigation. However, similarly to the Budapest Convention, Article 27 does not explicitly authorise unilateral direct co-operation or extraterritorial cross-border data access. The provision is tied to the principle of territoriality and sovereignty, as the service provider must have a presence within the jurisdiction by virtue of offering services there. Therefore, Article 27 must be read in conjunction with the Convention's sovereignty principles (Article 5), which affirm that enforcement powers are fundamentally territorial.

[66] G Priyandita and B Hogeveen, 'The UN cybercrime convention: a victory for state sovereignty' (*The Strategist*, 16 August 2024), available at www.aspistrategist.org.au/the-un-cybercrime-convention-a-victory-for-state-sovereignty/.

3.2.3.3. *International Soft Law Instruments*

International soft laws could play an essential role in shaping cross-border data-access rules. In this regard, three statements of principle – the Global Privacy Assembly (GPA) Resolution on Government Access to Data (2021), the Organisation for Economic Co-operation and Development (OECD) Declaration on Government Access to Personal Data Held by Private Sector Entities (2022), and the International Chamber of Commerce (ICC) White Paper on Trusted Government Access to Data (2022) – can be considered foundational for legitimate, responsible, and rights-respecting government access to data across borders.[67] The convergence towards key principles demonstrated in these documents reflects common positions shared among governments, businesses, and data protection authorities.

In particular, the OECD has been instrumental in setting international standards for data protection, privacy, and the broader digital economy. Its 1980 Privacy Guidelines – a pivotal global instrument – have shaped many national laws, and its recent Principles on Artificial Intelligence have been incorporated into the EU's AI Act. The December 2022 Declaration on Government Access to Personal Data Held by Private Sector Entities could similarly influence common cross-border data-access norms.[68] The Declaration is regarded as a significant achievement, given its international political weight and the high level of consistency in data-access safeguards employed by governments in developed countries.[69] It recognises that OECD countries uphold shared norms and safeguards regarding government access to personal data held by private sector entities, summarising these in a set of principles. The Declaration outlines the following seven principles:

(a) Government access to individual data must be provided for and regulated by a legal framework that sets out purposes, conditions, limitations, and safeguards for such access (legal basis).
(b) Government access to individual data must be necessary and proportionate to achieve a legitimate purpose (legitimate aim).
(c) Government access to individual data must be subject to prior approval by independent authority (approval).
(d) Personal data acquired through government access must be processed and handled only by authorised personnel (data handling).

[67] Global Privacy Assembly, Resolution on Government Access to Data, Privacy and the Rule of Law: Principles for Governmental Access to Personal Data held by the Private Sector for National Security and Public Safety Purposes, October 2021; ICC White Paper on Trusted Government Access to Personal Data Held by the Private Sector, 22 August 2022.

[68] OECD, Declaration on Government Access to Personal Data Held by Private Sector Entities (n 4).

[69] K Propp, 'Gentlemen's Rules for Reading Each Other's Mail: The New OECD Principles on Government Access to Personal Data Held by Private Sector Entities' (*Lawfare*, 10 January 2023), available at www.lawfaremedia.org/article/gentlemens-rules-reading-each-others-mail-new-oecd-principles-government-access-personal-data-held.

(e) Transparency mechanisms regarding government access to personal data should be put in place, including public reporting by oversight bodies and procedures to request access to government records (transparency).
(f) Mechanisms must exist for effective and impartial oversight to ensure that government access complies with the legal framework (oversight).
(g) The legal framework must provide individuals with effective judicial and non-judicial redress to identify and remedy violations of the national legal framework (redress).

These principles are articulated drawing upon the existing laws and practices of OECD members, and apply when government access to data is undertaken within the governments' respective territories. At first glance, the phrase 'within their respective territories' appears to limit investigative measures to domestic operations, thereby excluding actions in foreign jurisdictions. However, the text does not exclude the possibility of extraterritorial production orders for data. Indeed, the Declaration expressly clarifies that its principles extend to 'situations where countries have the authority under their national legal framework to mandate that private sector entities provide data to the government when the private sector entity or data are not located within their territory'. This inclusion reflects contemporary legal developments, as evidenced by instruments such as the CLOUD Act and e-Evidence Regulation.

The GPA resolution and ICC White Paper also articulate consistent themes, demonstrating an emerging convergence towards key principles. For instance, the GPA resolution foregrounds the rule of law, requiring a clear legal basis and authorisation for government access to private- held data. It also prescribes protection of human rights, respect for privacy and data protection, and meaningful safeguards such as ex ante and ex post oversight mechanisms. Similarly, the ICC White Paper, while expressly endorsing the OECD framework, elaborates additional principles, including the resolution of conflicts of law. Recognising that government requests for access to data held by a private company in another jurisdiction might pose conflicts of law that are difficult to navigate, the ICC calls for the establishment of frameworks through which such conflicts or inconsistencies can be raised and resolved.

3.2.3.4. New Institutional Design for Cross-Border Data Access?

In their 2016 report, the Internet & Jurisdiction Policy Network founders, Bertrand de La Chapelle and Paul Fehlinger, highlighted an 'institutional gap' in the existing model of international legal co-operation on the Internet.[70] Similarly, the former UN special rapporteur on the right to privacy, Joseph Cannataci, in his 2017 report, criticised the Budapest Convention for not creating a mechanism like an

[70] de La Chapelle and Fehlinger, 'Jurisdiction on the Internet' (n 27).

international body with the authority to authorise international data access.[71] A survey by the Internet & Jurisdiction Policy Network revealed this gap, with only 15 per cent of over 150 respondents believing in the adequacy of existing institutions to address the cross-border legal challenges on the Internet.[72]

Efforts to address this institutional gap include the UN special rapporteur's 2018 proposal of an international legal instrument, introducing a human rights perspective to the cross-border data-access conversation and advocating for safeguards against government surveillance overreach.[73] This proposal included drafting a 'blueprint' for future legal frameworks, detailing rules for electronic surveillance and cross-border data access, and, uniquely, suggesting an International Data Access Authority. This authority would be responsible for issuing an International Data Access Warrant, enforceable in participating countries, and balancing law enforcement needs and privacy protection.[74] Similarly, the Global Network Initiative (GNI) commissioned a report proposing a comparable institutional arrangement, an 'Independent Clearinghouse', to manage cross-jurisdictional data-access requests.[75] However, this report lacks specifics on the clearing-house's structure and operational procedures, and it is unclear whether it would be anchored in an international agreement.

Despite these proposals, no concrete multilateral initiative has adopted such institutional arrangements. The Budapest Convention, the OECD Declaration, and the UNCC lack specific institutional mechanisms for implementation. While the UNCC establishes a Conference of the States Parties to improve co-operation,[76] it does not create an authority for authorising and overseeing cross-border data-access requests, as envisaged by the UN Special Rapporteur and GNI.

3.2.4. A Nuanced Approach to Cross-Border Data Access

A nuanced approach is emerging alongside the policy initiatives previously discussed, representing a new generation of cross-border data-access regimes. This approach attempts to realistically address the jurisdictional and conflicts-of-law issues associated with cloud data through bilateral data-sharing agreements based on the principle of reciprocity, the rule of law, and privacy protection. It involves reciprocal cross-border data-access agreements between like-minded countries, allowing law enforcement authorities in each participating country to

[71] 'Report of the Special Rapporteur on the Right to Privacy, Joseph A. Cannataci' (2017) A/HRC/34/60 para 46c.

[72] Svantesson, 'Internet & Jurisdiction Global Status Report' (n 6) 33.

[73] UN Special Rapporteur on the right to privacy, 'Working Draft Legal Instrument on Government-Led Surveillance and Privacy' (2018).

[74] ibid, art 16.

[75] Woods, 'Data Beyond Borders' (n 12); see also M Hohmann and S Barnett, 'Improving Cross-Border Access to Electronic Evidence' (Global Public Policy Institute, Policy Brief January 2019).

[76] Art 57, A/AC.291/22/Rev.1.

compel or request data from service providers in other participating countries, subject to specific conditions and safeguards.

The emerging frameworks are nuanced in the sense that each agreement would be tailored to each participating country, grounded in baseline requirements. Unlike unrestrained unilateral assertion of extraterritorial jurisdiction, production orders under this nuanced approach can only be served on service providers located in a country with a cross-border data-access agreement, targeting data of nationals or legal residents of the investigating country. Participating governments are allowed to utilise domestic legal processes to compel service providers within their jurisdiction to produce electronic evidence within the providers' possession, custody, or control, irrespective of where the providers might choose to store that data. This approach differs from the MLAT system in four key aspects:

(a) It shifts the focus from the data's location to the target person's location and nationality.
(b) It contrasts with the MLAT system, which de facto imposes the law of the recipient country, by allowing data disclosure to be governed by the issuing/requesting country's legal standards and the specific data-sharing agreement.
(c) It eliminates the need for intervention by authorities in the receiving country, reassigning the responsibility to verify government requests' legality to the issuing/requesting country.
(d) It assigns new roles to service providers to receive, assess, and respond to foreign law enforcement requests.

The new framework introduced under the CLOUD Act exemplifies this nuanced approach. It lifts the blocking provisions for 'qualified' foreign governments, creating a foundation for a new generation of agreements.[77] It aims to address the challenges that law enforcement authorities around the world are facing when investigating criminal activities involving data held by US service providers. Once an executive agreement is in place, qualified foreign governments can order data production directly from US service providers without going through the MLA process. The CLOUD Act also allows service providers to challenge government requests under strict procedures. The first agreement under this framework, between the US and the UK, was signed in 2019, enabled by the UK's Crime (Overseas Production Orders) Act 2019. A similar agreement was signed between the US and Australia in 2021, while other jurisdictions, including the EU and Canada, are currently engaging with the US to negotiate similar arrangements. The subsequent chapters will explore these initiatives in more detail.

[77] B Smith, 'The CLOUD Act Is an Important Step Forward, but Now More Steps Need to Follow' (*Microsoft on the Issues*, 3 April 2018), available at https://blogs.microsoft.com/on-the-issues/2018/04/03/the-cloud-act-is-an-important-step-forward-but-now-more-steps-need-to-follow/; Clarifying Lawful Overseas Use of Data (CLOUD) Act 1625, 115th Cong. div. V (2018) s 102 (1)–(6); see also PM Schwartz, 'Legal Access to the Global Cloud' (2018) 118 *Columbia Law Review* 1681, 1742.

3.3. A Critical Appraisal of the Policy Responses

Addressing the cross-border data-access problem requires reconciling multiple potentially conflicting interests. According to the European Commission, the challenges in cross-border data access affect society in general, victims, suspects in criminal investigations, users of services offered by service providers, service providers, and public authorities.[78] In addressing these interests, four overarching principles have become pervasive in academic and policy discussions.[79] Accordingly, the following foundational principles should underpin any initiative aimed at addressing the cross-border data-access problem and serve as criteria for evaluating its efficacy.

Provide effective and efficient access to cross-border data: As discussed in previous chapters, the inability to get timely access to electronic evidence held by foreign service providers for a legitimate law enforcement purpose poses significant risks for public safety and security and the rule of law. Given the rising need for electronic evidence, cross-border data-access frameworks should enable competent public authorities to have the necessary tools to access such evidence effectively and in a timely manner.

Safeguard human rights and due process: Cross-border data access by law enforcement authorities poses a significant threat to fundamental rights and freedoms, including the privacy and data protection rights. Any framework governing law enforcement access to personal data held by service providers must embed adequate human rights and due process standards to prevent potential abuse of power and unjustifiable intrusions into individual rights and freedoms. Such a framework should enshrine safeguards ensuring that law enforcement access is legally grounded, necessary, and proportionate, subject to independent authorisation and oversight, transparent in practice, and accompanied by effective redress mechanisms.

Address conflicts of laws: Multinational service providers and the data that they control often fall under the jurisdiction of multiple countries' laws, making conflicting legal obligations inevitable. The laws of one country may require the disclosure of specific data which, at the same time, is prohibited by the laws of another country. Cross-border data-access frameworks must provide mechanisms to mitigate and resolve potential conflicts of law for service providers.

Respect sovereignty: The increasing disregard for the existing system of international legal co-operation and the increasing trend in unilateral cross-border

[78] P Swire and J Hemmings, 'Stakeholders in Reform of the Global System for Mutual Legal Assistance' in FH Cate and JX Dempsey (eds), *Bulk Collection: Systematic Government Access to Private-Sector Data* (Oxford University Press, 2017) 395–407.

[79] See, for instance, Smith, 'A Call for Principle-Based International Agreements' (n 43); 'Working Draft Legal Instrument' (n 73); Internet & Jurisdiction Policy Network, 'Framing Access to User Data Across Jurisdictions' (12 May 2017); Woods, 'Data Beyond Borders' (n 12); European Commission, 'Impact Assessment' (n 18).

data-access powers could be viewed as intrusions into the territorial and digital sovereignty of other countries. As the US Deputy Assistant Attorney General put it, 'even as so many countries reach *out* beyond their borders for evidence vital to their criminal investigations, they also, perhaps instinctively, are wary when other countries reach into their jurisdictions'.[80] Therefore, cross-border data-access frameworks should recognise and respect the sovereignty of the countries involved.

These principles collectively provide a common language to establish comprehensive frameworks for addressing cross-border data-access challenges, encompassing efficient access to law enforcement, human rights protection, conflict resolution, and respect for sovereignty. Each principle contributes to a balanced and responsible approach to navigating the complexities of the cross-border data-access issues. Below is a comparative analysis of the emerging cross-border data-access policies against these principles.

3.3.1. Reforming Existing Cross-Border Data-Access Tools is Necessary but Insufficient

The MLAT system was developed precisely to mitigate conflicts of law and reconcile competing interests that could unfold due to the jurisdictional limits of law enforcement and criminal investigations involving cross-border elements. A key aspect of its design was the respect for the sovereignty of the countries involved, embedding procedures and safeguards to uphold the fundamental rights of individuals in these processes. MLA procedures, therefore, ensure that the appropriate authorities are involved, and that requisite safeguards are considered in both the requesting and receiving countries.[81]

Given these functionalities, many commentators concur that updating the MLAT system is essential in addressing the challenges of cross-border data access. This consensus leads to critical inquiries: what extent of reform is necessary for the MLAT system to effectively manage the growing demands for cross-border data access? Can MLAT reform adequately tackle the 'loss of location' problem and the difficulties governments encounter in accessing cross-border data, especially when such data pertains to their nationals and is crucial for investigation of purely local crimes? The answer to these questions predominantly relies on the structural design of the MLAT system. Viewing MLAT issues as purely administrative and procedural issues leads to suggestions like procedural streamlining, digitalisation, stakeholders' training, and resource augmentation. In this respect, the practical and legislative initiatives, as discussed previously, are steps in the right direction.

[80] Remarks of Deputy Assistant Attorney General Richard W. Downing at the International Symposium on Cybercrime Response (13 September 2023), available at www.justice.gov/criminal/cloud-act-resources.

[81] Swire and Hemmings, 'Mutual Legal Assistance in an Era of Globalized Communications' (n 3).

However, the problem with the MLAT system transcends these administrative and procedural aspects. A perfectly functioning MLAT system might still struggle with the scalability and speed required to keep up with the rapidly increasing cross-border data-access demands. A more critical issue is the structural design of the system. The MLAT system operates on the assumption that law enforcement authorities always know where the required evidence is located. This assumption becomes problematic as certain cloud computing architectures make the physical location of data, and consequently its normative significance, irrelevant.[82] This situation challenges the law enforcement authorities' ability to determine which foreign authorities to approach with MLA requests. Hence, focusing solely on procedural and administrative aspects of the MLAT system results in a process that is not only cumbersome and inefficient but also, at times, of no practical relevance. This makes the reformist approach inherently incomplete.

Another aspect of the reformist approach that requires attention is the informal and voluntary co-operation between public authorities and foreign service providers. This form of co-operation, while directly impacting on issues like conflict of law and sovereignty, holds significant implications for law enforcement and human rights. The primary limitation of this voluntary co-operation model is its evolution without a clear legal framework. It is predominantly governed by the internal policies of service providers, leading to a regulatory void. As a result, the voluntary co-operation between public authorities and service providers is ineffective in crime investigation and prosecution, lacking both enforcement mechanisms and predictability. Additionally, this form of co-operation is limited in scope, often allowed only by certain countries (notably the US and Ireland), and applicable only to specific types of data, such as subscriber information.

From a privacy and data protection standpoint, significant questions linger regarding the legal authority of service providers to voluntarily disclose users' personal data to foreign government authorities. European authorities assert that the companies, in their role as data controllers, typically lack the legal authority to disclose personal data.[83] The legal intricacies surrounding the informal co-operation between law enforcement authorities and foreign service providers cannot be sufficiently resolved through the practical and operational reforms previously discussed.

Therefore, while the practical and operational reform initiatives taken by various stakeholders have led to notable short-term improvements, their impact remains limited to being a temporary solution. These initiatives should be perceived as interim measures, granting additional time for countries and other stakeholders to develop more sustainable and effective co-operative mechanisms for managing

[82] *cf* J Daskal, 'The Un-Territoriality of Data' (2015) 125 *Yale Law Journal* 326; AK Woods, 'Against Data Exceptionalism: Jurisdictions in the Cloud' (2016) 68 *Sandford Law Review* 748.

[83] Article 29 Working Party, 'Data Protection and Privacy Aspects of Cross-Border Access to Electronic Evidence' (29 November 2017).

cross-border data-access challenges. The need for long-term, comprehensive, and sustainable solutions remains critical in the evolving landscape of cross-border data access.

3.3.2. Unilateralism is not Sustainable

Unilaterally asserting extraterritorial jurisdiction by governments is appealing for several reasons. It facilitates cross-border access to electronic evidence irrespective of the global location of data. This approach becomes viable for governments who have the power to exercise jurisdiction over service providers controlling the data. Such unilateral action aligns with the 'un-territoriality of data' or the 'loss of location' concept.[84] This strategy seems feasible, particularly for powerful jurisdictions capable of enforcing their laws extraterritorially, such as the US and EU.[85]

However, in the long term, and if implemented on a global scale, unrestrained access to extraterritorial data could prove counter-productive. One significant risk of unilateralism policies is that they could incentivise governments with weaker human rights protections to adopt similar unilateral measures. As many experts observe, the rise of 'unilateral disclosure obligations will lead to other unilateral disclosure obligations'.[86] This trend poses a significant threat to the privacy and data protection rights of individuals, especially concerning data pertaining to non-residents of the requesting country. For instance, the substantive and procedural safeguards in the requesting country may be less robust than those in the target individuals' country of residence. A related issue is the differential treatment of non-residents, compared with residents and citizens, under the domestic laws of the requesting country. For example, US constitutional protections do not extend to non-US persons, potentially leading to what Lisa M. Austin has described as a 'constitutional black hole'.[87] In such cases, the privacy of the affected individual may be insufficiently protected under both the laws of the requesting country and those of the country of residence, as neither the home country nor the individual concerned is informed of the data-access or surveillance measures undertaken by a foreign government.

The unilateral assertion of extraterritorial jurisdiction also overlooks the sovereign interests of other nations, thereby compromising international co-operation and hindering the development of co-operative frameworks. This approach undermines international comity and disregards the location of data

[84] Daskal, 'The Un-Territoriality of Data' (n 83); JJ Schwerha, 'Law Enforcement Challenges in Transborder Acquisition of Electronic Evidence from "Cloud Computing Providers"' (Council of Europe Project on Cybercrime Discussion Paper, 15 January 2010).

[85] Svantesson, 'Internet & Jurisdiction Policy Network Global Status Report' (n 6) 67.

[86] Brief of Former Law Enforcement, National Security, and Intelligence Officials, *US v Microsoft* (n 26).

[87] LM Austin, 'Technological Tattletales and Constitutional Black Holes: Communications Intermediaries and Constitutional Constraints' (2016) 17 *Theoretical Inquiries in Law* 451.

as a critical factor in legal jurisdiction.[88] The lack of international consensus on alternative connecting factors for enforcing jurisdiction over cloud data creates legal uncertainty for users and service providers, potentially escalating tensions between countries. Unilateral extraterritorial jurisdiction assertions could provoke the enactment of countervailing blocking statutes. As unilateral laws compelling the production of data stored in foreign servers proliferate, there may be a concurrent rise in laws that prohibit or restrict service providers from disclosing user data to foreign governments. Consequently, such unilateral assertion of extraterritorial jurisdiction makes conflicts of law inevitable. The emergence of mutually exclusive legal requirements – disclosure obligations and prohibitions – places service providers in a position of irreconcilable legal obligations. Complying with one country's laws could necessitate violating those of another. It becomes impractical for a service provider to operate globally while adhering to the national requirements of every country. Furthermore, unilateral extraterritorial jurisdiction adversely impacts on the free flow of data, potentially spurring protective measures like data localisation.

Data localisation is another common unilateral response to the cross-border data-access problem. As discussed earlier in this chapter, this approach is particularly appealing to governments that lack the authority to force foreign service providers to comply with local authorities. By enforcing data localisation, these measures aim to simplify government access and counter unilateral requests from foreign governments. However, the effectiveness of data localisation is questionable. In the era of cloud computing, completely preventing data from exiting a nation is a formidable challenge, as it may require severing Internet connectivity altogether. This strategy might also inadvertently encourage wrongdoers to migrate to less compliant, more secretive services.[89]

Data localisation does not serve security and privacy purposes either. It can inadvertently make foreign surveillance efforts easier by limiting service providers' ability to employ robust, globally competitive security measures.[90] Paradoxically, it may also centralise user information within a jurisdiction, thereby aiding foreign surveillance.[91] Data localisation policies, often based on an outdated, location-centric view of data protection, fail to guarantee security solely based on data's physical storage location within a country.[92] In less democratic countries, data localisation can be misused for domestic surveillance and censorship.

From an economic point of view, there are well-documented studies that show how data localisation affects both domestic and global digital economies. Studies

[88] M Böse, 'An Assessment of the Commission's Proposals on Electronic Evidence' (European Parliament, Policy Department for Citizens' Rights and Constitutional Affairs, 2018).

[89] Chander and Lê, 'Data Nationalism' (n 36) 732.

[90] ibid 716.

[91] ibid 717.

[92] D Castro, 'The False Promise of Data Nationalism' (*The Information Technology & Innovation Foundation*, 9 December 2013), available at www.itif.org/publications/2013/12/09/false-promise-data-nationalism/.

across jurisdictions, including Brazil, China, the EU, India, Indonesia, South Korea, and Vietnam, have shown that data localisation strategies are counter-productive, placing countries at a comparative disadvantage.[93] These policies also put service providers in a difficult position, forcing them to choose between exiting important markets or complying with localisation mandates detrimental to their customers and business interests.[94] The growing trend towards data localisation has raised concern about potential 'internet fragmentation' or 'balkanisation'.[95] Some fear that widespread adoption of data localisation policies could fundamentally alter the Internet as we know it, though others dismiss those concerns as exaggerated.[96] Therefore, while data localisation might offer a sense of control and digital sovereignty, its broader implications, particularly regarding effectiveness, security, privacy, and economic impact, suggest a need for careful consideration. Its potential to disrupt the seamless functioning of the global Internet further underscores the complexity of employing such measures.

3.3.3. Recent Global Frameworks are Insufficient

It is commonplace to describe digital technology as a global phenomenon: data flows seamlessly across national borders, and the architecture of the Internet largely escapes the jurisdiction of any single state. In light of this perspective, proposals for an international framework to address the cross-border data-access problem have significant theoretical appeal. A coherent global regime could advance the universality of the right to privacy and other international human rights by establishing common substantive and procedural safeguards.[97] It would also benefit service providers by eliminating conflict between divergent domestic obligations while discouraging unilateral practices such as data localisation. In theory, this internationalist approach aligns with the rhetoric of open and borderless Internet.

However, despite its conceptual promise, recent multilateral initiatives have proven insufficient. The OECD principles, though potentially influential, are non-binding. They reflect consensus among Member States but lack legal force, rendering their practical impact uncertain. The principles primarily emphasise domestic data access by governments while failing to address the core issues of

[93] M Bauer and others, 'The Costs of Data Localization: Friendly Fire on Economic Recovery' (2014) ECIPE Occasional Paper No 3/2014.

[94] ibid.

[95] E Fraser, 'Data Localisation and the Balkanisation of the Internet' (2016) 13 *SCRIPTed: A Journal of Law, Technology & Society* 359; J Daskal, 'Law Enforcement Access to Data Across Borders: The Evolving Security and Rights Issues' (2016) 8 *Journal of National Security Law & Policy* 473, 475.

[96] *cf* International Conflicts of Law and Their Implications for Cross Border Data Requests by Law Enforcement: Hearing before the H. Comm. on the Judiciary, 114th Cong. Serial No. 114–84 (2016) 106; M Mueller, *Will the Internet Fragment? Sovereignty, Globalization and Cyberspace* (Polity, 2017).

[97] Many human rights experts argue that the same privacy rights should apply across borders and regardless of nationality. For instance, see 'Report of the Special Rapporteur on the Right to Privacy' (n 71); Milanovic, 'Human Rights Treaties and Foreign Surveillance' (n 46).

cross-border data access. Notably, the Declaration provides no mechanism for resolving conflicts of law. It also remains unclear whether they can influence practice beyond the OECD membership. Despite representing a remarkable degree of normative convergence, these soft-law instruments remain aspirational rather than operational.

By contrast, the UNCC signifies an ambitious attempt at global legal harmonisation in cybercrime. It requires States Parties to criminalise core cyber offences and adopt procedural powers analogous to those in the Budapest Convention. Beyond its harmonisation effect, the core function of the UNCC is the facilitation of international co-operation between States Parties. It offers states a legal basis for sharing digital evidence, extraditing suspects, and ensuring mutual assistance. In addition to enabling co-operation under the Convention itself, it actively encourages bilateral and multilateral agreements that could supplement or strengthen co-operation (Article 47). Each State Party must appoint a central authority for the receipt and execution of requests and a 24/7 contact network to ensure round-the-clock co-operation.

Nevertheless, while these measures are essential to fight cybercrime, they fail to address the core cross-border data-access problem, namely how law enforcement authorities can obtain data stored outside their territorial jurisdiction or held by foreign service providers. The Convention focuses on data exchange directly between public authorities on the basis of MLA procedures, as opposed to direct co-operation between public authorities and private service providers. By relying on MLA procedures, the Convention fails to provide a legal basis for direct co-operation between competent authorities and foreign service providers. As highlighted above, Article 27 is fundamentally anchored in the principle of territoriality; it applies only to providers with a nexus to the requesting state. Thus, when a service provider is situated abroad, law enforcement authorities remain dependent on MLA, with all its attendant limitations. The Convention's fundamental orientation is towards deference to the sovereign discretion of states. It not only compels States Parties to comply with the principle of sovereignty but also preserves each state's right to refuse mutual legal assistance requests on grounds of sovereignty (Article 40). Compounding this problem, the Convention fails to offer meaningful mechanisms for resolving conflicts of law, especially where service providers find themselves caught between mutually inconsistent obligations under different jurisdictions.

The question of human rights safeguards emerged as one of the most divisive aspects of negotiations surrounding the UNCC. The Convention's origins under Russian initiative drew significant scepticism from Western countries, civil society, and technology companies, who feared an authoritarian influence on global cybercrime governance. Critics warned that efforts to establish a common international standard risked a 'lower common denominator' of protection, thereby weakening due process in pursuit of efficient law enforcement co-operation. Concerns centred on the potential erosion of privacy and free expression, as over 100 civil society organisations jointly warned that the treaty could produce disastrous consequences for human rights. They cited the vague and expansive language as enabling authoritarian states to misuse the Convention's enforcement powers for political or repressive ends. Among the most contested provisions were Article 6 on the respect for human rights, Article 24 on safeguards and conditions for procedural powers, and Article 36 on personal data protection. Disputes over these provisions were so sharp that seven rounds of voting were required to dismiss some countries' proposals to remove or water down the proposed human rights safeguards.[98] The fact that some states still supported these proposals, and later reiterated objections even after adoption, underscored persistent divisions over the Convention's normative foundations.

Because of these tensions, the final text includes only a nominal set of human rights safeguards. Article 6 explicitly requires that the implementation of the Convention must be consistent with a state's obligations under international human rights law. It also establishes that no provision of the Convention may be interpreted to permit the suppression of fundamental freedoms. However, this provision does not go beyond nominally requiring consistency with international human rights law and fails to provide specific protections. This means that the minimum consistency requirement can be satisfied by whatever baseline exists in a given State Party's domestic law.

Article 24 attempts to operationalise the human rights guarantees by mandating that any procedural powers and international co-operation measures granted under the Convention be subject to domestic legal conditions consistent with human rights law and the principle of proportionality. It requires judicial or independent oversight, effective remedy, justification of application, and limits on scope and duration of such powers. However, these requirements apply when 'appropriate', allowing States Parties wide discretion in determining when these protections are necessary. Furthermore, the Convention allows these protections to be defined almost entirely by national law. In practice, this could result in superficial or ineffective judicial oversight in jurisdictions lacking independent courts. Although the provision nods to the principle of proportionality, it stops short of imposing binding or uniform standards. Notably, the principle of proportionality under Article 24 fails to explicitly reference the principles of legality and necessity.[99] While these principles were included in the draft text, they were later removed for lack of consensus, after some States Parties argued that the principles of 'proportionality, necessity, and legality' should be omitted, since they are not uniformly recognised across domestic systems.

Article 36 governs cross-border sharing of personal data between competent authorities. It requires that any transfer of personal data must comply with each

[98] K Poireault, 'UN Adopts Controversial Cybercrime Treaty (*Infosecurity Magazine*, 12 August 2024), available at www.infosecurity-magazine.com/news/un-adopts-controversial-cybercrime/.

[99] 'Joint Statement on the Signing of the UN Convention on Cybercrime' (*Human Rights Watch*, 24 October 2025), available at www.hrw.org/news/2025/10/24/joint-statement-on-the-signing-of-the-un-convention-on-cybercrime.

state's data protection laws, and that onward transfers occur only with authorisation from the original transferring state. However, consistent with the broader approach of the Convention, it defers to domestic standards and fails to prescribe substantive transnational data protection requirements, thereby creating significant potential for misuse. Negotiation records show that some states argued that references to the 'protection of personal data' should be removed from the draft text, maintaining that privacy protections are already covered under general human rights provisions, and that personal data protection does not constitute a right formally recognised in the UN system. This position reveals a persistent reluctance among certain states to acknowledge data protection as an autonomous fundamental right, resulting in the Convention leaving the scope and enforcement of the safeguards to domestic law. Consequently, data protection levels remain contingent on national discretion, undermining the Convention's capacity to ensure consistent safeguards in cross-border co-operation.

In summary, the UNCC prioritises the protection of national sovereignty. For this reason, it heavily focuses on co-operation between competent authorities but lacks a clear framework for direct co-operation between authorities and service providers across jurisdictions. This deficiency means that it fails to effectively address the crucial challenges of cross-border data access in today's digital environment. Because it operates through state-to-state requests, the UNCC does not fully address the issues that leave the MLAT system ineffective and, at times, dysfunctional. Additionally, the UNCC does not provide a mechanism to resolve conflicts of law, an omission that becomes problematic given the possible broader interpretations and applications of Article 27, which inevitably give rise to conflicting obligations. Most critically, the human rights safeguards within the Convention are weak and insufficient, potentially allowing authoritarian states with weak judicial independence and oversight to misuse the provisions for surveillance purposes.

Compared with the UNCC, the Budapest Convention and its Second Additional Protocol provide a more suitable framework for an internationalist approach to cross-border data access. These instruments incorporate specific measures to balance law enforcement needs, state sovereignty, and human rights, while also offering mechanisms to resolve conflicts of law involving service providers. The Second Additional Protocol is specifically designed to address the persistent problems of cross-border data access, thereby remedying a key shortcoming of the original Convention.

From a law enforcement perspective, the Second Additional Protocol offers a more effective tool against cybercrimes than the UNCC, as it enables data access through procedures and co-operative mechanisms that the UN framework lacks. It establishes an expanded legal basis for direct co-operation between competent authorities in one State Party and service providers located in another. This co-operation may occur even in the absence of a territorial nexus such as the 'offering of services', and location of data, and does not require reliance on mutual assistance channels. Moreover, the Protocol obliges the receiving State Party to give effect to production orders issued by another State Party by taking reasonable steps to comply with them. Specifically, the receiving state must require the service provider within its jurisdiction to produce the requested data within the prescribed time.

While this enhancement strengthens law enforcement capacity, the Protocol also safeguards national sovereignty and human rights by subjecting these powers to defined protections and conditions. From a sovereignty perspective, particularly that of the receiving state (where the service provider is located), the Protocol introduces several safeguards. Direct co-operation with service providers is restricted to basic subscriber information, which, while vital for cybercrime investigations, is generally considered less intrusive. A State Party retains the right to require that production orders be accompanied by simultaneous notification to its authorities, a right that can be exercised at any time by informing the Secretary General of the Council of Europe. Additionally, a State Party may oblige service providers in its territory to consult authorities prior to disclosing data, and these authorities may instruct the service providers not to release subscriber information for specific reasons. Finally, a State Party may, at the time of signature of the Protocol, reserve the right not to apply the measures concerning cross-border production orders for subscriber information. By allowing States Parties to require notification or consultation – or even to refuse cross-border production orders – the Protocol prevents foreign authorities from gaining unrestrained access to data held within another territory.

As highlighted above, the Protocol also establishes mechanisms to resolve conflicting legal obligations faced by service providers, by requiring each State Party to introduce legislative measures enabling service providers in its territory to directly comply with production orders issued by competent authorities in another party. These measures effectively eliminate blocking provisions in the receiving state.

Lastly, while the Budapest Convention and its Protocol have drawn criticism from civil society organisations, they collectively represent a more advanced regulatory framework for human rights and data protection than the UNCC. Specifically, the Protocol imbeds principles of lawfulness, fairness, transparency, and proportionality, ensuring cross-border data access only for legitimate criminal justice purposes. Through requirements for judicial or independent oversight, data subject remedies, and safeguards against excessive or unauthorised use, the Protocol strengthens accountability and privacy protection within transnational law enforcement co-operation. However, despite these crucial steps, the Budapest Convention and its Protocol replicate some of the structural weaknesses of the UN framework by granting broad discretion to national laws and thereby risking fragmentation of standards and weaker protections across differing domestic frameworks.

Beyond these normative limitations, the Budapest Convention also faces significant practical and political challenges that could constrain its global legitimacy and reach. Although its structure is scalable and well suited to addressing the cross-border data-access problems, the Convention remains politically contentious. Several influential states, most notably China, Russia, India, and Brazil, have refused to accede, citing concerns over sovereignty and unequal participation in norm-setting. Their absence could weaken the Budapest Convention's universality, and curtails its effectiveness as a global framework for cybercrime governance.

3.3.4. The Nuanced Approach has Scalability Problems

The new generation of cross-border data-access agreements envisioned by the CLOUD Act (the nuanced approach) could offer less ambitious but more tailored and realistic alternatives to address the jurisdictional and conflicts-of-law challenges of the cloud. Generally, this approach considers all the principles delineated above, although the scope and substantive details of the agreements will be tailored to each participating country. If implemented on a broad scale, the nuanced approach could remove barriers to effective law-enforcement access to data and mitigate conflicts of laws, while also respecting the territorial sovereignty of each participating country and upholding the privacy protections of the individual whose data is being sought. However, this approach also has limitations and gives rise to some new risks.

From a law enforcement perspective, a CLOUD Act agreement would provide participating countries with direct and rapid access to data no matter where the sought-after data happens to be stored. It would do so in two ways. First, the agreement would eliminate the multiple formal approvals and involvement of multiple actors in the receiving country.[100] The CLOUD Act envisions the elimination of these processes altogether. Instead, the agreement would authorise the requesting government to obtain data directly from service providers in the receiving country. Second, the agreement would require each participating country to lift domestic legal restrictions otherwise preventing service providers subject to its jurisdiction from disclosing data directly to the authorities in the other participating country.[101]

The removal of blocking statutes in each participating country would also help alleviate potential conflicts of laws. Once a cross-border data-access agreement is in place, a service provider can directly respond to legitimate requests issued by foreign governments subject to the agreement without the risk of violating the law of the country where the service provider is incorporated. Perhaps the most significant step undertaken by the CLOUD Act framework is the creation of a

[100] For details on how the MLA procedure works, see Swire and Hemmings, 'Mutual Legal Assistance in an Era of Globalized Communications' (n 3); T Lin and M Fidler, 'Cross-Border Data Access Reform: A Primer on the Proposed U.S.-U.K. Agreement' (A Berklett Cybersecurity publication, Berkman Klein Center for Internet & Society, 2017).

[101] CLOUD Act, s 103(b) (codified at 18 USC, s 2703[h][5]; s 105 [b] [codified at 18 USC, s 2523(b)(4)(I)].

judicial review mechanism in case a clash between the laws of the participating countries arises.[102]

The framework envisioned by the CLOUD Act also has the potential to provide sufficient protections because only countries that meet baseline privacy and civil liberties standards regarding the sharing of data across borders can be eligible to participate. In this regard, the CLOUD Act prescribes four-phase requirements that must be met by a foreign country. Chapter four sets these out in detail, but it suffices to say here that these requirements include: (i) domestic law that affords robust substantive and procedural protections for privacy *(eligibility)*; (ii) a written certification by the US Attorney General that the foreign country meets these baseline requirements *(qualification)*; (iii) specific conditions and safeguards that the qualifying foreign government should follow in every request *(implementation)*; and (iv) an ex post periodic review of the process to ensure compliance with the requirements of the agreement *(review and accountability)*.

Another significant safeguard envisaged under the nuanced approach is that participating countries can negotiate a reciprocal agreement restricting one party from targeting data of the nationals and legal residents of the other party. The US–UK Agreement, for instance, prohibits law enforcement authorities in the UK from using the agreement to obtain data on the citizens and legal residents of the US, and vice versa. The focus on the nationality of the target serves at least two purposes: (i) it respects the sovereign interest of each participating country to protect the privacy and security of its citizens from foreign governments; and (ii) it creates legal certainty for users by ensuring that their privacy and other fundamental rights are protected by the laws of their country, and that these protections do not vary as their data moves across border.[103]

By making the location of data irrelevant for determining jurisdiction over data, this approach also takes into account current technological realities and is compatible with the borderless nature of the Internet. Moreover, this approach could help mitigate the growing trend in unilateral measures such as expansive extraterritorial authorities and forced data localisation. However, despite these promises, the nuanced approach, as exemplified by the US–UK agreement, should also serve as a cautionary tale. More importantly, if not pursued with caution, the CLOUD Act framework could lead to unintended consequences, as outlined in chapter four. Specifically, the CLOUD Act faces significant challenges in scalability. It was not designed for widespread global use; instead, it primarily targets high-priority and trusted partners who share American values, which may restrict its broader applicability. This limitation risks creating a divide where only a select group of countries benefit from the framework.

[102] ibid, s 2703(h).

[103] OS Kerr, 'The Next Generation Communications Privacy Act' [2013] *University of Pennsylvania Law Review* 373, 417.

3.4. Conclusion

As the US Department of Justice observes, 'the international community continues to struggle with the critical question of how to provide law enforcement agencies efficient and effective access to electronic evidence needed to protect public safety while preserving respect for sovereignty and privacy'.[104] The shortcomings of the traditional system of cross-border legal co-operation, combined with the surging demand for digital evidence, have created both urgency and frustration among law enforcement authorities worldwide. The inability to access data stored outside their territorial jurisdiction in a timely and effective manner has prompted many governments to take matters into their own hands by introducing unilateral measures. Among these unilateral responses, bilateral and regional initiatives have multiplied, while multilateral organisations have intensified their efforts to address these challenges, most notably through the modernisation of the Budapest Convention and adoption of the UN Cybercrime Treaty.

This chapter advances four approaches that help explain the current and emerging initiatives and assesses their effectiveness in addressing the cross-border data-access problem. Although these policy responses vary in form and scope, they all seek to resolve an overarching question: can domestic legal frameworks legitimately compel the production of data stored on foreign soil without the consent of the host state? Conversely, can the host state invoke territorial sovereignty to block such access simply because the data resides within its borders?

Emerging international practice increasingly suggests that unilateral cross-border data access does not, in itself, constitute an infringement of territorial sovereignty of the state where data is stored. This evolving practice challenges the suitability of traditional sovereignty-based mechanisms, which rely heavily on the physical location of data, for today's technological realities. However, this increasing shift does not authorise states to use unilateral measures at will to access data across borders. Despite the growing international acceptance of cross-border data-access frameworks, unrestrained unilateral action risks being perceived as a violation of sovereignty under international law. Consequently, extraterritorial measures must be subject to clear conditions, restrictions, and safeguards. A fundamental prerequisite is that the requesting state must establish territorial or personal jurisdiction over the service provider controlling the data, based on a substantial connection. Such a connection may exist, for instance, when the service provider has an establishment in the requesting state or offers services there, even if headquartered overseas. Even when jurisdiction over the service provider is established, cross-border data-access requests must be constrained by substantive and procedural safeguards.

[104] US Department of Justice, 'Promoting Public Safety, Privacy, and the Rule of Law Around the World: The Purpose and Impact of the CLOUD Act' (White Paper, April 2019), available at www.justice.gov/CLOUDAct.

For instance, the Budapest Convention and UN Cybercrime Treaty restrict production orders to subscriber information, reflecting a cautious approach to extraterritorial data requests. Likewise, the OECD Declaration on Government Access to Personal Data outlines extensive principles governing such access. It mandates that government access to individual data be regulated by a legal framework that clearly defines the purposes, conditions, limitations, and safeguards, ensuring that access is necessary and proportionate to a legitimate aim, and subject to prior approval by an independent authority. While measures remain insufficiently robust, they nonetheless signify a gradual normative convergence towards establishing shared standards and safeguards governing government access to data across borders.

4

The United States' Approach: The CLOUD Act

The US wields significant influence over major global cloud service providers and, by extension, over the vast majority of data they manage worldwide. This influence means that any regulatory changes in the US can directly affect how these providers co-operate with law enforcement worldwide. The CLOUD Act was introduced to address the jurisdictional, privacy, and sovereignty challenges faced by US and foreign law enforcement authorities in accessing electronic evidence stored outside their respective territorial jurisdictions. This legislation positions the US at the forefront of global cross-border data-access reform, establishing a new model of international co-operation. Under this model, US technology companies are permitted to disclose user data directly to 'qualified foreign governments' in response to their requests to assist investigations into serious crimes. Given its substantial impact on shaping international standards for law enforcement access, the CLOUD Act warrants closer examination. This chapter provides an overview of the background leading to the CLOUD Act's adoption, explores the extraterritorial reach of US government law enforcement powers, and evaluates how the statute regulates foreign governments' access to data held by US service providers. It also assesses whether the statute effectively meets its stated objectives.

4.1. Blocking Statutes and the CLOUD Act

The US law governing law enforcement access to electronic data was originally enacted in 1986, when the Internet was in its infancy. The Stored Communications Act (SCA), part of the Electronic Communications Privacy Act (ECPA), aims to achieve two key public policy objectives: protecting the privacy of electronic communications stored with providers of electronic communications and remote computing services, and ensuring legitimate law enforcement access to data stored by such providers. The legislation governs how and under what conditions US and foreign law enforcement authorities can access user data held by US-based technology companies. However, because the SCA did not contemplate the scale of cross-border data-access issues presented by the ubiquity of cloud computing, it has failed to adequately address either of the following scenarios: (1) American law enforcement authorities seeking access to data held by US service providers; and (2) foreign governments seeking access to data held by US service providers.

In fact, the SCA has created more problems than it solves. It has been the primary source of international conflicts of law, creating challenges for US law enforcement authorities, foreign governments, service providers, and users' privacy.

While the statute authorises US law enforcement authorities to obtain certain categories of communications data stored in the US, through specific requirements, such as warrants and subpoenas, it is not explicit whether these powers extend to obtaining data held abroad. This lack of clarity led to inconsistent interpretations of the statute. This ambiguity led US authorities to face jurisdictional and conflicts-of-law challenges in accessing user data held by US-based service providers in overseas databases. Nothing illustrates the jurisdictional conundrum before the adoption of the CLOUD Act more than the five-year-long dispute between Microsoft and the US government concerning the reach of a search warrant issued under the SCA.[1] Following the Second Circuit's decision in *Microsoft Ireland*, which held that enforcing the warrant for information stored abroad would constitute an impermissible extraterritorial application of the SCA, several US service providers refused to comply with judicial orders requiring the disclosure of data stored overseas. Before the adoption of the CLOUD Act, the US Department of Justice (DOJ) reportedly identified close to 100 cases that involved similar situations – service providers declining to comply with judicial orders even where the victim, the offender, and the account holder were all within the US.[2]

The challenges created by the SCA have been more pronounced when it comes to the interests of foreign governments seeking access to data held by US-based technology companies. The statute explicitly prohibits US-based service providers from disclosing certain types of user data (such as email content and text messages) to foreign governments without a valid legal process issued by a US court. Service providers that comply with foreign-government requests for these types of data in violation of these blocking provisions of the SCA risk criminal sanctions.

The SCA's blocking provisions were designed with good intentions to advance legitimate public policy goals. As with any other government, the US government has a legitimate interest in overseeing the actions of companies operating within its jurisdiction, which includes ensuring that these companies do not infringe upon the privacy and civil liberties of US citizens while conducting business abroad. The blocking statute serves to protect US citizens from having their data accessed by foreign governments, and it allows US technology companies to assert that they are legally barred from directly assisting those foreign governments.[3] Blocking

[1] This chapter builds on a previous article by the author: see H Abraha, 'Regulating law enforcement access to electronic evidence across borders: the United States approach' (2020) 29 *Information and Communication Technology Law* 324. See also Per Curiam No 17–2 *United States v Microsoft Corp* (584 US, 17 April 2018).

[2] House Judiciary Hearing on Law Enforcement Access to Data Stored Across Borders: Facilitating Cooperation and Protecting Rights (24 May 2017).

[3] M Perault and R Salgado, 'Untapping the Full Potential of CLOUD Act Agreements' (Center for Strategic and International Studies, 2024), available at www.csis.org/analysis/untapping-full-potential-cloud-act-agreements.

statutes like this are not exclusive to the US; many other countries have enacted similar laws.

However, the SCA's blanket prohibition is ill-suited to today's interconnected world, where even purely domestic criminal investigations often require access to electronic evidence across borders. This prohibition applies even where the US has nothing to do with the investigation, except that the data in question happens to be stored on US soil due to the business decisions of the service provider or the online activities of the user. Furthermore, it does not matter whether the request comes from a government that respects the rule of law, even if the data pertains to that government's own citizens.[4] For these reasons, the SCA's blocking provisions have often been criticised as inflexible and arbitrary, forcing foreign governments to seek alternative measures.[5]

The DOJ summarised the arbitrariness of the blocking provisions and their implications as follows:

> Foreign governments investigating criminal activities abroad increasingly require access to electronic evidence from U.S. companies that provide electronic communications services to millions of their citizens and residents. Such data is often stored or accessible only in the United States, where U.S. law, including the ECPA, limits the companies' ability to disclose it. Our companies may face conflicting legal obligations when foreign governments require them to disclose electronic data that U.S. law prohibits them from disclosing. This legal conflict can occur even though the request is made pursuant to lawful process in the foreign country, involves communications between foreign nationals abroad, and concerns criminal activities outside the United States with no relation to this country other than the fact that the service provider stores the data in the United States.[6]

Addressing the SCA's domestic and international challenges required legislative intervention. The first attempt, known as the Law Enforcement Access to Data Stored Abroad (LEADS) Act, was introduced in 2014 by Senator Orrin Hatch, aiming to tackle the issues raised in the *Microsoft Ireland* case. However, the proposal did not gain traction in Congress. The push for legislative intervention intensified after the US Court of Appeals for the Second Circuit ruled in 2016 that the SCA did not authorise the issuance of a warrant to obtain data stored abroad. The case then proceeded to the Supreme Court, creating a precarious situation for both the DOJ and Microsoft: a victory for Microsoft would impose territorial restrictions on data, fuelling data localisation, while a government win could enable nations to unilaterally access global data, setting a dangerous precedent.[7] The potential implications of the Supreme Court upholding this decision, particularly those concerning public safety and privacy, prompted the DOJ to

[4] ibid.

[5] See ch 3.

[6] Letter from PJ Kadzik, Assistant Attorney General, US Department of Justice Office of Legislative Affairs, 15 July 2016.

[7] J Daskal, 'The Un-Territoriality of Data' (2015) 125 *Yale Law Journal* 326.

introduce the initial draft of the CLOUD Act on 15 July 2016, just one day after the Second Circuit's ruling. In a covering letter accompanying the legislative proposal, Assistant Attorney General Peter Kadzik emphasised the urgency of avoiding a Supreme Court decision on the matter:

> Yesterday, the United States Court of Appeals for the Second Circuit held in *Microsoft Corp. v. United States* that section 2703 of ECPA does not authorize our courts to issue and enforce warrants served on U.S. providers to obtain electronic communications stored abroad. If the decision stands, or is extended to other parts of the country, the U.S would not have … access to data necessary to advance important U.S investigations that protect the safety of Americans and could not obtain reciprocal benefits from other countries. The Administration intends to promptly submit legislation to Congress to address the significant public safety implications of the *Microsoft* decision.[8]

The CLOUD Act was enacted against this backdrop. It employs a two-step approach to address the challenges associated with cross-border data access. The first step (Part I) focuses on domestic challenges by clarifying the extraterritorial reach of US judicial orders for the disclosure of data stored overseas.

The novelty of the CLOUD Act lies in its second part (Part II). This part amends the SCA and permits US-based technology companies to disclose 'communications content' to foreign governments who would enter into bilateral agreements with the US government. As a result, US service providers would no longer face conflicting obligations when responding to requests from foreign countries that have established such agreements. If conflicts do arise, the CLOUD Act creates a new statutory right for service providers to challenge government requests in court. Additionally, the statute outlines a series of substantive and procedural requirements that must be fulfilled at each stage of the bilateral agreement and during any legal processes initiated to obtain user data. The following sections provide detailed analysis of the two parts of the CLOUD Act.

4.2. Fortifying the Long Arms of US Law Enforcement Powers

The first part of the CLOUD Act addresses the inability of US law enforcement authorities to obtain electronic evidence stored overseas in a timely fashion.[9] Prior to the CLOUD Act, and until challenged by Microsoft, the SCA was used to compel US-based service providers to produce data under their possession, custody, or control regardless of where the data was located.[10] The US government argued

[8] Letter from PJ Kadzik (n 6).

[9] Clarifying Lawful Overseas Use of Data (CLOUD) Act 1625, 115th Cong div V (2018), s 102 (1)–(2).

[10] US Department of Justice, 'Promoting Public Safety, Privacy, and the Rule of Law Around the World: The Purpose and Impact of the CLOUD Act' (White Paper, April 2019).

that relying on the SCA to compel service providers subject to its jurisdiction to disclose data under their control was consistent with Article 18 of the Budapest Convention.[11] The CLOUD Act clarifies the ambiguities in the SCA, explicitly stating that US law enforcement agencies can access data stored abroad, provided that the company controlling the data is subject to US jurisdiction. Thus, the enactment of the CLOUD Act rendered the *Microsoft Ireland* case moot, and precludes US service providers from using data location or network architecture as grounds to refuse compliance with US judicial orders.

The new provision added in Chapter 121 of Title 18 of the United States Code requires service providers to disclose their customers' data to US authorities regardless of where such data is located. One significant clarification is that, by authorising law enforcement agencies to compel a service provider to disclose user data irrespective of the location of the provider and the data in question, the CLOUD Act establishes that a search warrant issued under the SCA extends beyond US borders. The jurisdictional locus shifts from the location of data to that of the service provider's degree of control ('controller doctrine'). Furthermore, the CLOUD Act introduces a new framework to address the potential conflicts with the laws of foreign nations. Each of these measures will be examined below.

4.2.1. Location-Agnostic Approach to Jurisdiction Over Cloud Data

The extent to which the physical location of data should serve as a basis for asserting jurisdiction over cloud data has been the subject of intense academic debate.[12] There have been extensive calls to move away from pre-Internet conceptions of territoriality and pursue alternative frameworks that reflect the realities of the cloud era. The CLOUD Act represents a significant response to these calls. It directly addresses the central issues in *Microsoft Ireland* and *Google Pennsylvania* by requiring US service providers to comply with the obligation to

> disclose the contents of a wire or electronic communication and any record or other information pertaining to a customer or subscriber within such provider's possession, custody, or control, regardless of whether such communication, record, or other information is located within or outside of the United States.[13]

Informed by the theory of 'un-territoriality of data', the CLOUD Act effectively shifts jurisdictional focus from the physical location of data to the service

[11] ibid.

[12] *cf* Daskal, 'The Un-Territoriality of Data' (n 7); AK Woods, 'Against Data Exceptionalism: Jurisdictions in the Cloud' (2016) 68 *Sandford Law Review* 748; PM Schwartz, 'Legal Access to the Global Cloud' (2018) 118 *Columbia Law Review* 1681.

[13] CLOUD Act, s 103(a) (codified at 18 USC, s 2713).

provider's control over that data. Consequently, US-based service providers cannot evade the reach of the CLOUD Act by merely relocating data out of the country.

Concerns regarding this location-agnostic approach to jurisdiction include:

1. Given that US companies manage the vast majority of data globally, and thus fall under US jurisdiction, focusing on data controllership may confer universal status on US law without regard to the legitimate interest and sovereignty of other countries.
2. Following the same logic, other nations, including those with weaker substantive and procedural safeguards, could unilaterally demand user data from service providers regardless of where the data is located.
3. Conflicts of law may be inevitable.

Cognisant of these concerns, the US Congress established a new regime allowing the US government to enter into reciprocal executive agreements with like-minded foreign governments. Congress has aptly noted that 'international agreements provide a mechanism for resolving these potential conflicting legal obligations where the United States and the relevant foreign government share a common commitment to the rule of law and the protection of privacy and civil liberties'.[14]

Once an executive agreement is in place, the expansive power of the US government to seek data regardless of its location will be counterbalanced by the service provider's ability, in certain circumstances, to challenge legal processes issued under the SCA (as amended by the CLOUD Act).[15] This enables partner foreign governments to negotiate reciprocal agreements that restrict the US government from targeting data belonging to their nationals and residents.[16] In addition to the applicable domestic statutory and constitutional limitations, these factors can be considered as meaningful restraints on the US government's access to global cloud data.

4.2.2. Data Controllership as the Locus of Jurisdiction Over Cloud Data

There is a clear global trend towards disregarding the location of data as a determining factor to assert jurisdiction. Instead, increasing emphasis is placed on the service providers who control the required data. Consistent with this global trend, the CLOUD Act renders location of data immaterial and establishes the test of 'possession, custody, or control' as the determining factor for whether the service provider must disclose the required data.

[14] ibid, s 102(6).
[15] ibid, s 103(b) (codified at 18 USC, s 2703[h]).
[16] US Department of Justice, 'Promoting Public Safety, Privacy, and the Rule of Law' (n 10).

Any service provider subject to US jurisdiction is required to comply with government legal requests to disclose user data within its possession, custody, or control.[17] Prior to issuing a disclosure order under the CLOUD Act, the US government must identify the service provider in 'possession, custody, or control' of the data in question and determine whether that service provider is subject to the US jurisdiction. However, these steps are not straightforward in practice, and give rise to three critical questions:

1. What constitutes 'possession, custody, or control' within the meaning of the CLOUD Act?
2. How will the US government determine which service provider is in 'possession, custody, or control' of the required data in 'multi-layered cloud services' and 'Data Trust clouds'?
3. Can foreign service providers be subject to US jurisdiction within the meaning of the CLOUD Act?

The CLOUD Act does not define what constitutes 'possession, custody, or control'. Instead, it mirrors the language of the US Federal Rules of Civil Procedure, and that of the Budapest Convention, to which the US is a party.[18] Under the Federal Rules of Civil Procedure, a domestic subsidiary or affiliate of a foreign entity may be subpoenaed to produce records within its 'possession, custody, or control'.[19] While the terms 'possession' and 'custody' amount to physical possession, there is no uniform standard to determine whether a company has 'control' over the required material. US courts apply one of two tests to determine whether control exists over subpoenaed documents: (a) the 'legal right' test; or (b) the 'practical ability' test.[20]

In *US v Int'l Union of Petro Indus*, the Ninth Circuit Court of Appeals defined 'control' as 'the legal right to obtain documents upon demand'.[21] Based on this interpretation, a company that does not have legal entitlement over a document cannot be compelled to produce that specific document, regardless of whether it has a practical ability to do so.[22] The Court observed that 'ordering a party to produce documents that it does not have the legal right to obtain will oftentimes be futile, precisely because the party has no certain way of getting those documents'.[23]

In contrast to the Ninth Circuit Court of Appeals, several district courts have applied the 'practical ability' theory. This theory assumes that a company

[17] CLOUD Act, s 103(1)(b).

[18] Federal Rules of Civil Procedure, Rule 34 and 45; Art 18, Convention on Cybercrime of the Council of Europe CETS No 185.

[19] Federal Rules of Civil Procedure, Rule 45.

[20] JD Jordan, 'Out of "Control" Federal Subpoenas: When Does a Nonparty Subsidiary Have Control of Documents Possessed by a Foreign Parent?' (2016) 68 *Baylor Law Review* 190.

[21] *US v Int'l Union of Petro Indus Wkrs* 870 F.2d 1450 (9th Cir 1989).

[22] *In Re Citric Acid Litigation* 191 F.3d 1090, 1106 (9th Cir 1999).

[23] ibid.

with the ability to demand and access a document in the ordinary course of business has 'control' over that document regardless of its legal entitlement.[24] In *Dietrich v Bauer*, for instance, the District Court of New York defined 'control', for the purpose of Rule 45 of the Federal Rules of Civil Procedure, as 'the legal right, authority, or practical ability to obtain the materials sought upon demand'.[25] What constitutes 'practical ability' generally depends on the totality of the circumstances in each case. Courts often use multi-factor analysis to evaluate whether a company has the practical ability over required documents.[26]

Despite this legal–practical distinction, however, a requested party does not need to have actual possession of documents to be deemed in control of them within the meaning of Rule 45. The Budapest Convention requires signatories to adopt legislative and other measures that would empower their respective law enforcement agencies to 'order a person in their territory to submit specified computer data in that person's possession or control'.[27] Within this context, the term 'possession or control' extends beyond mere physical possession and includes situations in which the data is outside the person's physical possession but can, nonetheless, be freely controlled by them.[28] However, the mere technical ability to access remotely stored data without legitimate control does not necessarily constitute 'control' under the Convention.[29]

While the requirement of 'possession or control' under Article 18(1) of the Budapest Convention generally corresponds with US law, a mere 'practical ability' to obtain data without a corresponding legal right is not applicable under the Convention. To establish 'control' within its meaning, both the 'legal right' and 'technical ability' tests must be satisfied. Therefore, even though focusing on 'control' over data aligns with the Convention principle, it remains uncertain which test (legal right test, practical ability test, or both) US courts will apply when interpreting the CLOUD Act.[30]

The second question concerns the difficulties law enforcement agencies may face in determining which service provider has the 'possession, custody, or control' over the required data in cases involving 'Data Trust clouds' and 'multi-layered cloud services'.[31] Paul M. Schwartz defined a Data Trust cloud as 'one in which a non-US entity manages the cloud as a trustee for a US-headquartered provider'.[32]

[24] Jordan, 'Out of "Control" Federal Subpoenas' (n 20); W Maxwell, MW Brennan, and AA Sura, 'Demystifying the U.S. CLOUD Act: Assessing the Law's Compatibility with International Norms and the GDPR' (Hogan Lovells, 2019).

[25] *Dietrich v Bauer* 198 FRD 397 (SDNY 2001).

[26] Maxwell, Brennan, and Sura, 'Demystifying the U.S. CLOUD Act' (n 24).

[27] Art 18, Convention on Cybercrime.

[28] See Explanatory Report of the Convention on Cybercrime, para 173.

[29] ibid.

[30] For a detailed analysis, see J Hemmings, S Srinivasan, and P Swire, 'Defining the Scope of "Possession, Custody, or Control" for Privacy Issues and the CLOUD Act' (2020) 10 *Journal of National Security Law & Policy* 631.

[31] See ch 1.

[32] Schwartz, 'Legal Access to the Global Cloud' (n 12) 1687.

Under this arrangement, a US-based service provider could relinquish effective 'possession, custody, or control' over data to circumvent US jurisdiction; thus, the CLOUD Act may not adequately address such issues. This situation is not hypothetical. As highlighted in chapter one, Microsoft has introduced a 'data trustee' model, whereby it places user data beyond US authorities' jurisdictional reach by partnering with foreign companies. Since Microsoft itself cannot access data held under this arrangement, applying the 'possession, custody, or control' test under the CLOUD Act may not work in practice. Although scalability of Microsoft's model remains uncertain, it could pose challenges for effectively enforcing the CLOUD Act.

The other challenge involves multi-layered cloud services. In cloud computing environments, the delivery of services often depends on complex multi-layered arrangements between various providers.[33] Furthermore, multinational cloud service providers can have affiliates and branches worldwide.[34] Different providers may be involved in particular cloud service offerings with varying degrees of control over underlying technologies and stored data. This complicates law enforcement agencies' efforts to identify who is in 'possession, custody, or control' of data when serving subsequent disclosure orders. As a result, the CLOUD Act may target service providers (such as infrastructure service providers) who do not have sufficient 'possession, custody, or control' over the sought-after data.

A similar problem arises when government agencies demand that service providers disclose data that belongs to corporate customers' employees. In such situations, the DOJ advises prosecutors to request data directly from the 'controller' (in this case, the corporate customer) rather than the cloud infrastructure provider, 'if doing so will not compromise the investigation'.[35] The DOJ has confirmed that the CLOUD Act does not change this practice.[36]

The final question concerns how far foreign service providers can be subjected to US jurisdiction under the CLOUD Act. As indicated above, merely having 'possession, custody, or control' is insufficient for issuing legal orders under this Act; targeted providers must also fall under the personal jurisdiction of US courts. The CLOUD Act does not change long-standing US principles dictating that foreign companies with 'sufficient contact' with the US are subject to its jurisdiction. What constitutes 'sufficient contact' remains fact-specific and depends on each company's nature and quality of contacts with the US-based entities.[37] Accordingly, any service provider offering services in the US can be subject to the CLOUD Act regardless of whether it is established in the US or abroad.

[33] WK Hon and C Millard, 'Cloud Technologies and Service' in C Millard (ed), *Cloud Computing Law* (Oxford University Press, 2014).

[34] OS Kerr, 'The Next Generation Communications Privacy Act' (2014) 162 *University of Pennsylvania Law Review* 373.

[35] US Department of Justice, 'Seeking Enterprise Customer Data Held by Cloud Service Providers' (December 2017).

[36] US Department of Justice, 'Promoting Public Safety, Privacy, and the Rule of Law' (n 10).

[37] ibid.

4.2.3. Resolving Conflicts of Law

The US Congress recognised that service providers are facing conflicting legal obligations when a foreign government orders production of electronic data that US law may prohibit, and vice versa.[38] To address this potential conflict, Congress created a new statutory right that allows service providers to challenge law enforcement requests, provided that specific substantive and procedural requirements are met.

Although the prerequisites for invoking this statutory right are strict in both substance and procedure, and limited in scope,[39] they serve as a starting point for resolving conflicting legal obligations. Under the CLOUD Act, service providers have the right to challenge US law enforcement requests when the following three cumulative requirements are satisfied: (a) the provider reasonably believes that the investigative target whose data is being sought is not a US person and does not reside in the US; (b) the provider reasonably believes that disclosure would create a material risk of violating a foreign nation's law; and (c) the foreign country whose law may be violated has entered into an executive agreement with the US as envisaged in the CLOUD Act.[40] Each of these requirements will be examined below.

4.2.3.1. The Nationality and Residence Requirement

According to the first requirement, a service provider can invoke the statutory right to challenge a disclosure order for user data only when the US government seeks the data of a national and resident of a foreign country with which the US has an executive agreement. This statutory right has no immediate effect, as it becomes applicable only once the US government enters into an executive agreement with a foreign partner.[41] Once such an agreement is in place, the 'nationality and residence' requirement will serve as the basis for cross-border data access.

As highlighted in chapter three, the shift in focus from the location of data to the location of the investigative target serves at least two purposes: (1) it ensures that the sovereign interests of qualifying foreign governments in protecting their citizens' privacy from US government actions are respected; and (2) it creates legal certainty for users by ensuring that the substantive and procedural safeguards remain consistent as their data moves across borders.[42] The need to focus on the

[38] CLOUD Act, s 102(4)–(5).

[39] J Daskal, 'Privacy and Security Across Borders' (2019) 128 *The Yale Law Journal Forum* 1029.

[40] CLOUD Act, s 103(b) (codified at 18 USC, s 2703[h]).

[41] The statutory right is not applicable if the US authorities order the disclosure of data pertaining to a target outside the jurisdiction of the partner foreign government, in which case the service provider can consider comity claims only under 'common law'. See CLOUD Act, s 103(c).

[42] See Brief Amicus Curiae of UN Special Rapporteur on the Right to Privacy Joseph Cannataci in Support of Neither Party, *United States v Microsoft (2017)* No 17-2 (2017) (noting that, 'to the extent that lay people think of these matters at all, they likely believe that their privacy rights in cyberspace are the same as in whatever physical place they reside').

user's place of residence or nationality rather than on the location of data had been advocated by various scholars long before the CLOUD Act was enacted. For instance, Orin S. Kerr recommended that the US Congress adopt a new Privacy Act based on the location of the user, arguing that 'privacy protections should follow the user instead of the data'.[43]

Although the shift from the location of data to 'nationality and residence' of the user is a positive development, it is important to note that its practical application may not be straightforward, particularly in the context of cloud computing. The requirement assumes that service providers always know the nationality and residence of their users. The statutory right to challenge government requests for data is meaningful only when service providers can reasonably ascertain where users reside at the time of the disclosure request. However, this is not often the case. There are situations where a user's identity and location cannot be determined or can only be ascertained with little certainty. This challenge arises largely due to how cloud services operate and how service providers manage user data.

For instance, some cloud service providers often store data physically closer to the user to minimise network latency, among other benefits.[44] This raises the question, how do service providers determine their users' physical locations? Some cloud data management practices illustrate that service providers try to ascertain user locations automatically and often arbitrarily. For instance, Microsoft determines a user's physical location based on 'information provided by the user during account registration process'.[45]

The automatic selection of user location without verification could lead to complex legal questions. Users can easily remain anonymous or provide a false identity and location.[46] Additionally, there is a significant chance that a user's location at the time of a disclosure order differs from what was identified during account registration. Consequently, determining whether the user is a national and resident of a qualifying foreign government could become an arbitrary decision.

For instance, would it be 'reasonable', as required by the CLOUD Act, for a service provider to rely solely on information provided by users to decide whether those users are US persons? Can a service provider that relies on automatic determination of user location reasonably ascertain that an investigative target is a national and resident of a qualifying foreign government so that it can challenge a legal process issued under US law? Does it make any difference if the service provider complies with a disclosure order and later finds that the user was residing in the territory of a qualifying foreign government at the time of request and disclosure?

[43] Kerr, 'The Next Generation Communications Privacy Act' (n 34).

[44] Brief for 51 Computer Scientists as Amici Curiae in Support of the Respondent, *United States v Microsoft* (2017) No 17-2 (2018); Petition for Writ of Certiorari at 14–18, *United States v Microsoft*, No 17-2-01 (US 23 June 2017).

[45] Petition for Writ of Certiorari at 14–18, *US v Microsoft* (n 44).

[46] Anonymity networks operate by allowing users to access the Internet while hiding their identity, including their nationality and residence.

This challenge takes us to the next concern created by the CLOUD Act's focus on nationality and residence of the user for cross-border data access – what Paul Schwartz refers to as the 'know-your-customer' regime. In his work 'Legal Access to the Global Cloud', Schwartz illustrates how this focus could 'create strong incentives for cloud providers to know who their users are', ultimately imposing costs on user privacy.[47] The statutory basis for a service provider to file a motion to modify or quash a disclosure order depends, among other factors, on its ability to reasonably demonstrate the nationality and residence of its users.[48] In other words, 'cloud providers would need to document their customers' nationality and location to benefit from the executive agreements developed under the CLOUD Act'.[49] This requirement will likely encourage cloud service providers to collect and document detailed identification information about users similar to what banks and other financial service entities are required to do.[50]

4.2.3.2. Material Risk of Violating the Laws of a Qualifying Foreign Government

The mere fact that the user whose data is being sought by US authorities resides within the jurisdiction of a qualifying foreign government does not suffice to challenge a disclosure order under the CLOUD Act. To move to quash or modify a legal disclosure order, the service provider must also 'reasonably believe' that the required disclosure would create a material risk of violating the laws of a qualifying foreign government.[51] Although the CLOUD Act does not define what constitutes 'reasonable belief' and 'material risk', these terms depend on how courts apply the requirements in their comity analysis.

Some issues are worth noting regarding the new statutory right. The first issue concerns the time limit within which the service provider must move to court to object to the disclosure order. The CLOUD Act stipulates that this statutory right can only be invoked within 14 days after the service provider has been served with the disclosure order.[52] This time limitation can only be extended with government consent or court permission. Given the difficulties in determining the location of the user, and the time and resources required to evaluate whether the US legal request violates foreign laws, concerns may arise regarding the adequacy of this time limitation. The strict time limit, coupled with the threat of sanctions for non-compliance, may incentivise service providers to disclose user data without a thorough assessment of the CLOUD Act's requirements.

[47] Schwartz, 'Legal Access to the Global Cloud' (n 12).
[48] CLOUD Act, s 103(b) (codified at 18 USC, s 2703[h][2][i]).
[49] Schwartz, 'Legal Access to the Global Cloud' (n 12).
[50] ibid 1688.
[51] CLOUD Act, s 103(b) (codified at 18 USC, s 2703[h][2][ii]).
[52] ibid.

The second issue is whether the qualifying foreign government can object to a disclosure order issued by US authorities under the CLOUD Act. Schwartz suggests that the purpose of focusing on the nationality and location is to allow qualifying foreign governments to contest the extraterritorial use of a CLOUD Act warrant.[53] Furthermore, the CLOUD Act allows service providers to notify qualifying foreign governments when US authorities issue a legal process seeking the disclosure of data of nationals or residents of those governments.[54] The sole purpose of such notification is to enable qualifying foreign governments to take appropriate action, which may include objecting to the legal process. Such objection could also be weighed against US interests by courts in their comity analyses, as discussed below. The specific grounds on which qualifying foreign governments may object to disclosure orders issued by US authorities, and vice versa, should be subjects of future executive agreement negotiations. As clarified by the DOJ, foreign governments are free, in negotiations, to seek restrictions that would prevent the US from using orders to target data of their nationals or residents.[55] Despite its limitations, the US–UK cross-border data-access agreement supports this approach by prohibiting the UK from targeting data of US persons and reciprocally prohibiting the US government from targeting the data of persons located in the UK.[56]

4.2.3.3. Comity Analysis

The effectiveness of the statutory right for service providers to challenge a warrant in a court of law depends much on how courts will apply the required comity analysis.[57] The CLOUD Act allows two types of comity claims: new statutory comity, and common law comity analysis. Regarding the new statutory comity, the CLOUD Act outlines the standards that courts should follow upon receiving a motion filed by a service provider to challenge a disclosure order. For the court to decide in favour of the service providers (ie approve the motion to quash or modify a legal order), it must find the following:[58]

1. The required disclosure would cause the provider to violate the laws of a qualifying foreign government.
2. The interests of justice dictate that the legal process should be modified or quashed; and

[53] Schwartz, 'Legal Access to the Global Cloud' (n 12) (noting that 'the ability of a foreign country to object to the extraterritorial use of an SCA warrant is present only when the cloud provider can reasonably point to the nationality and location of the user').

[54] CLOUD Act, s 103(b) (codified at 18 USC, s 2703[h]).

[55] US Department of Justice, 'Promoting Public Safety, Privacy, and the Rule of Law' (n 10).

[56] Art 7, Agreement between the Government of the United States of America and the Government of the United Kingdom of Great Britain and Northern Ireland on Access to Electronic Data for the Purpose of Countering Serious Crime 2019.

[57] Schwartz, 'Legal Access to the Global Cloud' (n 12).

[58] CLOUD Act, s 103(b) (codified at 18 USC, s 2703[h][2][i]–[iii]).

3. The investigative target whose data is being sought is not a US person and does not reside in the US.

Determining whether 'the interests of justice dictate that the legal process should be modified or quashed' requires a fact-specific inquiry and the balancing of different interests. In this way, the totality of the circumstances of each case would dictate whether the court should ban or change a disclosure order issued under the CLOUD Act.[59] The CLOUD Act specifies several factors that courts should consider when engaged in this balancing test, including the relative interest of the US and those of the qualifying foreign government, the interest of the service provider, the location and nationality of the target, and the existence of other less harmful, timely, and effective means to access the data being sought.[60] Surprisingly, the CLOUD Act does not explicitly include the interests of the target (such as the right to privacy) among these factors. While one might expect that courts would take into account the privacy and other human rights interests when analysing the competing interests of the US and the qualifying foreign government, this omission represents a legislative gap in terms of privacy protections.

This new statutory comity framework applies once a CLOUD Act executive agreement is in place but does not apply when the conflict of law arises between the US law and a foreign country with which the US government does not have a CLOUD Act agreement. However, the CLOUD Act also preserves the existing common law comity analysis, under which service providers can challenge US legal processes even in the absence of such an agreement.[61]

4.3. Foreign Governments and US Service Providers

The second part of the CLOUD Act envisages a new reciprocal data-sharing agreement. The legal initiative allows law enforcement agencies from partner countries to access US-held data without going through the MLAT process. By creating the new framework, the CLOUD Act takes three profound measures to address the source of conflict and frustration for foreign governments in their efforts to obtain data held by US service providers, and vice versa:

1. It removes the provisions of the SCA that prohibit US service providers from disclosing communications content to qualifying foreign governments.
2. It requires partner foreign governments to afford reciprocal rights by taking similar measures (such as removing blocking statutes) so that service providers operating in the qualifying foreign government can respond to orders from US authorities without facing conflicting legal obligations.[62]

[59] ibid.
[60] ibid (codified at 18 USC, s 2703[h][3][A]–[H]).
[61] ibid.
[62] ibid (codified at 18 USC, s 2523[b][4][I]).

3. It mandates that qualifying foreign governments offer service providers the statutory right to challenge the legal process should conflicting legal obligations arise.[63]

The new legal regime is not self-executing; it requires an executive bilateral agreement between the US government and eligible foreign countries. Once an executive agreement has been signed, the benefits for the foreign government are principally twofold: it will be able to (a) gain streamlined access to user data held by US service providers; and (b) provide greater privacy protection for its citizens and residents when the US law enforcement seeks their data.[64]

However, the new framework also raises new concerns. By allowing partner countries to bypass the MLAT process, questions arise regarding the adequacy of the substantive and procedural safeguards in addressing the overreaching powers of foreign governments. For instance, the envisaged executive agreements may lower the threshold for law enforcement access to data (eg by removing the probable cause requirement). The following paragraphs examine in detail the powers and limits of foreign governments in accessing user data held by US service providers, identifying and analysing four phases of a CLOUD Act executive agreement.

The eligibility phase: The CLOUD Act outlines baseline requirements for a foreign government to be eligible for the executive agreement negotiations. The primary requirement is that the foreign government must have a domestic law that 'affords robust substantive and procedural protections for privacy and civil liberties in light of the data collection and activities of the foreign government'.[65] A foreign government whose domestic laws governing law enforcement access to electronic data prima facie fail to meet the eligibility criterion would not be considered as a prospective partner under the CLOUD Act. Consequently, the first determining factor for a potential partner country to negotiate an executive agreement is the adequacy of its own rule of law and privacy protections.[66] This requirement is critical, as access to data held in the US will primarily be governed by that foreign country's domestic laws once the executive agreement is in place.

Congress also specifies an extensive set of baseline rules as to what constitutes 'robust substantive and procedural protections' and how these requirements can be demonstrated. These requirements include: (a) the adequacy of substantive and procedural laws on cybercrime and electronic evidence; (b) respect for the rule of law and principles of non-discrimination; (c) adherence to applicable international human rights obligations; and (d) accountability and transparency regarding the collection and use of electronic data by law enforcement agencies.[67]

[63] ibid, s 103(b) (codified at 18 USC, s 2703[h]).
[64] B Barnett and others, 'Forecasting the Impact of the New US CLOUD Act' (Dechert LLP, 2018).
[65] CLOUD Act, s 105(a) (codified at 18 USC, s 2523[b][1]).
[66] ibid (codified at 18 USC, s 2523[b][4][D][iii]).
[67] The adequacy of substantive and procedural laws on cybercrime and electronic evidence can be demonstrated by being a party to the Cybercrime Convention, or through domestic laws that are consistent with the Convention. See ibid s, 105(a) (codified at 18 USC, s 2523[b][1][B][i]).

Therefore, the first step for a foreign government that wants to be part of an executive agreement is to review its domestic laws to ensure they fulfil the minimum criteria set forth by the CLOUD Act. The prospective partner country should not only incorporate these 'substantive and procedural protections' into its domestic law but also demonstrate their effective implementation. From a human rights perspective, the eligibility requirements serve as an initial layer of protection, and could minimise concerns that political and foreign policy interests may unduly influence executive agreements under the CLOUD Act.

The negotiation, certification, and qualification phase: The US government can negotiate CLOUD Act agreements only with foreign governments that satisfy the eligibility criteria. The Attorney General, with the concurrence of the Secretary of State, is tasked with evaluating and determining whether the domestic laws of a foreign government meet the baseline requirements highlighted above.

The CLOUD Act also prescribes several requirements that delineate what the US government can negotiate and what it cannot, in addition to the baseline requirements. Satisfying the baseline criteria alone is insufficient to achieve a qualifying foreign government status. For instance, the foreign government must agree to adopt procedures that minimise the acquisition, retention, and dissemination of information concerning US persons, and to afford reciprocal rights of data access to the US government.[68]

Another critical requirement at this stage is that any executive agreement entered by the US government should not undermine encryption. The CLOUD Act specifies that 'the terms of the [executive] agreement shall not create any obligation that providers be capable of decrypting data or limitation that prevents providers from decrypting data'.[69] This approach is 'encryption-neutral' in that the executive agreement will neither 'create any new authority for law enforcement to compel service providers to decrypt communications' nor 'prevent service providers from assisting in such decryption'.[70] This is a positive step towards privacy protection, especially in light of increasing pressure from law enforcement and intelligence agencies to regulate encryption technologies in ways that could undermine privacy and security.[71]

Once an executive agreement is reached between a foreign government and the US Attorney General, the latter must submit a written certification to Congress explaining how the foreign government meets each requirement stipulated under the CLOUD Act.[72] It is only at this stage that the requirements of the CLOUD

[68] ibid (codified at 18 USC, s 2523[b][2]).
[69] ibid (codified at 18 USC, s 2523[b][3]).
[70] US Department of Justice, 'Promoting Public Safety, Privacy, and the Rule of Law' (n 10).
[71] Schwartz, 'Legal Access to the Global Cloud' (n 12).
[72] CLOUD Act, s 105 (a) (codified at 18 USC, s 2523[b]).

Act are considered satisfied, and that the qualifying foreign government status is conferred on the foreign government.[73]

Executive agreements under the CLOUD Act come into force through a simple signature of the US executive branch.[74] Congress has a limited oversight role; its power is restricted to issuing a joint resolution of disapproval rather than affirmatively approving the agreement and setting the baseline requirements that foreign countries must meet to qualify for the agreement. Given Congress's limited power of issuing joint resolutions,[75] there is a high likelihood that executive agreements will enter into force without strict congressional scrutiny. Furthermore, the authority entrusted to the executive branch to determine and certify foreign governments is exempt from any judicial or administrative review.[76] While eliminating congressional approval or independent oversight may streamline the process of reaching executive agreements, it potentially introduces a susceptibility to political and foreign policy influences.

Therefore, the determination and certification of a foreign government constitutes the most crucial part of this process from a human rights perspective, for several reasons:

1. Once a foreign government obtains the qualifying status, its domestic laws – not those of the US – will govern the proceeding and enforcement of disclosure and interception orders issued by that qualifying foreign government.
2. The domestic laws of qualifying foreign governments are not required to meet US standards as long as they satisfy baseline requirements.
3. The determination and certification process neither requires congressional approval, nor is subject to judicial review; and
4. The US government has no means to verify whether each request meets the requirements set out in the CLOUD Act; this responsibility is shifted to domestic institutions within qualifying foreign governments and service providers. The US government can only make a periodic review of compliance.

Consequently, the determination and certification process by the Attorney General must be carried out with greater prudence. The process should be as transparent as possible, and must benefit from expert inputs as envisaged under the CLOUD Act.[77]

[73] The CLOUD Act defined 'qualifying foreign government' as a foreign government with which the US has an executive agreement, and the laws of which provide to service providers substantive and procedural opportunities to challenge a law enforcement request for user data. See ibid, s 103(b) (codified at 18 USC, s 2703[h][1][A][i]–[ii]).

[74] For a comprehensive analysis on the problem of executive agreements in general, see OA Hathaway, CA Bradley, and JL Goldsmith, 'The Failed Transparency Regime for Executive Agreements: An Empirical and Normative Analysis' (2020) 134 *Harvard Law Review* 632.

[75] Schwartz, 'Legal Access to the Global Cloud' (n 12).

[76] CLOUD Act s 105(a) (codified at 18 USC, s 2523[c]).

[77] ibid (codified at 18 USC, s 2523[b][1][A]).

The implementation phase: The fact that a foreign government affords robust substantive and procedural protections for privacy and civil liberties and achieves qualifying foreign government status under the CLOUD Act does not grant that government the power to make direct requests to US service providers at will. Instead, the CLOUD Act outlines at least four conditions that the qualifying foreign government must follow before issuing a request, and after data is obtained.

The first requirement specifies *target limitations*, detailing whose data can be requested by the foreign government and under what conditions. Specifically, the qualifying foreign government is permitted to request only data belonging to non-US citizens located outside the US. At the same time, the qualifying foreign government is prohibited from directly or indirectly targeting US citizens and residents (US persons).[78] To access data of a US person, the qualifying foreign government must go through the MLAT process.[79] Furthermore, the qualifying foreign government cannot target any person outside the US if the purpose is to obtain information concerning a US person.[80] It also cannot request data on its citizens and residents if that data will ultimately be used to target a US person. Thus, the qualifying foreign government is not only legally restrained from targeting US persons but also required to adopt procedures designed to minimise the acquisition, retention, and dissemination of information concerning US persons.[81] Reciprocally, the qualifying foreign government may negotiate similar restrictions that would prevent the US from targeting its nationals and residents.

The protection of third-country nationals and residents under the CLOUD Act also needs to be mentioned. Although the CLOUD Act lacks clarity in this regard, the US–UK cross-border data-access agreement illustrates this issue well. In cases where an order subject to this agreement is issued for data of a person reasonably believed to be located in a third country, the agreement contains an explicit requirement that the issuing party notify the appropriate authorities in the third country where the person is located.[82] By imposing a prior notification requirement on the issuing party, the agreement recognises the territorial sovereignty and privacy interests of third countries. While this notification requirement is a valuable addition to the CLOUD Act and could serve as a useful baseline for future negotiations, it does have significant limitations, as discussed below in the context of UK–US data-sharing agreement.

The second requirement is *order-specific*, detailing both substantive and procedural requirements that qualifying foreign governments must adhere to when

[78] ibid (codified at 18 USC, s 2523[b] [4] [A]–[B]); See also s 103(b) (codified at 18 USC, s 2703[h] [5]).

[79] J Daskal, 'Unpacking the CLOUD Act' [2019] *eucrim* 220.

[80] CLOUD Act, s 105 (a) (codified at 18 USC, s 2523[b][4][B]).

[81] ibid (codified at 18 USC, s 2523[b][2]).

[82] Art 5(10), US–UK Agreement.

issuing disclosure orders under their domestic law.[83] Specifically, the CLOUD Act outlines essential criteria regarding the type of crime being investigated, the subject of the order, the standard of proof required, and judicial oversight. The CLOUD Act restricts its application to the prevention, detection, investigation, or prosecution of 'serious crime', including terrorism. For other types of crimes, qualifying foreign governments must utilise the MLAT process or alternative mechanisms. However, the term 'serious crime' remains undefined within the Act, creating potential ambiguity. A clear definition would have been beneficial from a human rights perspective, as it would have delineated the scope of requests strictly to serious crimes. The lack of definition may lead to uncertainty about which crimes are covered, and could undermine protections traditionally afforded under cross-border co-operation frameworks, such as the 'dual criminality' requirements found in MLAT agreements.

The CLOUD Act also mandates that each order issued by a qualifying foreign government must specify a particular individual, account, address, personal device, or other specific identifier as the object of the order.[84] This particularity requirement is derived from the Fourth Amendment principles[85] and prohibits broad powers such as 'bulk data collection'.[86] Additionally, each order must meet a factual standard that deviates from traditional norms; it must be based on 'articulable and credible facts' rather than the stricter 'probable cause' standard used in MLAT processes. This means that qualifying foreign governments are not required to demonstrate a probable cause standard equivalent to that in US law for issuing production or an interception order against US-based companies. Instead, orders should comply with domestic laws of the qualifying foreign government while being grounded in articulable and credible facts regarding the conduct under investigation.[87]

Critics argue that omitting a probable cause standard diminishes protections, compared with the MLAT system.[88] Under the MLAT process, data requests from foreign governments undergo scrutiny by the DOJ, requiring a US judge to establish probable cause. The CLOUD Act replaces this with a lower threshold – 'reasonable justification based on articulable and credible facts' – which aligns more closely with standards governing requests for subscriber information rather than content disclosure under US law. Proponents of eliminating the probable cause requirement argue that it facilitates co-operation with foreign governments without compromising human rights protections. They contend that imposing a US-specific standard on crimes unrelated to US jurisdiction undermines legitimate

[83] CLOUD Act, s 105 (a) (codified at 18 USC, s 2523[b][4][D][i]–[vi]).

[84] ibid, s 2523(b)(4)(D)(ii); See also Kerr, 'The Next Generation Communications Privacy Act' (n 34); Daskal, 'Privacy and Security Across Borders' (n 39).

[85] See US Constitution, Amendment IV.

[86] US Department of Justice, 'Promoting Public Safety, Privacy, and the Rule of Law' (n 10).

[87] CLOUD Act, s 105(a) (codified at 18 USC, s 2523[b][4][D][iv]).

[88] See, for instance, a coalition letter of opposition from 24 privacy, civil liberty, and human rights organisations, available at http://bit.ly/2Xk5MCr.

interests of foreign governments and could incentivise them to pursue invasive options to obtain data stored in the US.[89]

The absence of a probable cause requirement in a foreign jurisdiction does not inherently suggest an inferior standard compared with US law. For instance, research indicates that both the US and EU systems exhibit strictness in different aspects without necessitating a general probable cause requirement for search or evidence requests in the EU.[90] Rather than imposing US standards on foreign requests or demanding alignment with US legal frameworks, the CLOUD Act aims to foster procedural and due process interoperability between US and foreign systems involved in data-access agreements. Lastly, each order issued by a qualifying foreign government must undergo review or oversight by an independent authority.[91] The inclusion of 'other independent authority' has raised concerns among privacy advocates, who fear that it may allow non-judicial entities to approve disclosure or interception orders. The CLOUD Act recognises that different countries maintain varying checks and balances within their legal systems.

The third requirement of the CLOUD Act at the implementation phase concerns *real time interception* of data. Beyond access to stored communications content, the CLOUD Act also allows qualifying foreign governments to issue orders for real-time interception. This marks the first instance where foreign governments, under an executive agreement, are legally permitted to collect real-time communications in the US. Paul Schwartz describes these real-time interception powers as the 'most expansive element of the CLOUD Act',[92] suggesting that they necessitate more stringent standards of necessity and proportionality than those required for ordinary disclosure orders.

Due to its intrusive nature, the CLOUD Act imposes 'time' and 'necessity' constraints for real-time interceptions that must be satisfied in addition to the previously discussed restrictions. Accordingly, an interception order issued under the executive agreement must be for a fixed, limited duration, should not last longer than is reasonably necessary to accomplish the approved purposes of the order, and must be issued only if the same information cannot reasonably be obtained through a less intrusive method.[93] The 'necessity' requirement is empirical; the issuing authority must demonstrate that all other alternatives have been exhausted, and that no less intrusive but equally effective means are available.

[89] AK Woods, 'Data Beyond Borders: Mutual Legal Assistance in the Internet Age' (Global Network Initiative, 27 January 2015); J Daskal and AK Woods, 'Cross-Border Data Requests: A Proposed Framework' (*Lawfare*, 24 November 2015), www.lawfareblog.com/cross-border-data-requests-proposed-framework.

[90] P Swire and D Kennedy-Mayo, 'How Both the EU and the U.S Are "Stricter" than Each Other for the Privacy of Government Requests for Information' (2017) 66 Emory Law Journal 617; S Vergnolle, P Swire, and JD Hemmings, 'A Mutual Legal Assistance Case Study: The United States And France' (2017) 34 *Wisconsin International Law Journal* 324.

[91] CLOUD Act, s 105(a) (codified at 18 USC, s 2523[b][4][D][v]).

[92] Schwartz, 'Legal Access to the Global Cloud' (n 12).

[93] CLOUD Act (codified at 18 USC, s 2523[b][4][D][vi][III]).

Despite these additional requirements for real-time interception, the standards imposed on qualifying foreign governments may be lower than those stipulated under the Wiretap Act, which governs real-time interception in the US. Beyond requiring a probable cause, real-time interception under the Wiretap Act necessitates more stringent justifications, commonly known as 'super warrants' or 'probable-cause-plus'.[94]

Among other stipulations, each application for real-time interception under the Wiretap Act must include: (1) a particular description of the nature and location of the facilities from which or the place where the communication is to be intercepted; (2) a complete statement regarding whether other investigative procedures have been attempted and failed or why they are unlikely to succeed if attempted; and (3) a statement indicating the duration for which the interception is required.[95] Furthermore, the Wiretap Act mandates that interception be conducted in a manner that minimises capturing communications not covered by the order,[96] and targets must be notified within 90 days following the termination of the order.[97] These requirements are not included in the CLOUD Act, rendering it a lesser standard of protection compared with the Wiretap Act. This discrepancy raises significant concerns regarding privacy and oversight.

The final implementation phase requirement of the CLOUD Act addresses the *security*, *use*, *handling*, and *dissemination* of user data obtained by qualifying foreign governments.[98] In this respect, the Act stipulates that: (1) disclosed data should be promptly reviewed; (2) unreviewed data should be stored in a secure system; (3) access to that system should be limited to individuals trained in applicable procedures; and (4) data deemed irrelevant to the purposes of the order should be segregated, sealed, or deleted, employing minimisation procedures similar to those outlined in the Foreign Intelligence Surveillance Act.[99] However, the specifics of how these requirements are operationalised are left to the discretion of the qualifying foreign government. While the CLOUD Act mandates that qualifying foreign governments store data in a 'secure system', it does not establish any specific security standard for this requirement.

The review and accountability phase: The CLOUD Act mandates periodic evaluation by the executive US government to determine whether qualifying foreign governments meet the Act's requirements. The Attorney General, in concurrence with the Secretary of State, is responsible for conducting this review every five

[94] 18 USC, s 2518 (2012); Swire and Kennedy-Mayo, 'How Both the EU and the U.S Are "Stricter" than Each Other' (n 90); Schwartz, 'Legal Access to the Global Cloud' (n 12).
[95] 18 USC, s 2518 (1)(b–d) (2012).
[96] ibid, s 2518(5).
[97] ibid, s 2518(8)(d)(1).
[98] CLOUD Act, s 105(a) (codified at 18 USC, s 2523[b][4][F]–[H]).
[99] ibid.

years and reporting findings and decisions to Congress.[100] Depending on the results, the review may lead to either the recertification of the foreign government or the unilateral annulment of the agreement, resulting in the loss of eligibility for that government. In the renewal report, the Attorney General must detail the reasons for the renewal, any substantive changes to the agreement or the relevant laws or procedures of the foreign government, and how the agreement has been implemented, among other considerations.[101]

This periodic compliance review may be inadequate, as requests from qualifying foreign governments are not subject to individual case-by-case evaluations within the US. The CLOUD Act delegates the assessment of each request – typically conducted by US authorities (including the DOJ, Attorney General, and US judges) – to the domestic procedures and institutions of the qualifying foreign government. This arrangement can be perceived as granting service providers excessive power to balance their business interests alongside human rights and law enforcement concerns. Service providers are tasked with evaluating each request on a case-by-case basis to determine whether it complies with the CLOUD Act, domestic laws of the requesting government, and their internal policies. This situation effectively grants service providers quasi-judicial powers, raising questions about their capacity to make such determinations when their business interests are at stake.

4.4. The Unfulfilled Promises of the CLOUD Act

Three interrelated problems dominated the literature, policy discourse, and courtroom debates preceding the CLOUD Act. First, the increasing global trend in unilateral assertions of extraterritorial jurisdiction over data. In *Microsoft Ireland*, for instance, numerous amicus briefs cautioned against the far-reaching consequences of the US government's practice of unilaterally compelling the production of data stored overseas, arguing that this could encourage other governments with weak protections to follow suit. Second, the global trend towards data localisation. Third, the conflict-of-law issue, which the US Congress summarised as potential conflicting legal obligations for service providers when foreign governments order production of electronic data that US law may prohibit disclosure of, and vice versa.[102]

The CLOUD Act aimed to address these problems by allowing foreign governments streamlined access to data hosted by US service providers, providing mechanisms to mitigate and resolve potential conflicts between US law and foreign law, reducing data localisation incentives, and setting privacy

[100] ibid (codified at 18 USC, s 2523[e][1]–[2]).
[101] ibid (codified at 18 USC, s 2523[e][2][A]–[C]).
[102] CLOUD Act, s 102(1–6).

safeguards for cross-border law-enforcement access to data. Consequently, the statute is often portrayed as a 'new paradigm for international law enforcement cooperation'.[103]

This section challenges these claims, arguing that the CLOUD Act could produce the opposite results. Contrary to its stated policy objectives, the CLOUD Act could incentivise unilateralism, generate new conflicts of law, reinforce the governments' desire to control data through data localisation, and ultimately undermine privacy. While the CLOUD Act offers a relatively realistic option to address jurisdictional and conflicts-of-law problems through a bilateral approach based on reciprocity and shared commitment to the rule of law and privacy protection, its positive aspects should not overshadow its shortcomings. This analysis challenges the statute's portrayal in literature and in policy discourse, concluding that it may not alleviate the problems it was designed to address.

4.4.1. CLOUD Act's Scalability Challenge

The success of the CLOUD Act framework depends on the number of countries willing to enter data-sharing agreements and meet baseline requirements. Nearly seven years after its adoption, the US has concluded only two agreements – with the UK (October 2019) and Australia (December 2021) – with negotiations underway with the EU and Canada.[104] These initial agreements were facilitated by similar legal systems and existing intelligence-sharing relationships.[105] Under this new arrangement, the UK and Australia have more options to obtain data held by US-based companies. The US–UK agreement has particularly shown promising results. In its first year (2022–23), over 10,000 requests were submitted under the terms of the agreement to obtain evidence held by US companies, providing critical data to UK law enforcement and intelligence agencies for combatting serious crimes.[106] The Home Office report shows that the agreement has significantly enhanced the ability to tackle serious crime, such as terrorism, child exploitation, drug trafficking, and organised crime. These outcomes underscore the agreement's efficacy in streamlining access to crucial data for combatting serious crimes, an outcome that would have been unattainable without this cross-border co-operation mechanism.

However, the limited number of agreements raises concerns about the Act's scalability to countries with different legal systems. The CLOUD Act appears

[103] Remarks of Deputy Assistant Attorney General Richard W Downing at the International Symposium on Cybercrime Response (13 September 2023), www.justice.gov/criminal/cloud-act-resources.

[104] CLOUD Act Resources, available at www.justice.gov/criminal/cloud-act-resources.

[105] Australia, Canada, the UK, the US, and New Zealand have formed the 'Five Eyes' alliance for intelligence-sharing.

[106] 'UK-US Data Access Agreement: first year of use (Written Statements by Tom Tugendhat, Statement UIN HCWS152' (UK Parliament), available at https://questions-statements.parliament.uk/written-statements/detail/2023-12-19/hcws152.

designed for high-priority and trusted partners sharing American values, potentially limiting its global applicability. Congressional hearings leading to its adoption reveal a narrow focus, primarily addressing the *Microsoft Ireland* case and enabling the UK–US agreement, the negotiation of which was completed before the Act.[107]

Furthermore, the UK was the only foreign government invited to testify in Congress about the importance of the CLOUD Act.[108] The US administration also confirmed that it will 'consider the new approach for other like-minded countries only if the US-UK agreement proves successful'.[109] Consequently, critics argue that the US has not considered countries unable to participate in emerging global systems for electronic evidence transfer.[110]

This scalability issue could create a divide, with only a few countries benefiting from the new framework. This means that the CLOUD Act risks creating a perception of a 'fast lane' for a privileged club.[111] Such exclusivity might exacerbate frustrations among countries unable to access data held by US companies, potentially spurring unilateral measures such as data localisation. Ultimately, this limited scalability could undermine the effectiveness, legitimacy, and sustainability of the system envisioned by the CLOUD Act, potentially hindering global co-operation in cross-border data access for law enforcement.

4.4.2. Unilateralism in Disguise

Contrary to its stated objective, the CLOUD Act promotes unilateralism through two mechanisms. Firstly, Part I of the Act codifies existing practices, and permits US authorities to compel US-based technology companies to produce data regardless of its global storage location or the user's nationality. Given the dominance of US-based companies in the global cloud infrastructure, this provision effectively enables the US government to unilaterally access worldwide data without notifying foreign governments or users. The only limitation to this unilateral power is

[107] 'Legislation to Permit the Secure and Privacy-Protective Exchange of Electronic Data for the Purposes of Combatting Serious Crime Including Terrorism' (*US Department of Justice*, 15 July 2016), available at https://www.aclu.org/sites/default/files/field_document/doj_legislative_proposal.pdf.

[108] The UK deputy national security adviser testified twice in Congress. See Written Testimony of Paddy McGuiness, UK Deputy National Security Advisor, before the US Senate Committee on the Judiciary's Subcommittee on Crime and Terrorism, at a Hearing entitled 'Law Enforcement Access to Data Stored Across Borders: Facilitating Cooperation and Protecting Rights' (10 May 2017).

[109] International Conflicts of Law and Their Implications for Cross Border Data Requests by Law Enforcement: Hearing before the H Comm on the Judiciary, 114th Cong Serial No 114–84 (2016) (Statement by David Bitkower, principal deputy assistant Attorney General United States Department of Justice).

[110] M Fidler, 'Africans Want Cross-Border Data Access Reform, But They Might Get Left Out' (*Council on Foreign Relations*, 26 October 2016), www.cfr.org/blog/africans-want-cross-border-data-access-reform-they-might-get-left-out.

[111] Perault and Salgado, 'Untapping the Full Potential of CLOUD Act Agreements' (n 3).

the service provider's ability to invoke common-law principles of comity, which can be challenging to enforce in practice.[112]

From the US perspective, the CLOUD Act merely reinforces pre-existing practices. In the *Microsoft Ireland case*, the company challenged the US government's unilateral exercise of extraterritorial law enforcement power, arguing that the SCA did not authorise the government to go around the world and vacuum up emails under a search warrant.[113] The adoption of the CLOUD Act does not address this concern; rather, it codifies the US government's position.

Furthermore, Part II of the CLOUD Act, which envisages reciprocal data-sharing agreements, may not effectively constrain US government unilateralism, for a couple of reasons. First, the lack of scalability highlighted above means that only a few countries would qualify for CLOUD Act agreements. Second, even with a CLOUD Act agreement in place, the US government could continue using Part I of the Act to compel service providers to disclose data without regard to the user's nationality or residence.

The US–UK CLOUD Act agreement exemplifies this issue by preserving the parallel application of domestic laws, even for obtaining data of persons covered by the agreement. This arrangement provides little incentive for US authorities to use the executive agreement over the CLOUD Act itself.[114] Moreover, the agreement allows both parties to unilaterally target third-country nationals and residents, potentially enabling UK law enforcement authorities to compel US-based service providers to disclose personal data of, for example, a German citizen residing in Germany, without the German authorities' knowledge and permission.

In essence, the international implications of US law remain largely unchanged post-CLOUD Act. Compliance with the Act may still lead to violations of foreign laws, potentially prompting countries to enact new blocking statutes to protect their data from the reach of the CLOUD Act. Most critically, other nations might emulate the US approach, introducing laws that allow their law enforcement authorities to access data across borders without regard for other states' sovereign interests. This scenario would create new conflicting legal obligations for service providers, further complicating the global data governance landscape.[115]

[112] E Mignon, 'The CLOUD Act: Unveiling European Powerlessness' (*Le Grand Continent*, 5 September 2020), available at https://legrandcontinent.eu/fr/2020/09/05/the-cloud-act-unveiling-european-powerlessness/.

[113] International Conflicts of Law and Their Implications for Cross Border Data Requests by Law Enforcement: Hearing before the H Comm on the Judiciary, 114th Cong Serial No 114–84 (2016).

[114] N Kushwaha, P Roguski, and BW Watson, 'Up in the Air: Ensuring Government Data Sovereignty in the Cloud', 2020 12th International Conference on Cyber Conflict (NATO CCDCOE Publications, 2020) 52; T Christakis, '21 Thoughts and Questions about the UK/US CLOUD Act Agreement: (And an Explanation of How It Works – with Charts)' (*European Law Blog*, 17 October 2019), available at www.europeanlawblog.eu/pub/21-thoughts-and-questions-about-the-uk-us-cloud-act-agreement-and-an-explanation-of-how-it-works-with-charts/release/1.

[115] SA Morris, 'Rethinking the Extraterritorial Scope of the United States' Access to Data Stored by a Third Party' (2018) 42 *Fordham International Law Journal* 183.

4.4.3. The CLOUD Act could Generate New Conflicts of Law

The extraterritorial reach of the CLOUD Act has triggered diplomatic and legislative responses from foreign countries, particularly the EU and its Member States. The Act has reinforced calls for digital sovereignty and blocking statutes in Europe. Shortly after the CLOUD Act's passage, the European Parliament adopted a resolution calling for the suspension of the EU–US Privacy Shield – a framework later invalidated by the CJEU.[116] The resolution expressed strong concerns regarding the CLOUD Act's implications for EU data protection laws. The French government has been particularly vocal in opposing the CLOUD Act, characterising it as a threat to 'digital sovereignty'.[117] Two French government reports highlighted this stance. The first report, ordered by Prime Minister Edouard Philippe, explored measures to protect French companies against extraterritorial legal actions.[118] This 26 June 2019 report, entitled *Restore the Sovereignty of France and Europe and Protect our Companies from Laws and Measures with Extraterritorial Scope*, found, among other things, that France is ill-equipped to protect French companies against the CLOUD Act, as the GDPR applies only to personal data. It proposed several counter-measures to counter the impacts of the CLOUD Act, most notably the reforming and strengthening of the 1968 French blocking statute.[119] A second report, released by the French Senate in October 2019, also characterised the CLOUD Act as aggressively extraterritorial, and called for the modernisation and strict enforcement of the blocking statute.[120]

These developments make conflicts of law inevitable. Service providers operating in France would find it challenging to comply with the CLOUD Act without violating the French blocking statute and the GDPR. Furthermore, until a cross-border data-access agreement is signed between the EU and the US, the new conflict-of-law resolution mechanism envisaged by the CLOUD Act would remain irrelevant to this problem. The conflict between the GDPR and the CLOUD Act is discussed in detail in chapter six.

[116] European Parliament resolution on the adequacy of the protection afforded by the EU-US Privacy Shield (2018/2645(RSP)), available at www.europarl.europa.eu/doceo/document/B-8-2018-0305_EN.html?redirect.

[117] Hemmings, Srinivasan, and Swire, 'Defining the Scope of "Possession, Custody, or Control"' (n 30) 632.

[118] R Gauvain, 'Rétablir la souveraineté de la France et de l'Europe et protéger nos entreprises des lois et mesures à portée extraterritoriale' (Rapport à la demande de Monsieur Édouard Philippe, Premier Ministre, 26 June 2019).

[119] ibid.

[120] Commission d'enquête sur la souveraineté numérique, Rapport de Gérard LONGUET sur la souveraineté numérique, fait au nom de la commission d'enquête, Rapport n° 7 (2019–2020), 1 October 2019.

4.4.4. The CLOUD Act could Spur, not Counter, Data Localisation

The CLOUD Act aimed to counter the global trend towards data localisation laws, which was a chief concern underlying discussions leading to its enactment.[121] Through a new generation of cross-border data-access agreements, the statute promised to provide a substantial incentive for countries to avoid adopting data localisation policies. However, this approach may be overly simplistic and potentially counter-productive.

The primary issue with the argument that CLOUD Act agreements will reduce the incentives for data localisation is that claim's narrow framing of such policies as merely a law-enforcement access issues. This framing lacks a holistic view of the diverse motivations driving global data-localisation trends. Data localisation policies pursue a wide range of objectives, including preventing foreign surveillance, protecting the privacy of citizens, promoting domestic economic development, and ensuring digital sovereignty. Facilitating domestic law-enforcement access to data is only one aspect of these policy objectives, and rarely the primary motivation. For instance, European calls for data localisation are largely prompted by concerns related to data protection, privacy, and fear of foreign access to European personal and industrial data.[122]

The increasing global trend to assert digital sovereignty further undermines the CLOUD Act's promise to disincentivise data localisation. Digital sovereignty policies, while varied in form, share the common goal of reasserting control over data generated in or passing through national Internet and cloud infrastructure, and subjecting data flows to national jurisdictions.[123] This aligns with what Milton Mueller described as the process of subjugating cyberspace to local jurisdiction.[124] The discourse on digital sovereignty is broader in scope but increasingly marked by data localisation requirements.[125]

Paradoxically, the CLOUD Act itself has incentivised data localisation rather than deterring it. It has prompted European countries to adopt standards and policies that would exclude US companies from government and company cloud storage. For example, the proposed European Cybersecurity Certification Scheme for Cloud Services (EUCS) aims to make cloud computing firms eligible for

[121] International Conflicts of Law and Their Implications for Cross Border Data Requests by Law Enforcement: Hearing before the H Comm on the Judiciary, 114th Cong Serial No 114–84 (2016).

[122] T Christakis, '"European Digital Sovereignty" Successfully Navigating Between the "Brussels Effect" and Europe's Quest for Strategic Autonomy' (Multidisciplinary Institute on Artificial Intelligence/ Grenoble Alpes Data Institute, December 2020).

[123] R Vatanparast, 'Data Governance and the Elasticity of Sovereignty' (2020) 46 *Brooklyn Journal of International Law* 1; Kushwaha, Roguski, and Watson, 'Up in the Air' (n 114); C Hobbs (ed), *Europe's Digital Sovereignty: From Rulemaker to Superpower in the Age of US-China Rivalry* (European Council on Foreign Relations, Essay Collection 2020) ECFR/336.

[124] M Mueller, *Will the Internet Fragment? Sovereignty, Globalization and Cyberspace* (Polity, 2017) 77.

[125] Christakis, 'European Digital Sovereignty' (n 122) 65.

certification only if they are immune from foreign laws such as the CLOUD Act. This effectively requires cloud service providers to have their headquarters within the EU, store European data in Europe, and restrict data access to EU personnel only.[126]

As highlighted above, the French government has been considering data localisation requirements specifically to counter the extraterritorial reach of the CLOUD Act. A 2019 French government report discussed data localisation as a tool to protect French companies from the long arms of the CLOUD Act.[127] The report suggested that data localisation could play a crucial role in securing France's digital sovereignty in three instances: (i) protecting sensitive data (sovereign public processing, private financial or strategic commercial data); (ii) guaranteeing enhanced accessibility (including access to data by courts or national regulators); and (iii) supporting the industrial ecosystem of cloud players and development of data processing capacities.[128] This approach would require French companies to avoid using American cloud hosting companies altogether.[129] Swedish authorities have already prohibited outsourcing public sector data to US cloud service providers subject to the CLOUD Act.[130] Some European policy-makers have even equated the storage of European data by US cloud services companies abroad to a loss of sovereignty.[131] French lawmakers argue that the CLOUD Act 'must be a wakeup call for Europe to accelerate its own, sovereign offer in the data sector'.[132] In conclusion, the CLOUD Act's approach to countering data localisation may be fundamentally flawed. By fortifying the long arms of US law enforcement authorities, the statute may inadvertently spur, rather than counter, the global trend towards data localisation policies.

4.4.5. Undermining Privacy and Other Human Rights

The CLOUD Act, despite its promises to create a privacy-enhancing framework in cross-border data-sharing, could ultimately undermine user privacy in several ways. By enabling US authorities to unilaterally access data stored overseas, the Act creates a precedent for other nations to adopt similarly extraterritorial measures, potentially leading to a global patchwork of conflicting data-access laws. This

[126] Z Meyers, 'Can the EU Afford to Drive out American Cloud Services?' (*Centre for European Reform*, 2 March 2023), available at www.cer.eu/insights/can-eu-afford-drive-out-american-cloud-services.

[127] Commission d'enquête sur la souveraineté numérique, Rapport de Gérard LONGUET (n 120).

[128] ibid.

[129] L Cerulus, 'France Wants Cyber Rule to Curb US Access to EU Data' (Politico, 13 September 2021), available at www.politico.eu/article/france-wants-cyber-rules-to-stop-us-data-access-in-europe/.

[130] K Propp, 'Waving the Flag of Digital Sovereignty (Atlantic Council, 11 December 2019), available at www.atlanticcouncil.org/blogs/new-atlanticist/waving-the-flag-of-digital-sovereignty/.

[131] F Burwell and K Propp, 'The European Union and the Search for Digital Sovereignty: Building "Fortress Europe" or Preparing for a New World?' (Atlantic Council Issue Brief 1, 2020).

[132] J Hemmings and N Swire, 'The Cloud Act Is Not a Tool for Theft of Trade Secrets' (*Lawfare*, 23 April 2019).

could result in a race to the bottom, where countries compete to assert jurisdiction over data, eroding privacy protections worldwide. Paradoxically, the push for data localisation in response to the CLOUD Act could lead to reduced cybersecurity protections, as localised data centres may lack the robust security measures of global cloud providers. Consequently, the CLOUD Act's approach to cross-border data access may inadvertently create a less secure, more fragmented digital landscape that compromises user privacy.

4.5. Conclusion

Compared to other alternatives, Part II of the CLOUD Act offers a relatively realistic option to deal with the jurisdictional and conflicts-of-law problems associated with cloud computing. It employs a bilateral approach premised on the principle of reciprocity and a shared commitment to the rule of law and the protection of privacy. While not perfect, this approach has several advantages compared with alternatives.

For instance, the CLOUD Act is realistic in the sense that it does not require partner countries to have identical legal frameworks as long as they fulfil the threshold requirements. Instead of subjecting foreign requests to US standards or requiring foreign governments to harmonise their national laws with the US system, the CLOUD Act tries to establish procedural and due process interoperability between the US system and those of foreign governments. At the same time, the statute has built-in substantive and procedural safeguards that foreign governments should satisfy at different stages of the process.

However, these positive aspects should not overshadow the shortcomings of the CLOUD Act. Contrary to its stated policy objectives and the claims of its advocates, the Act could potentially incentivise unilateralism, generate new conflicts of law, reinforce governments' desire to have control over data through data localisation, and ultimately undermine privacy. These potential negative outcomes warrant careful consideration and ongoing evaluation of the Act's implementation and impact on global data governance and privacy protection.

5

The EU Way: The e-Evidence Package

On 13 June 2023, the EU Parliament ushered in a new era of criminal justice access to electronic evidence across borders with the adoption of the Regulation on the European Production and Preservation Orders for electronic evidence in criminal matters ('the e-Evidence Regulation' or 'the Regulation').[1] Often characterised as the EU version of the CLOUD Act, this landmark legislation establishes a framework empowering law enforcement authorities to directly access stored data across borders. Complementing the Regulation is a Directive designed to harmonise rules concerning the appointment of legal representatives by non-EU service providers, streamlining evidence-gathering in criminal proceedings.[2]

This legislative package is the culmination of nearly a decade of intense debate and consultation, reflecting the high priority that improving cross-border access to electronic evidence for criminal investigations has held on the EU policy agenda since at least 2015.[3] In its June 2016 Conclusions, the Justice and Home Affairs Council urged the Commission to explore a common EU approach encompassing three areas: (i) streamlining judicial co-operation proceedings; (ii) developing a unified EU framework for co-operation with service providers; and (iii) exploring the contours of enforcement jurisdiction in cyberspace.[4] The e-Evidence Package directly responds to these imperatives, promising a more efficient and cohesive approach to criminal justice access to electronic evidence across borders.

This chapter delves into the EU's response to the complex cross-border data-access problem, critically examining the jurisdictional theories underpinning the e-Evidence Regulation and its implications for the sovereign interests of third countries, the operational realities of non-EU service providers, and the fundamental rights of individuals whose data is now within reach of EU law enforcement.

[1] Regulation (EU) 2023/1543 of the European Parliament and of the Council on European Production Orders and European Preservation Orders for electronic evidence in criminal proceedings and for the execution of custodial sentences following criminal proceedings (e-Evidence Regulation) [2023] OJ L191/118.

[2] Directive (EU) 2023/1544 laying down harmonised rules on the designation of designated establishments and the appointment of legal representatives for the purpose of gathering electronic evidence in criminal proceedings (e-Evidence Directive) [2023] OJ L191/181.

[3] Communication from the Commission to the European Parliament, the Council, the European Economic and Social Committee and the Committee of the Regions: The European Agenda on Security, COM (2015) 185 final.

[4] Council Conclusions on Improving Criminal Justice in Cyberspace (9 June 2016).

5.1. Compelling Factors Behind the e-Evidence Package

Prior to the introduction of the E-evidence Package, the legal landscape governing the cross-border gathering of electronic evidence by EU authorities was characterised by a fragmented array of national, regional, and international legal frameworks. Six sets of legal frameworks were particularly relevant in this context.

Bilateral and multilateral MLATs *with third countries* provided one of the main frameworks through which Member States could request digital evidence stored outside the EU. Several such bilateral and multilateral agreements, including the EU–US MLA agreement, set out procedures and conditions for co-operation between competent authorities.

A second layer of complexity stemmed from the patchwork of bilateral and multilateral MLATs operating *within* the EU itself. These legal frameworks include EU-level instruments such as the 2000 Convention on Mutual Assistance in Criminal Matters between the Member States of the EU, as well as various bilateral agreements between the Member States. Although the European Investigation Order (EIO) Directive replaced the Mutual Assistance in Criminal Matters between the Member States and other MLA channels within the EU, the older instruments remain applicable for co-operation with Member States not bound by the EIO Directive, such as Ireland and Denmark, which have opted out. Third, national regimes of Member States often include their own provisions for cross-border data access. These unilateral legal instruments empower national authorities to compel the disclosure of data held by foreign service providers, operating independently of the MLA system.

Equally important are the national regimes of *third countries*, which shape EU authorities' ability to access electronic evidence across borders. Any MLA request issued by an EU Member State to a third country is subject both to the domestic laws of that third country and to the applicable treaty provisions. Similarly, co-operation between EU law enforcement authorities and service providers in third countries is often determined by the data protection and disclosure laws of the provider's country. For instance, the European Commission has noted that the US and Ireland account for a large proportion of the total volume of requests from European law enforcement authorities.[5] Because the legal rules of the third country in which the service provider is established typically define the limits of co-operation with foreign governments, US law directly affects EU authorities' capacity to obtain data from service providers under their jurisdiction.

The Budapest Convention on Cybercrime is another instrument that plays a crucial role in this landscape. Together with its Additional Protocol, the Budapest

[5] Improving Cross-Border Access to Electronic Evidence: Findings from the Expert Process and Suggested Way Forward (Non-paper from the Commission services, 8 June 2017).

Convention introduces several cross-border data-access mechanisms that operate independently of existing MLAT frameworks. As discussed in chapter three, the Budapest Convention is the first international instrument to establish concrete rules for obtaining electronic evidence from service providers abroad, and has become a cornerstone of global co-operation. All EU Member States, with the exception of Ireland and Sweden, are parties to this Convention, and the EU holds observer status within the Cybercrime Convention Committee, which oversees the implementation, monitoring, and further development of the Convention.

Finally, the EIO Directive represents a major step forward in facilitating the gathering and transfer of evidence among EU the Member States bound by it. The EIO Directive, in application since 2017, enables an authority in one Member State (the 'issuing authority') to request specific criminal investigative measures be carried out by an authority in another Member State (the 'executing authority'). Its scope encompasses all investigative measures, including gathering electronic evidence, with exceptions for joint investigation teams and cross-border surveillance as provided for in the Schengen Agreement.[6] The EIO Directive introduces a more efficient system for gathering cross-border evidence, replacing previous mechanisms and setting the stage for further developments in this area. It aims 'to create a single, efficient and flexible instrument for obtaining evidence located in another Member State in the framework of criminal proceedings'.[7] The Directive improves upon the MLAT system by reducing co-operation obstacles and grounds for refusal, setting strict response deadlines, and introducing standardised formalities for production orders. It streamlines co-operation procedures by creating a direct communication between judicial authorities, bypassing central authorities as required in the MLAT system.

While the Directive differs from the MLAT system in many aspects, both frameworks rely on a 'mediated access model', requiring the involvement of relevant competent authorities in both the issuing and executing states.[8] Like the MLAT system, the EIO Directive does not authorise direct co-operation between law enforcement authorities and service providers, nor does it allow unilateral transborder data access. Judicial scrutiny in both the countries involved remains crucial to ensure that every order is executed in accordance with the procedures and safeguards prescribed under the different legal systems concerned. However, the EIO Directive has several salient features distinguishing it from the MLAT system, as described below.

Recognition and execution: The EIO Directive requires the executing state to recognise an EIO issued by another Member State without any further formality,

[6] Art 3, Directive 2014/41/EU of the European Parliament and of the Council regarding the European Investigation Order in criminal matters (EIO Directive) [2014] OJ L130/1.

[7] Explanatory Memorandum Relating to the Initiative by a Group of Member States for a Directive of the European Parliament and of the Council Regarding the European Investigation Order in Criminal Matters (Council of the European Union, 2010).

[8] S Carrera and others, 'Access to Electronic Data by Third-Country Law Enforcement Authorities: Challenges to EU Rule of Law and Fundamental Rights' (Centre for European Policy Studies, 2015).

and execute it as if ordered by its own authority, except for on specific grounds highlighted below.[9] This contrasts with the MLAT system, which imposes the law of the recipient country. The EIO Directive provides limited grounds for refusal and sets a strict time limit for recognition and execution.[10]

Responsibility for fundamental rights compliance: The issuing state's competent authorities are exclusively responsible for ensuring that each EIO meets the requirements of legality, necessity, and proportionality. The EIO Directive assumes that the issuing authorities, as opposed to the executing authorities, are best placed to assess the substantive merits of the case, on the basis of their knowledge of the details of the investigation concerned. For instance, the legality requirement prevents the issuing authorities from using EIOs to obtain evidence from another Member State through an investigative measure that does not exist under the issuing state's national law or would not be available in a similar domestic case.[11] The EIO Directive relieves the executing authorities from the responsibility of assessing the legality, necessity, and proportionality of EIOs. Instead, the executing authorities have to trust the assessment performed by the issuing state.

Applicable law: The law of the issuing state primarily governs the investigative measures, with the executing state recognising and executing the EIO without further scrutiny.[12] This approach eliminates the requirement of dual criminality for 32 specific offences (listed in Annex D of the Directive), making a significant departure from the MLAT system. However, the relevance of the national legislation of the executing state is not excluded altogether. The EIO Directive provides for several situations where the national law of the executing state should prevail. For instance, in addition to the grounds for refusal, the executing authorities should ensure that the formalities and procedures specified in the EIO are consistent with the fundamental principles of law of the executing state and that the investigative measures exist under the national law of the executing state. In cases where the investigative measures do not meet these requirements, the executing authority may take different measures, including, but not limited to, opting for a less intrusive investigative measure than the one indicated in an EIO, or consult the issuing authority.

These features stem from the foundational principle of 'mutual recognition', first implemented in the field of evidence at the EU level through the 2008 Framework Decision on the European Evidence Warrant (EEW).[13] The European Council regards this principle as 'the cornerstone of judicial co-operation' in

[9] Art 9, EIO Directive.

[10] Subject to specific grounds for postponement and refusal, the executing state is required to recognise a request within 30 days and execute it within 90 days (Art 12). In situations where the sought-after evidence is vulnerable to destruction, transformation, removal, transfer, or disposal, the Directive allows the executing state to take provisional measures within 24 hours (Art 32).

[11] Art 6(1)(b), Recital 10, EIO Directive.

[12] See ibid, Art 9.

[13] Council Framework Decision 2008/978/JHA on the European evidence warrant for the purpose of obtaining objects, documents, and data for use in proceedings in criminal matters [2008] L350/72.

criminal matters within the Union.[14] It requires Member States to accept each other's judicial decisions without further formalities and procedures, signifying a high degree of trust in each other's legal systems. This trust distinguishes the EIO Directive's mutual recognition approach from the traditional mutual legal assistance regime.

While the EIO Directive represents an improvement over previous mechanisms for cross-border data access, it has several shortcomings. First, the EIO, like the MLAT system, relies on inter-state co-operation. This means that it requires the involvement of competent authorities in both the issuing and executing states. It does not authorise direct co-operation between law enforcement authorities and service providers. This mediated access model can be slower and more cumbersome than direct access mechanisms. Second, law enforcement authorities cannot use the EIO Directive to compel service providers in other Member States to hand over data. They must go through the judicial authorities in the other Member State, which adds time and complexity to the process.

Third, while the EIO Directive aims to streamline co-operation through mutual recognition, the executing state can still refuse to execute an EIO under specific circumstances. These caveats can potentially limit the effectiveness of the EIO. Fourth, even with the established time limits, the process of issuing, transmitting, recognising, and executing an EIO can still be time-consuming, particularly when compared with the speed at which electronic evidence can be created, moved, or deleted.

Lastly, and crucially, the EIO Directive does not apply to obtaining electronic evidence from third countries or non-participating Member States. Consequently, the primary frustration for EU law enforcement – the fact that majority of criminal investigations involving digital evidence require cross-border requests to non-EU service providers – remains unaddressed. These legislative gaps and practical challenges prompted the European Commission to propose a new instrument less than a year after the deadline for the EIO Directive's implementation had passed.

5.2. Towards a New Approach

The EU and its Member States have long expressed significant concern over, and called for action to address, the challenges of cross-border data access in judicial proceedings.[15] One of the main challenges EU authorities face regarding cross-border data access is the refusal by service providers to make the required data available. This often occurs in at least three common scenarios: (i) the authority in question lacks jurisdiction over the location where the service

[14] See Recital 2, EIO Directive.
[15] COM (2015) 185 final (n 3).

provider's headquarters are established; (ii) the authority in question lacks jurisdiction based on the nationality of the individual person whose data has been requested; or (iii) a case is connected with the legal system of a third country (outside the EU), given that the largest service providers are based in the US.

In response to these concerns, the Commission released its legislative proposals for e-evidence, accompanied by a lengthy impact assessment report.[16] Drawing on considerable consultations, the impact assessment report provided a detailed description of the problem and outlined potential policy options. Specifically, the Commission argued that the borderless nature of the Internet, coupled with the increasing prevalence of cloud computing, has rendered the traditional frameworks of obtaining electronic evidence across borders ineffective.[17] The Commission identified slow judicial co-operation procedures, inefficient co-operation between private service providers and public authorities, and lack of clear definition of enforcement jurisdiction in cyberspace as obstacles to effective cross-border investigation and prosecution in the EU. These challenges were characterised as a 'regulatory failure', indicating that a significant proportion of crimes involving cross-border access to e-evidence cannot be effectively investigated or prosecuted within the EU, and thereby necessitating new regulatory measures.

Regarding policy solutions, the Commission considering several legislative options (along with practical measures) and ultimately proposed that *new international agreements* and *common EU legislation* on direct co-operation between public authorities and foreign service providers should constitute the preferred EU policy. The Commission deemed these policy options the most feasible (legally, technically, and politically), coherent with other EU instruments, and effective, relevant, and proportional to tackling the problem.

5.2.1. Negotiating New International Agreements

The Commission explored the possibilities of the EU entering into bilateral and multilateral international agreements to address judicial co-operation and/or direct co-operation with service providers. In this regard, the Commission suggested that '[t]he EU could seek to conclude international agreements coherent with EU-internal solutions to provide a basis for closer international cooperation with safeguards comparable to those of the EU-internal solution with regard to individuals' rights, including judicial redress'.[18]

The Commission further observed that international agreements (whether bilateral or multilateral) would ensure international comity, provide appropriate conditions and safeguards, institute mutually compatible approaches, and reduce

[16] SWD (2018) 118 final.
[17] ibid.
[18] ibid 47.

conflicts of law.[19] It identified a bilateral agreement with the US as a 'priority', given that a large majority of European data is stored within the US or held by service providers based in the US. The Commission rejected the CLOUD Act's bilateral agreements on a country-by-country basis, arguing that this approach could lead to a fragmented response for the Member States and hamper international co-operation in investigations and prosecutions.[20] Instead, the Commission prefers the EU to act *en bloc* in negotiating a cross-border data-sharing agreement with the US (see chapter six).

At a multilateral level, the Commission's first and preferred option is for the EU to actively participate in the Council of Europe's Second Additional Protocol to the Budapest Convention. One of the reasons that the Budapest Convention has become the EU's instrument of choice is that important third countries, such as the US, are parties to the Convention. However, the Commission also acknowledged the Second Additional Protocol would not be sufficient to adequately address the cross-border data-access problem. While the Additional Protocol could significantly improve the MLA process, the direct co-operation between public authorities and foreign service providers does not extend to content data. Further, the Convention and its Second Additional Protocol lack an institutional mechanism to enforce cross-border data requests.

5.2.2. A Common EU Legislation on Direct Co-operation with Service Providers

The Commission's impact assessment revealed that direct co-operation between the Member States' authorities and US-based service providers has de facto become the main channel for law enforcement and judicial authorities to obtain non-content data.[21] However, this channel of co-operation between EU Member States and foreign-based service providers is limited to non-content data only, and has evolved without any clear legal framework. Its voluntary nature is not regulated by domestic law or relevant international law.[22] Such legal uncertainty poses challenges for service providers, law enforcement authorities, and individuals alike.[23]

An additional challenge arises from the fragmented nature of responses by the Member States and service providers. The absence of a common approach to

[19] ibid 48.
[20] ibid 78.
[21] ibid 163.
[22] I Walden, 'Law Enforcement Access to Data in Clouds' in C Millard (ed), *Cloud Computing Law* (Oxford University Press, 2013).
[23] For instance, the European Commission identified eight general and practical shortcomings of direct co-operation between European authorities and service providers headquartered in third countries, including lack of transparency, accountability, reliability, and predictability. See SWD (2018) 118 final, 220–23.

obtaining data from foreign service providers means that each service provider must assess requests under the diverse laws and practices of Member States. Simultaneously, service providers maintain varying policies and respond differently to requests from governments.[24] This variation impedes effective criminal investigation and prosecution, exacerbates conflicting obligations for service providers, and creates risks for the fundamental rights of the individuals whose data is being sought. The Commission argues that, 'if each Member State were to continue or start its own individual approach, then this would further increase the diversity of approaches and lead to possible conflicts related to the different conditions and safeguards for access'.[25] Consequently, the Commission proposed a harmonised system for direct co-operation with service providers that would apply to all categories of data.

5.3. The e-Evidence Legislative Package Arrives

Faced with growing challenges in cross-border data access for criminal investigations, the EU launched the e-Evidence Package in April 2018, shortly after the US CLOUD Act came into effect. This package comprises a Regulation and a Directive, and seeks to modernise and streamline the process by which law enforcement authorities of a Member State can obtain electronic evidence directly from service providers, while simultaneously strengthening safeguards for fundamental rights. The e-Evidence Regulation, set to take effect in August 2026, introduces European Production and Preservation Orders, designed to compel service providers in other Member States or third countries to directly produce or preserve data, bypassing traditional MLAT channels. The accompanying Directive (Directive 2023/1544) aims to harmonise rules obliging service providers that offer services in the EU in more than one Member State, and non-European service providers active in the EU market, to appoint legal representatives in the EU. Directive 2023/1544 would serve as an enforcement tool for production and preservation orders. The combined objective of the twofold legislative package is to facilitate European law enforcement authorities' access to electronic evidence and streamline co-operation with service providers.

This chapter focuses not on the substance, but rather on the international implications of, the e-Evidence Regulation and its accompanying Directive. Specifically, this chapter examines the extraterritorial reach of the Regulation and its underlying theories of jurisdiction, the implications for fundamental rights, potential conflicts with third-country laws and sovereignty interests, and the mechanisms the Regulation provides to address these concerns.

[24] 'Developments in the Law – More Data, More Problems' (2018) 131 *Harvard Law Review* 1714, 1717.

[25] SWD (2018) 118 final, 38.

5.3.1. The Extraterritorial Reach of the e-Evidence Regulation

One of the challenges the EU seeks to address through the e-Evidence Regulation is determining the 'connecting factors' sufficient for the Member States to exercise 'enforcement jurisdiction' over cloud data.[26] Addressing this issue inevitably impacts on the sovereign interests of third countries, on non-EU service providers, and on the fundamental rights of targeted individuals. Traditionally, the EU has relied on three connecting factors to justify asserting jurisdiction over individuals or entities: conduct within the EU, physical or legal presence within the EU, or possession of EU Member State nationality.[27] These connecting factors are strongly linked to the principle of territoriality, the normative significance of which has been increasingly challenged by the advent of cloud computing.

Furthermore, the e-Evidence Regulation aims to mitigate the legal uncertainty arising from disparate national laws that apply varying connecting factors to regulate cross-border data access via production orders. For instance, some EU Member States consider the storage or processing location of the data (ie the location of the infrastructure used for storage or processing), while others focus on the location of the service provider's seat or another establishment, and still others rely on the place where a service provider offers services. The absence of a common EU approach complicates the determination of what constitutes a cross-border situation and impedes the ability to determine when a country can exercise enforcement jurisdiction over data.

In this regard, the Commission was requested to determine 'which connecting factors can provide grounds for enforcement jurisdiction in cyberspace' and 'which investigative measures can be used regardless of physical borders'.[28] A common EU approach was particularly needed in situations where:

> a number of information systems are used simultaneously in multiple jurisdictions to commit one single crime, situations where relevant e-evidence moves between jurisdictions in short fractions of time, or where sophisticated methods are used to conceal the location of e-evidence or the criminal activity, leading to loss of location.[29]

However, the e-Evidence Regulation appears to focus less on prescribing which connecting factors should determine enforcement jurisdiction in cyberspace and more on delineating issues that should *not* be considered valid connecting factors. Consequently, the e-Evidence Regulation grants EU law enforcement authorities the power to order the production or preservation of data held by service providers irrespective of: (a) the location of data; (b) the location or nationality of the target;

[26] The Commission defined 'enforcement jurisdiction' as the competence of the relevant authorities to undertake an investigative measure. ibid 6.

[27] J Scott, 'The New EU "Extraterritoriality"' (2014) 51 *Common Market Law Review* 1343, 1344.

[28] SWD (2018) 118 final.

[29] ibid (internal quotations removed).

and (c) the establishment of the service provider, subject to certain conditions. In this regard, the e-Evidence Regulation operates similarly to the US CLOUD Act. This unilateral extension of enforcement jurisdiction has significant implications for the sovereignty of third countries where the required data is stored or the service provider is established, as well as the fundamental rights of non-EU citizens.

5.3.1.1. *Disregarding the Location of Data*

Similar to the US CLOUD Act, the e-Evidence Regulation departs from data storage as the determining factor for enforcement jurisdiction. The Regulation empowers competent authorities in Member States to compel service providers to produce or preserve electronic evidence regardless of the location of the data.[30] Consequently, data stored in a third country can be targeted by the extraterritorial reach of the e-Evidence Regulation. Like the CLOUD Act, this approach is informed by the ubiquity of cloud computing, and the theoretical concept of un-territoriality of data. This rationale is reflected in Recital 21 of the Regulation, which states that:

> data are no longer stored or otherwise processed on a user's device but made available on a cloud-based infrastructure enabling access from anywhere. … Thus, the application of this Regulation should not depend on the actual location … of the data processing or storage facility.

This is further justified by the fact that much of the data needed for criminal investigation and prosecution in the EU resides in the cloud, on servers outside the EU. Provided that the required data is needed for a criminal proceeding for which the issuing EU authority is competent, and is related to a service offered in the Union, the location of the server is deemed immaterial.

Drawing on the unique characterisation of data, including 'mobility', 'divisibility', and 'un-territoriality', the Commission questions whether the traditional mechanisms designed to protect the sovereignty of another country (such as considering the location of data) are appropriate for today's technological realities. It argues that '[s]tates de facto have no control over data as it crosses borders into or from their territory'.[31] This assertion challenges the long-standing principle of territoriality and suggests that making location of data a determinative factor to exercise enforcement jurisdiction fails to serve any normative interest.[32] Law enforcement access to data stored in another territory would not necessarily constitute an interference with the territorial sovereignty of the foreign country in whose territory the data is stored, as states may not 'exercise authority over

[30] Art 1, e-Evidence Regulation.
[31] SWD (2018) 118 final 13.
[32] J Daskal, 'The Un-Territoriality of Data' (2015) 125 *Yale Law Journal* 326, 373.

data, even when it is located within their borders'.[33] This perspective implies that a country may not legitimately object to or prohibit foreign law enforcement access on the mere ground that the sought-after data happens to be stored in its territory. The decision of where to store data, in most cases, is made by the service provider, based on business considerations, and for reasons often unrelated to the user or public interest. For this reason, the EU lawmakers concluded that using location of data as a connecting factor would give the power to the service providers to decide 'whether and where access to data should be granted and what rights apply'.[34]

5.3.1.2. Disregarding Service Provider's Establishment

The e-Evidence Regulation applies to non-EU service providers that offer services within the Union, irrespective of their physical location or establishment.[35] This broad scope and extraterritorial jurisdiction stem from the unique characteristics of cloud-based services, as detailed in various recitals of the Regulation:

> Network-based services can be provided from anywhere and do not require physical infrastructure, premises or staff in the country where the relevant service is offered. Therefore, relevant electronic evidence is often stored outside of the investigating State or by a service provider established outside of that State, creating challenges regarding the gathering of electronic evidence in criminal proceedings.[36]

While service providers established in the Union clearly fall under the Regulation's scope, the primary objective is to establish mechanisms that enable competent authorities to issue binding production or preservation orders directly to non-EU service providers. There is a growing emphasis on the service providers who control the data in question. A country with personal jurisdiction over a service provider has the authority to unilaterally compel that provider to disclose data under its control, custody, or possession. Asserting legitimate jurisdiction over a service provider requires a substantial connection between the provider and the investigating state. However, in the absence of universally agreed-upon criteria for establishing this substantial connection and asserting enforcement jurisdiction, countries are continuously redefining the meaning of jurisdiction over service providers and the data they control, often based on their respective leverage.

Although both the US CLOUD Act and the e-Evidence Regulation use the service provider as a jurisdictional link, they differ in their criteria for establishing

[33] R Vatanparast, 'Data Governance and the Elasticity of Sovereignty' (2020) 46 *Brooklyn Journal of International Law* 1; see also Daskal, 'The Un-Territoriality of Data' (n 32) 379.

[34] SWD (2018) 118 final 53.

[35] The Regulation covers three categories of services, including electronic communications services, Internet domain name and IP numbering services, and other information society services that enable their users to communicate with each other or make it possible to store or otherwise process data on behalf of the users to whom the service is provided. See Art 3(3), e-Evidence Regulation.

[36] ibid, Recital 7.

a substantial connection between their respective territories and service providers, with the e-Evidence Regulation adopting a broader approach. The CLOUD Act's jurisdictional basis focuses on the service provider's establishment, which is logical, given that major technology companies are headquartered in the US. Regardless of their global operations, service providers headquartered or established or with subsidiaries in the US are subject to US legal process and compulsion under the CLOUD Act.[37] Despite the current dominance of US-based service providers in managing and controlling the majority of global data – a position that may not be permanent – the US leverages this historically unique position to require US-based companies to disclose customer data under their possession, custody, or control to the government regardless of where the companies operate in the world.[38]

The reality in the EU is different, with relatively few major service providers incorporated within its borders. American companies dominate Europe's cloud industry, hosting the large majority (around 80 per cent) of European data.[39] Consequently, EU law enforcement agencies frequently seek data from service providers established in foreign jurisdictions, primarily in the US. A European Commission survey conducted during the preparation of the e-Evidence Regulation revealed that nearly two-thirds of the investigations where electronic evidence is relevant require access to data held by service providers based in another jurisdiction.[40]

The scenarios discussed in chapter two provide good illustrations. The *Microsoft Ireland* and *Google Pennsylvania* cases involved domestic service providers, even though the sought-after data was stored in foreign jurisdictions. Conversely, in both the *Yahoo* and *Skype* cases, the service providers had no establishment (legal or physical presence) in Belgium, nor was the data stored on Belgian soil.

Therefore, the primary focus of the e-Evidence Regulation is to provide competent authorities in Member States with effective tools to obtain data held by foreign service providers. The EU lacks the leverage to rely solely on the 'establishment' requirement to exercise enforcement jurisdiction over major service providers. Furthermore, 'establishment' is susceptible to change by internal company policies.[41] As the Commission noted, solely relying on 'establishment', a subsidiary, or infrastructure would undermine the effectiveness of accessing electronic evidence across borders, as service providers could avoid establishing themselves in the EU.[42] Therefore, the EU has adopted a two-pronged approach to address this

[37] Even though the CLOUD Act only applies to service providers incorporated in the US, there is a possibility whereby foreign service providers could be subject to this statute.

[38] This approach appears to find international law support in the Budapest Convention, art 18(1)(a).

[39] A Wirth, G Tricco, and M Martinez, 'Clouds on the Horizon: Europe's Cloud Policy Threatens Transatlantic Digital Harmony' (CEPA, 10 May 2022).

[40] SWD (2018) 118 final 14.

[41] ibid 74.

[42] ibid 53.

problem: (a) virtual presence as a jurisdictional hook; and (b) forced localisation as an enforcement tool.

5.3.1.2.(a) Virtual Presence as a Jurisdictional Hook

The application of EU law is triggered by 'engaging in conduct in the EU'. However, the type of conduct that justifies the application of EU law remains controversial. To address emerging technological realities, the EU has been gradually adapting its definition of what constitutes conduct within its jurisdiction. One such development is the recognition of 'virtual presence' as a jurisdictional trigger.

A similar line of reasoning occurs in the Belgian case law, which introduced cross-border data-production orders based on the virtual presence of service providers. In the *Yahoo* and *Skype* cases, the Belgian courts found that, even if the service providers were not physically established on Belgian soil, they were virtually present in Belgium by offering their services to Belgian customers.[43] By actively participating in Belgium's economic life, the service providers voluntarily submitted themselves to the Belgian law.[44] This Belgian approach partly served as an inspiration for the e-Evidence Regulation.

The application of the e-Evidence Regulation does not, therefore, depend on the actual location of the provider's establishment. Even without any physical presence in the EU, foreign service providers that are 'virtually present' by 'offer[ing] services in the European Union' fall under the purview of the Regulation. If a foreign service provider avails itself of the European internal market and derives benefits from it, it is subject to EU law regarding that specific service. It is important to note that production and preservation orders under the e-Evidence Regulation can only be issued for data pertaining to services offered in the Union. Conversely, services offered exclusively outside the Union are not within the scope of the Regulation, even if the service provider is established in the Union.

The concept of virtual presence as a jurisdictional hook raises several questions: what factors are sufficient to exercise enforcement jurisdiction over foreign service providers that offer services in the EU without having establishment in the Member States? What would constitute 'offering [a] service' within the meaning of the e-Evidence Regulation? Could the mere accessibility of a website in the EU be sufficient to subject a non-EU service provider to the purview of the e-Evidence Regulation?

In the absence of establishment, EU competent authorities should apply a two-factor test when ascertaining whether a non-EU service provider is offering services in the Union: (i) the service provider is enabling legal or natural persons

[43] P de Hert, C Parlar, and J Thumfart, 'Legal Arguments Used in Courts Regarding Territoriality and Cross-Border Production Orders: From Yahoo Belgium to Microsoft Ireland' (2018) 9 *New Journal of European Criminal Law* 326.

[44] ibid.

in one or more Member States to use the services; and (ii) a substantial connection exists between the service provider and Member States based on specific factual criteria.[45] However, these elements are somewhat vague and require further clarification. For instance, the Regulation does not establish objective criteria for determining the existence of a 'substantial connection'. Instead, it identifies non-exhaustive instances from which the existence (or lack) of a substantial connection can be inferred. For instance, in the absence of establishment, substantial connection to the Union exists where the service provider has a significant number of users in one or more Member States or targets its activities towards one or more Member States.

5.3.1.2.(b) Forced Localisation as Enforcement Tool

The 'virtual presence' in the Union of a service provider would not necessarily guarantee the enforceability of the investigative measures issued under the e-Evidence Regulation. For instance, competent authorities may not know how to contact service providers that lack establishment in their jurisdiction, and whom to contact. Member States often employ varied approaches regarding obligations imposed on service providers which do not have establishment in their jurisdiction. As the Commission noted, such individualised and uncoordinated national approaches to enforcing production and preservation orders would create legal uncertainty for all stakeholders involved.[46] Such risk of legal uncertainty and lack of enforceability prompted the introduction of a forced legal representative model through the e-Evidence Directive.

The Directive addresses this fragmented approach by establishing harmonised rules that require non-EU service providers to localise their legal representatives for purposes of receiving, compliance with, and enforcement of production and preservation orders issued by competent authorities of the Member States under the e-Evidence Regulation. It imposes an obligation on non-EU service providers to designate at least one legal representative in the Union, who will be responsible for providing access to data stored outside the EU within 10 days of a request, or within six hours, in the case of an emergency.

The obligation for non-EU service providers to designate a legal representative is not new to the e-Evidence Initiative; a similar obligation exists in the EU digital rule book, such as in the GDPR, and in the national laws of some Member States. The practical effect of the forced representative localisation model is to extend the EU's power to mandate disclosure for data stored outside its territory, a principle analogous to the extraterritorial application of the CLOUD Act.

[45] Art 3(4), e-Evidence Regulation.

[46] Proposal for a Directive of the European Parliament and of the Council laying down harmonised rules on the appointment of legal representatives for the purpose of gathering evidence in criminal proceedings {SWD (2018) 118 final} – {SWD(2018) 119 final} 5.

However, the EU's approach of forced representative localisation is not without controversy. A key issue relates to the enforceability of the requirement. It is unclear how the EU will enforce this model on a large scale. Also unclear is how small-to-medium-sized foreign companies will make informed decisions in recruiting a trusted party to be their representative in the EU.[47] As the Commission acknowledges, 'the obligation to designate a legal representative in the Union would generate costs' and 'could represent an important burden', especially for SMEs not established in the Union.[48] The second issue regarding this form of (re)territorialisation is the risk of reciprocity. The model set by the EU could be emulated by other nations around the world, to the detriment of the EU's interests. For instance, European small-to-medium-sized service providers could be required by third countries to appoint legal representatives wherever in the world they offer their services. The problems of enforceability and reciprocity give rise to the third issue, which is the legitimacy of the system itself. As one report put it, the EU's model of 'rep localization' could lead to arbitrary enforcement, thereby undermining the legitimacy of the entire system.[49] This model could also widen the power imbalance between countries that enjoy personal jurisdiction over major service providers or have the regulatory power to enforce their laws extraterritorially and those who have neither the jurisdictional leverage nor regulatory power.

5.3.1.3. Disregarding Data Subject's Location, Place of Residence, or Nationality

Nationality and place of residence have long served as jurisdictional triggers for the application of EU law.[50] Service providers also often apply nationality-based criteria to decide whether to comply with law enforcement requests for data. For example, some service providers comply with foreign governments' requests only if the sought-after data concerns nationals of the requesting country.[51] In contrast, the e-Evidence Regulation mandates the disclosure of data located in third countries without regard to the nationality or residence of the person concerned, as long as the service provider offers services in the EU.

The Commission offered two justifications for rejecting place of residence or nationality as a jurisdictional trigger: (i) criminal investigations in the EU are not limited to certain nationals; and (ii) restricting the investigative measures to target only EU nationals or residents would undermine the effectiveness of the e-Evidence Regulation.[52] Consequently, the e-Evidence Regulation makes no

[47] DJB Svantesson, 'Internet & Jurisdiction Global Status Report 2019' (Internet & Jurisdiction Policy Network, 27 November 2019) 147.
[48] SWD (2018) 118 final 91.
[49] Svantesson, 'Internet & Jurisdiction Global Status Report 2019' (n 47) 147.
[50] Scott, 'The New EU "Extraterritoriality"' (n 27).
[51] SWD (2018) 118 final 74.
[52] ibid 74, 241.

distinction between production orders targeting European citizens and those targeting third-country nationals, even if they are located outside the Union. This means that the e-Evidence Regulation could be used to compel the production of data pertaining to a US person located in the US without the permission of US authorities, as long as the data is related to a service offered in the Union. The location, nationality, and place of residence of a non-EU person whose data is being requested may only play a role when the competent court of the issuing EU Member State establishes that the law of the third country prohibits disclosure of the data concerned and determines whether to uphold or lift the production order.[53] Specifically, the Regulation requires the competent court in the issuing EU Member State to consider the location, nationality, and residence of the person whose data is being sought, when weighing the degree of connection of the criminal case to the investigating state and the third country.

5.3.2. Implications

The EU e-Evidence Regulation represents a significant step towards streamlining cross-border access to electronic evidence for law enforcement purposes within the EU. However, the Regulation's unilateral extension of enforcement jurisdiction, granting EU authorities the power to order the production of data held by service providers regardless of data location, target location/nationality, or service provider establishment carries several risks.

Conflict with third-country laws: Service providers operating globally may be subject to data protection laws, national security laws, or other regulations in the countries where they are established or where their data is stored. Compliance with an EU production order under the e-Evidence Regulation could, therefore, place them in violation of these third-country laws, exposing them to legal sanctions. The service provider could face liability not only under the e-Evidence Regulation but also under the criminal and/or civil law of the relevant third country.

Intervention with sovereign interests: A state's ability to control data within its borders is often considered a matter of national sovereignty. This control may be related to national security, economic interests, or the protection of its citizens' fundamental rights. The e-Evidence Regulation's extraterritorial reach could be seen as an intrusion upon these sovereign interests, particularly if the data requested is related to sensitive matters or involves citizens of a third country.

Infringement of fundamental rights: Non-EU citizens may have different expectations of privacy and data protection from those of EU citizens. The e-Evidence Regulation, by allowing EU authorities to access their data, could subject them to standards and procedures that are inconsistent with their national laws and

[53] Art 17(6)(b), e-Evidence Regulation.

values, potentially infringing upon their fundamental rights. While the data subject notification requirement under Article 13 of the Regulation attempts to address some of these concerns, it also introduces new complexities, as will be discussed below.

5.3.3. Review Procedures in Case of Conflicting Obligations

Recognising the risks highlighted above, the e-Evidence Regulation includes mechanisms aimed at mitigating the extraterritorial implications. Specifically, the Regulation establishes review procedures for cases in which a non-EU service provider requested to produce data faces conflicting obligations from third-country laws prohibiting the disclosure of the requested data. Unlike the CLOUD Act, which restricts the conflicts-of-law resolution mechanism only to countries that have executive agreements with the US, the conflicts-of-law resolution mechanism under the e-Evidence Regulation is not conditioned by agreement with third countries. The e-Evidence Regulation allows service providers to challenge a production order on conflict-of-law grounds irrespective of the country affected and the location or nationality of the person concerned.

Interestingly, there is a significant discrepancy between the Commission proposal and the final text of the Regulation. Recognising the risks of a unilateral assertion of extraterritorial jurisdiction, the Commission proposed extensive review mechanisms, even to the extent of involving third countries' authorities in certain conflicting obligation situations. The Commission was particularly concerned about the risk of 'reciprocity'; that is, that the extraterritorial reach of the e-Evidence Regulation might legitimise 'similar production orders by non-EU countries with respect to data held in the EU or providers headquartered in the EU'.[54] The risk of reciprocity could be particularly acute if it involves third countries that do not have fundamental rights safeguards essentially equivalent to those guaranteed by EU law. These risks were also partly reflected in the Commission's amicus brief filed in the *Microsoft Ireland* case, stating that:

> any domestic law that creates cross-border obligations, whether enacted by the United States, the European Union, or another state should be applied and interpreted in a manner that is mindful of the restrictions of international law and considerations of international comity.[55]

Consequently, the Commission proposed two different review procedures to be caried out in the investigating (issuing) Member State: (i) review mechanisms

[54] SWD (2018) 118 final 58.

[55] Brief of the European Commission on behalf of the European Union as Amicus Curiae in Support of Neither Party, *United States v Microsoft* (2017) No 17-2 (2017) 7.

for conflicting obligations based on fundamental rights or fundamental interests of a third country; and (ii) review mechanisms for conflicting obligations based on other grounds. Under the first scenario, the Commission's proposal stipulates that if the service provider believes compliance with the production order would conflict with third-country law prohibiting the disclosure of the requested data, it must submit a reasoned objection to the issuing authority. If the issuing authority decides to uphold the order despite the objection, it must refer the matter to a competent court in the issuing state for review. The court would then determine whether a conflict of laws exists. If it finds that the third-country law is applicable and indeed prohibits disclosure of the requested data, it must notify the third country concerned, which would have a specified deadline to respond. Should the third country object, the order must be lifted.

This review mechanism would have constituted a robust 'jurisdictional safety valve' had it been adopted.[56] It could have prevented the jurisdictional overreach of the e-Evidence Regulation, reducing conflicting legal obligations and facilitating international co-operation and comity. The review mechanism could have been particularly useful in protecting fundamental rights or fundamental interests of a third country, as that country would have been involved in the process and could have objected to the production order.

Unfortunately, this review mechanism was excluded from the Council proposal, and consequently from the final text of the e-Evidence Regulation. Instead, the Regulation incorporates a review mechanism solely on the second ground, whereby the competent court in the issuing state is allowed, but not obliged, to consult with the third country if the court determines that conflicting obligations exist. This review process, established under Article 17 of the e-Evidence Regulation, involves several steps:

1. The service provider must file a reasoned objection to the issuing authority (the law enforcement agency in the EU Member State), including all relevant details regarding the third-country law, its applicability to the case, and the nature of the conflicting obligation. This places the initial burden on the service provider to identify and articulate the legal conflict. The reasoned objection cannot be based on the fact that similar conditions, formalities, and procedures for issuing an order for production do not exist in the applicable law of the third country, or on the sole fact that the data is stored in a third country. These strict requirements aim to prevent abuse of the conflicts-of-law clause by service providers.
2. The issuing authority must review the production order based on the reasoned objection.
3. If the issuing authority intends to uphold the production order, it must request a review by a competent court in the issuing state. The execution of the production order would be suspended pending this judicial review.

[56] Scott, 'The New EU "Extraterritoriality"' (n 27).

4. The competent court must assess whether a conflict of obligation exists. This involves determining whether the third-country law is applicable and, if so, whether it prohibits the disclosure of the data in the specific circumstances of the case. The court may seek appropriate external expertise, including consulting with the third country.
5. If the court finds that the third-country law prohibits disclosure, it must then determine whether to uphold or lift the production order. This assessment is based on a weighing of several factors, giving particular weight to the interests protected by the third-country law (including fundamental rights and national security) and the degree of connection between the criminal case and the two jurisdictions.

While the review procedures established under Article 17 represent a positive step towards addressing the extraterritorial implications of the e-Evidence Regulation, this review procedure raises several concerns.

First, it is regrettable that the review procedure excludes the third country whose fundamental interests, including the fundamental human rights of its citizens and its sovereignty, could be impacted by a production order under the Regulation. Even if the competent court in the investigating state finds that a production order conflicts with a third-country law prohibiting the disclosure of the data in the circumstances of the case on grounds of fundamental interests such as human rights and national security, the competent court can make an autonomous decision without informing the third-country authorities. Article 17(7) permits the competent court to 'request information from the competent authority of the third country', but does not oblige it to do so.[57] It is entirely at the discretion of the court in the investigating country whether or not to inform the third country. This means that the assessment of whether or not a conflict exists is solely carried out by the competent court of the investigating country. Furthermore, the Regulation does not require the investigating authorities or the competent court to lift the production order resulting in conflict of law, even if such conflict concerns fundamental rights or national security interests of the third country. As the Committee on Civil Liberties, Justice and Home Affairs aptly noted, leaving the assessment and interpretation of the third country's law only to the competent court in the investigating state ignores the complexities of the third-country law and the fact that the competent court in the investigating state is not a specialist on the substance of the third-country law.[58] Consequently, this unilateral approach marks a significant gap in the Regulation, in addressing its potential impact on the sovereignty of third countries and the fundamental rights of individuals.

[57] Committee on Civil Liberties, Justice and Home Affairs, 4th Working Document (C) on the Proposal for a Regulation on European Production and Preservation Orders for electronic evidence in criminal matters (2018/0108 (COD)) – Relation with third country law, DT\1179239EN.docx.
[58] ibid.

Second, the judicial review procedure established under Article 17 of the Regulation is limited in scope. The competent court is primarily tasked with determining whether a legal conflict exists and, if so, weighing the factors outlined in Article 17(6). The court does not appear to have the power to question the underlying justifications for the production order or to assess whether the request is proportionate or necessary in the first place.

Third, the factors outlined in Article 17(6) provide some guidance for the court's assessment, but they are inherently subjective and open to interpretation. The 'degree of connection' between the criminal case and the two jurisdictions (the investigating EU state and the third country) can be assessed in various ways, and the relative weight given to each factor can significantly influence the outcome. The explicit prioritisation of the third country's 'fundamental rights as well as other fundamental interests preventing the disclosure of the data' seems like an important safeguard to mitigate against unintended intervention in the sovereign interests of third countries. However, the degree to which particular weight is given to this may be determined by many factors not present in the provision, leading to inconsistent interpretations across the Member States.

A fourth shortcoming of the conflicts-of-law clause is the strict time limitation within which the service provider must inform the issuing authority that compliance with the production order conflicts with applicable laws of a third country. According to Article 17 of the e-Evidence Regulation, the service provider should file its objection within 10 days after the date on which the order was served. Expecting the service providers to provide a very detailed and extensive assessment of third countries' laws within such a limited time frame poses a significant challenge. As the Committee on Civil Liberties, Justice and Home Affairs noted, 'third country laws that include important protection of fundamental rights are not necessarily framed as laws intended to protect fundamental rights as such but might be hidden in all types of legislation'.[59] Service providers may lack the time and expertise to evaluate third countries' laws and determine whether they conflict with the production order. The strict deadline, coupled with sanctions for non-compliance, could lead to quasi-automatic compliance.

The final, and crucial, limitation of the review procedure is that it focuses primarily on the potential conflict between the EU law and third-country law, and does not explicitly address the rights of individuals whose data is being requested. It appears that the procedures are intended to safeguard the interests of third countries and service providers, leaving the affected individuals without equivalent protections. Article 13 of the Regulation requires the investigating authorities to inform the person whose data is being requested about the production order. This transparency requirement is essential for upholding due process and enabling individuals to exercise their rights, such as the right to challenge the

[59] ibid.

legality of the data access. However, Article 13(2) provides a significant exception to the transparency principles. It permits authorities to delay, restrict, or omit informing the data subject if specific conditions are met. The conditions, derived from the Law Enforcement Directive (EU) 2016/680, primarily relate to situations where informing the data subject could jeopardise investigations, prejudice national security, or risk obstructing justice. While these exceptions are intended to safeguard legitimate law enforcement objectives, they also pose a risk to the fundamental rights of individuals, particularly to third-country nationals. For example, there are no clear safeguards in place to ensure that these exceptions are applied only when strictly necessary and proportionate, nor are there safeguards that prevent the routine use of these exceptions to avoid transparency and accountability. If the EU authority invokes Article 13(2) and delays or omits the notification of the data subject, the affected person would not have the opportunity to challenge the request and exercise their right to an effective remedy.

The transparency requirement could have been strengthened by establishing 'notice-by-default' for persons targeted by production orders.[60] The e-Evidence Regulation could have balanced the interests of law enforcement with the rights of individuals by allowing service providers to notify their users of any production order, except when a judge has authorised a non-disclosure order. Instead, the Regulation leaves to the discretion of the investigating authorities the decision whether or not to notify the targeted person. This problem is further compounded because the person whose data is being requested is allowed to contest the legality of an order only in the issuing state. This would be particularly challenging for third-country nationals with a different judicial system.

5.4. Conclusion

The EU e-Evidence Regulation represents the latest effort towards modernising criminal justice access to data across borders. By granting EU authorities the power to directly access data held by service providers worldwide, the Regulation seeks to overcome the limitations of the traditional MLAT system. However, the expansive reach of the Regulation raises significant concerns about its extraterritorial implications, specifically regarding the sovereignty of third countries and the fundamental rights of individuals.

While the Regulation establishes review procedures for cases in which a non-EU service provider faces conflicting obligations from third-country laws

[60] J Frank and L Cossette, 'E-Evidence: Robust Fundamental Rights Protections Are Needed for European Law Enforcement Authorities' Access to Data' (*Microsoft EU Policy Blog*, 6 November 2019), available at https://blogs.microsoft.com/eupolicy/2019/11/06/e-evidence-fundamental-rights-protections-needed/.

prohibiting the disclosure of the requested data, it suffers from several shortcomings. The exclusion of affected third countries from the decision-making process, the narrow scope of judicial review, the absence of a requirement for service providers to notify data subjects, and the limited transparency and due process afforded to individuals all contribute to a system that risks undermining international comity and fundamental rights.

The next chapter will delve into the interplay between the EU and US approaches to cross-border data access. It will examine how, in the absence of a transatlantic cross-border data-access agreement, these approaches could exacerbate existing conflicts of law and jurisdictional competition and potentially give rise to new ones. Furthermore, it will explore the long-standing differences between the two jurisdictions regarding privacy and security, and how these disparities could further complicate the ongoing EU–US negotiations on a reciprocal cross-border data-access agreement.

6

The EU–US Jurisdictional Game and Fight for Norm-Setting

The transatlantic relationship between the US and the EU regarding cross-border data access constitutes one of the most complex and evolving areas in contemporary law and technology. At its core, this relationship is shaped by both convergence and divergence in regulatory philosophies, legal structures, and geopolitical objectives. While both jurisdictions acknowledge the necessity of facilitating law enforcement's timely access to electronic evidence in an increasingly digitalised, borderless environment, their approaches to privacy, data protection, and digital sovereignty differ markedly.

This fundamental divergence has fostered recurring tensions and legally fraught conflicts between the regimes, exemplified by the incompatibilities between the CLOUD Act and the General Data Protection Regulation (GDPR), as well as between the e-evidence Regulation and the Stored Communications Act (SCA). These overlapping and contradictory obligations produce regulatory uncertainty, threaten digital sovereignty, undermine digital privacy rights, and expose service providers to significant risks. Efforts to negotiate a comprehensive EU–US agreement on cross-border data access aim to resolve these tensions; however, the negotiation process faces intractable challenges and uncertainties.

This chapter compares the EU and US approaches to cross-border data access, highlighting the areas of convergence and divergence in their efforts to address law enforcement access to cloud-stored data. It demonstrates how the US CLOUD Act and the EU e-Evidence Regulation exacerbate existing conflicts of law and intensify jurisdictional competition in the absence of a transatlantic cross-border data-access agreement. Furthermore, this chapter examines the structural, procedural, and substantive challenges underpinning the EU–US negotiation process. Ultimately, these dynamics exemplify the ongoing jurisdictional games and norm-setting competition through which the US seeks to maintain its digital supremacy while the EU strives to assert digital sovereignty and independence from US technology companies.

6.1. Transatlantic Areas of Convergence and Divergence

The approaches of the US and the EU to the challenges of cross-border data access exhibit both significant overlaps and marked differences. A notable point of convergence is their mutual engagement with the concept of territorial sovereignty – each jurisdiction alternately links or decouples data governance from physical location of data. While both the US and the EU are often characterised as instituting 'extraterritorial' regulatory frameworks, a closer examination reveals a nuanced reality. Their respective legal regimes are flexible and resist categorisation within the strict territorial/extraterritorial binary.[1] Instead, each regime incorporates elements of both approaches. This flexibility reflects an evolving legal landscape where data flows and sovereignty are continuously renegotiated and redefined.

On the one hand, both US and EU regulatory models increasingly downplay the physical location of data, and in certain instances the location of the data subject, as the primary basis for enforcement jurisdiction. Departing from the procedures of traditional MLATs, both the US's CLOUD Act and the EU's e-Evidence Regulation pioneer models of direct co-operation between law enforcement authorities and private service providers. Under these models, service providers may be required to comply directly with law enforcement requests for data irrespective of the location where such data is stored. This mechanism can be regarded as a distinct expression of extraterritorial legal authority.

Conversely, both jurisdictions maintain structural links to the principle of territoriality within their law enforcement and privacy frameworks. In particular, each system imposes legal restrictions on the disclosure to foreign authorities of data stored within its territorial boundaries or belonging to its citizens or residents. For example, the EU prohibits: (1) the transfer of data to third countries that do not afford a level of protection essentially equivalent to that provided by EU law; and (2) the disclosure of EU data to third-country governments outside the framework of established international agreements.[2] This approach underscores the EU's commitment to territoriality in data governance and indicates that the EU views the extraterritorial application of third-country laws used to access EU data as a breach of international law.[3] Similarly, the US, through the SCA, restricts the direct disclosure of content data stored in the US to foreign governments, reaffirming the link between data and US territorial sovereignty. Thus, even as both legal systems embrace extraterritorial mechanisms for accessing data, they simultaneously invoke territorial limits to prevent foreign authorities from exercising comparable jurisdiction over data within their reach.

[1] R Vatanparast, 'Data Governance and the Elasticity of Sovereignty' (2020) 46 *Brooklyn Journal of International Law* 1–36.

[2] See Arts 44 and 48, Regulation (EU) 2016/679 of the European Parliament and of the Council on the protection of natural persons with regard to the processing of personal data and on the free movement of such data, and repealing Directive 95/46/EC (General Data Protection Regulation) [2016] OJ L119/1.

[3] ibid, Recital 115; Brief of the European Commission on behalf of the European Union as Amicus Curiae in Support of Neither Party, *United States v Microsoft* (2017) No 17-2 (2017).

These competing territorial and extraterritorial dimensions serve distinct regulatory objectives. The extraterritorial capacity empowers local law enforcement agencies in both jurisdictions to secure electronic evidence held abroad. By contrast, the territorial restrictions function as protective mechanisms shielding citizens' data from unfettered foreign access and asserting data sovereignty over domestic digital infrastructure. In practice, this approach is frequently operationalised through the selective use of blocking statutes or other legal instruments, under which authorities may authorise extraterritorial production of data for domestic purposes while actively restricting disclosures to foreign governments. Both jurisdictions adopt a dual standard in interpreting territorial sovereignty by applying flexible, expansive interpretations to justify their own extraterritorial production orders, recognising the de-territorialisation of cloud data while simultaneously taking a more restrictive stance towards foreign requests by invoking blocking statutes to prevent access.[4]

Roxana Vatanparast has aptly described this phenomenon as the 'elasticity of sovereignty' – a dynamic and continuous process in which states adapt and repurpose traditional concepts of territorial sovereignty to address new challenges in the digital environment.[5] Through this process, both the EU and the US deploy various justifications and connecting factors to support the extraterritorial application of their laws while simultaneously pursuing strategies to re-territorialise data in ways that best serve their own interests. Notably, the ultimate objective for both remains the assertion and preservation of regulatory control over cross-border data flows, even as they redefine jurisdictional boundaries to keep pace with changing technological realities.[6]

For instance, the EU's insistence that foreign service providers maintain local representation within its borders and recognise a 'virtual presence' as sufficient for regulatory oversight exemplifies a broader trend towards innovative interpretations of territorial sovereignty. However, if countries persist in seeking jurisdictional footholds to compel data production, the result may be what Dan Svantesson called 'jurisdictional hyper-regulation'[7] – a scenario in which global service providers are amenable to the legal claims of every nation in which their services are accessed, exacerbating the risk of regulatory fragmentation, increased international tension, and pervasive legal uncertainty. The proliferation of such overlapping claims could ultimately impede the development of coherent and predictable rules for transnational data governance, to the detriment of both individual rights and international commerce.

[4] Vatanparast, 'Data Governance and the Elasticity of Sovereignty' (n 1); C Ryngaert, 'Extraterritorial Enforcement Jurisdiction in Cyberspace: Normative Shifts' (2023) 24 *German Law Journal* 537.

[5] Vatanparast, 'Data Governance and the Elasticity of Sovereignty' (n 1).

[6] M Mueller, *Will the Internet Fragment? Sovereignty, Globalization and Cyberspace* (Polity, 2017) 41.

[7] D Svantesson, 'European Union Claims of Jurisdiction over the Internet: An Analysis of Three Recent Key Developments' (2018) 9 *Journal of Intellectual Property, Information Technology and Electronic Commerce Law* 113.

6.2. Recurring Tensions and Reciprocal Conflict

While the US and the EU share certain structural similarities in their approaches to cross-border data access, their most persistent and consequential divergence arises from deeply embedded differences in their legal and philosophical traditions concerning privacy, data protection, and surveillance laws. The US approach to privacy is rooted in market-based principles. This means that, traditionally, privacy protection in the US has been guided by the idea that the free market, through consumer choice and competition among businesses, can provide sufficient privacy protections. In this model, individuals are viewed as consumers who negotiate the terms of data disclosure in exchange for access to services, effectively commodifying personal data. Consequently, the US Constitution does not recognise a general or explicit right to data protection, and federal privacy and state rules are typically less comprehensive and more permissive. In stark contrast, the EU adopts a rights-based approach. Privacy and data protection are enshrined as fundamental rights under the EU Charter of Fundamental Rights, with the GDPR operationalising them.

These fundamental differences generate recurring tensions and reciprocal legal conflicts in the context of cross-border data access (and commercial co-operation). The rights-driven EU model requires that any transfer of personal data outside the EU satisfies strict Charter-based standards, meaning that international agreements and mechanisms involving such transfer are subject to close legal and political scrutiny. The fragmented and pragmatic US system, by contrast, may facilitate law enforcement access to data held by US-based service providers, even when such disclosures run afoul of European privacy rules.

A paradigmatic instance of reciprocal conflict arises when, for example, US law compels service providers to produce data located in the EU despite GDPR prohibitions, or when the EU expects compliance with its production orders served on US providers despite the SCA's restrictions in the US. Both regimes thus seek unilateral access to data held in the other's jurisdiction while simultaneously restricting disclosures of their own citizens' data to foreign authorities. These overlapping obligations generate intractable conflicts of law, erode digital sovereignty, and expose service providers to the risk of violating fundamental rights.

Importantly, while the stated aim of recent initiatives such as the CLOUD Act and the e-Evidence Regulation is to mitigate such conflicts through harmonised frameworks, the realisation of this objective is contingent upon a reciprocal, comprehensive transatlantic data transfer agreement – a solution which remains elusive in the contexts of both law enforcement and commercial co-operation. In the absence of such an agreement, regulatory uncertainty intensifies and the jurisdictional contest over cross-border data access persists.

As the figure below demonstrates, direct disclosures of data compelled under the CLOUD Act may contravene GDPR obligations, just as disclosures by a US service provider to an EU law enforcement entity pursuant to the e-Evidence

Regulation may violate the SCA. Adding complexity, while the GDPR does not fully govern data processed by law enforcement and intelligence entities, it does apply to personal data processed by commercial actors and subsequently requested by or disclosed to these public authorities.[8]

Figure 1 Schematic description of legal requirements prohibiting and compelling production of data

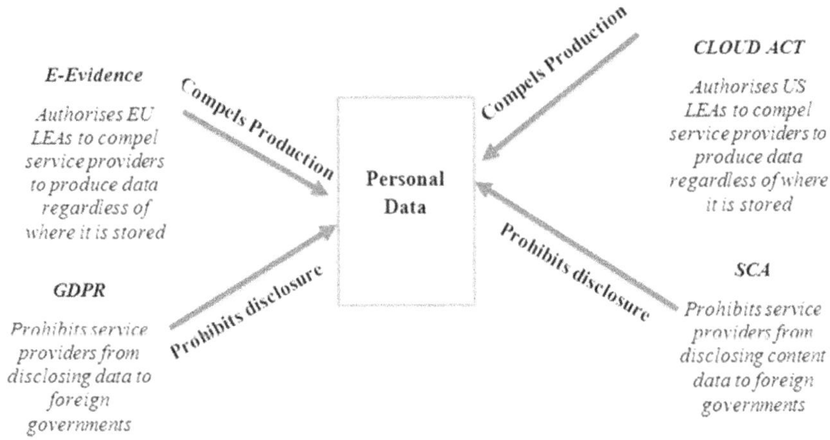

6.2.1. CLOUD Act v GDPR

In 2018, two major pieces of legislation – the US's CLOUD Act and the EU's GDPR – entered into force, establishing potentially conflicting obligations for service providers operating transatlantically. The CLOUD Act authorises US authorities to compel disclosure of data held by US-based service providers irrespective of where the data is physically stored, including on servers located in the EU. A salient illustration of such expansive authority is a scenario in which a US-based cloud service provider (such as Microsoft or Google) offers services within the EU. Such a provider could be ordered by US authorities, under the CLOUD Act, to produce EU residents' data, even if that data never leaves the EU or is stored exclusively in an EU data centre. In practice, this means that services like Microsoft Azure, which might process sensitive French health data on French soil, could still be subject to compelled disclosure under US law, due to corporate control headquarters' location.

Furthermore, the extraterritorial reach of the CLOUD Act can, in some situations, extend to EU-based entities owned or controlled by US parent

[8] *Facebook Ireland Ltd v Maximillian Schrems* C-311/18, ECLI:EU:C:2020:559, [2020] [86]–[89].

companies, broadening the potential for conflict. A memorandum prepared for the Dutch National Cyber Security Centre (NCSC) highlights that European companies, even when all data processing and storage occur within the EU borders, may be subject to a US legal demand for data disclosure under the CLOUD Act.[9] This is possible when the EU entity has sufficient connections to the US, such as being a subsidiary of a US parent company, relying on US cloud or technology providers, or otherwise maintaining a corporate relationship that gives the US company possession, custody, or control over data stored in the EU. The NCSC memorandum concludes that EU entities can only avoid the reach of the CLOUD Act if they process data exclusively through non-US-affiliated organisations that lack substantive US contacts – meaning no US parent company, no significant business in the US, and no US national with access to the data.[10] Any US corporate link is deemed to create a legal pathway for US authorities to assert jurisdiction, raising potential conflicts with EU data protection laws, particularly the GDPR.

The critical question, then, is whether a service provider can simultaneously comply with the CLOUD Act and the GDPR, or whether compliance with one inevitably results in a violation of the other. The prevailing answer, as will be detailed below, is negative.

The GDPR serves as a blocking statute by design, as illustrated by Article 48, which stipulates that:

> Any judgment of a court or tribunal and any decision of an administrative authority of a third country requiring a controller or processor to transfer or disclose personal data may only be recognised or enforceable in any manner if based on an international agreement, such as a mutual legal assistance treaty, in force between the requesting third country and the Union or a Member State, without prejudice to other grounds for transfer pursuant to this Chapter.

This provision accomplishes three critical functions. First, it clarifies that foreign court or administrative orders cannot, by themselves, serve as a lawful basis for data transfer from the EU. This specifically targets unilateral mechanisms like those codified in the CLOUD Act. GDPR Recital 115 reinforces that such extraterritorial demands may violate international law and hinder the GDPR's objective of providing robust data protection within the EU:

> Some third countries adopt laws, regulations and other legal acts which purport to directly regulate the processing activities of natural and legal persons under the jurisdiction of the Member States. This may include judgments of courts or tribunals or decisions of administrative authorities in third countries requiring a controller or

[9] 'How the CLOUD-Act works in data storage in Europe' (*National Cyber Security Centre*, 16 August 2022); Greenberg Traurig LLP, 'Memorandum-Application of the CLOUD Act to EU Entities' (Dutch Ministry of Justice and Security – NCSC, 2022), available at https://english.ncsc.nl/latest/weblog/weblog/2022/how-the-cloud-act-works-in-data-storage-in-europe?trk=public_post_comment-text.

[10] Greenberg Traurig LLP, 'Memorandum' (n 9).

> processor to transfer or disclose personal data … The extraterritorial application of those laws, regulations and other legal acts may be in breach of international law and may impede the attainment of the protection of natural persons ensured in the Union by the [GDPR].

Second, Article 48 prioritises the MLAT system or other equivalent agreements as the preferred lawful means for transferring data from the EU to third countries. The EU's rationale is that MLATs ensure compliance with EU law and judicial supervision within the Union.[11] In 2017, the Article 29 Working Party (WP29) explicitly warned that the 'circumvention of existing MLATs or other applicable legal basis under EU law by a third country's law enforcement authority is … an interference with the territorial sovereignty of an EU member state'.[12] Although Article 48 permits data transfer under international agreements other than the MLAT system, no EU–US agreement currently exists to facilitate such transfers.

Article 48 mentions a mutual legal assistance treaty as an example of an international agreement that may provide a legal basis for transferring personal data in response to third-country law enforcement requests. However, MLATs apply when data is exchanged directly between public authorities rather than through direct co-operation between authorities and service providers. The Council of Europe's Second Additional Protocol is currently the only international framework that provides for direct co-operation between private entities and public authorities. Once the Additional Protocol enters into force, it could be interpreted as an 'international agreement' within the meaning of Article 48 of the GDPR. Until then, the GDPR and the CLOUD Act remain on a collision course. Should a service provider operating within the European market, and thus subject to the requirements of the GDPR, be served with a US warrant requesting the disclosure of personal data of EU citizens or residents, the provider must refuse such direct request and refer the requesting authority to an existing MLAT.[13] However, this requirement would cause the service provider to violate the CLOUD Act, which is specifically designed to bypass the MLAT system.

Lastly, Article 48 allows for 'other grounds for transfer' as per GDPR Chapter V, primarily Articles 6 and 49. European data protection authorities, the European Data Protection Supervisor (EDPS), and the European Data Protection Board (EDPB) have jointly reviewed whether there are 'other legal bases' under which the GDPR allows the direct transfer of EU data in response to a request made under the CLOUD Act.[14]

[11] Brief of the European Commission, *US v Microsoft* (n 3) 14.

[12] Statement of the Article 29 Working Party, 'Data Protection and Privacy Aspects of Cross-Border Access to Electronic Evidence', 29 November 2017.

[13] Guidelines 2/2018 on Derogations of Art 49 under Regulation 2016/679, 25 May 2018.

[14] Initial Legal Assessment of the Impact of the US CLOUD Act on the EU Legal Framework for the Protection of Personal Data and the Negotiations of an EU–US Agreement on Cross-Border Access to Electronic Evidence, 10 July 2019.

In doing so, they applied a two-step test, that: (i) the transfer must rely on a legal basis as per Article 6 GDPR; and (ii) the transfer must rely on the derogations under Article 49 GDPR. Article 6(1)(c)–(f) sets out a list of 'necessary' interests that could be considered in relation to the legality of transfer to a third country, including transfer in response to a judicial order. After evaluating each criterion, the EDPS and EDPB concluded that only 'the vital interests of the data subject' (Article 6(1)(d) GDPR) could be cited as a legal basis to reply to a request under the CLOUD Act.[15] However, this interpretation would not solve anything because it is unlikely that a request issued under the CLOUD Act would qualify as 'necessary in order to protect the vital interests of the data subject' under the GDPR. Therefore, Article 6 would not offer a valid legal basis when it comes to requests from third-country authorities.[16]

The other possible legal basis for transferring personal data in response to a CLOUD Act order is Article 49 of the GDPR. In its amicus brief submitted to the US Supreme Court in the *Microsoft Ireland* case, the European Commission suggested that two 'grounds for transfer' under Article 49 could be relevant, depending on the precise circumstances. One such possible ground is if 'the transfer is necessary for important reasons of public interest'.[17] Article 49(4) of the GDPR provides that the requirement of 'public interest' must be recognised in Union or Member State law, not merely in the requesting third country. This raises the question of whether the investigation of a crime in a third country could also qualify as a public interest recognised in Union law or in the law of the Member State. Though it should be interpreted strictly, the Commission has taken the view that the answer to this question is in the affirmative, observing that:

> In general, Union as well as Member State law recognises the importance of the fight against serious crime – and thus criminal law enforcement and international cooperation in that respect – as an objective of general interest. … Article 83 of the TFEU identifies several areas of crime that are particularly serious and have cross-border dimensions, such as illicit drug trafficking.[18]

This articulation by the Commission lacks clarity. It did not clarify whether the investigation of serious crime in a third country could justify the transfer of EU data to that third country outside the MLAT system. The EDPS and EDPB also disagree with the Commission's interpretations, arguing that:

> it is not sufficient that the data transfer is requested (for example by a third country authority) for an investigation which serves a public interest of a third country which, in an abstract sense, also exists in EU or Member State law.[19]

[15] ibid.

[16] Some US scholars criticised this interpretation by the EDPS/EDPB as 'strikingly narrow'. See, for instance, P Swire, 'When Does GDPR Act as a Blocking Statute: The Relevance of a Lawful Basis for Transfer' (Georgia Tech Scheller College of Business Research Paper No 3473187, 2019).

[17] Art 49(1)(d), GDPR.

[18] Brief of the European Commission, *US v Microsoft* (n 3) 15.

[19] Initial Legal Assessment (n 14).

Another possible ground under which transfer can be permissible is when the transfer is 'necessary for the purposes of compelling legitimate interests pursued by the controller which are not overridden by the interests or rights and freedoms of the data subject'.[20] The Commission hinted that, subject to the strict requirements under the last paragraph of Article 49(1) of the GDPR, the controller's legitimate interests could possibly justify data transfer to a third country outside the MLAT procedure.[21] However, the EDPS and EDPB appear to take a slightly different view.

After arguing that the derogations set out under Article 49 of the GDPR should be interpreted strictly, the authorities concluded that these derogations are either very difficult to meet or insufficient to justify the transfer of personal data in response to CLOUD Act requests.[22] For instance, the requirements to 'notify both the supervisory authority and the data subject of the transfer' under the last paragraph of Article 49(1) are difficult, if not impossible, to meet, given the confidentiality requirements of CLOUD Act requests. Consequently, their assessment concluded that such derogations should be interpreted strictly and are rarely, if ever, met in the context of law enforcement requests.

The net effect is that it is generally impossible for a service provider to fully comply with both US CLOUD Act obligations and the EU GDPR without risking breaching one or the other regime. Attempts to circumvent the MLAT system are likely to run afoul of Article 48 and related GDPR provisions. The legal conundrum is further amplified by three aggravating factors:

1. While the CLOUD Act includes a 'comity' analysis mechanism through a new statutory right allowing service providers to challenge warrants that conflict with foreign law, this mechanism only applies where the conflicting jurisdiction has an executive agreement with the US. There is no such agreement between the EU and the US, rendering this pathway unavailable for EU-based data.
2. In addition to the GDPR, several EU Member States have supplementary laws prohibiting or restricting the transfer of certain categories of data abroad, increasing the likelihood of multi-layered legal exposure for service providers.[23]
3. As shall be detailed below, the *Schrems II* decision and subsequent invalidation of the Privacy Shield have further constrained the avenues for lawful data transfer from the EU to the US outside the MLAT process, narrowing the already slim margins of legal compliance.

[20] Art 49(1), GDPR.

[21] Brief of the European Commission, *US v Microsoft* (n 3) 15.

[22] Initial Legal Assessment (n 14).

[23] Explanatory Memorandum, 'Recommendation for a Council Decision authorising the opening of negotiations in view of an agreement between the European Union and the United States of America on cross-border access to electronic evidence for judicial cooperation in criminal matters' COM (2019) 70 final 2.

Therefore, the extraterritorial reach of the CLOUD Act and the strict transfer requirements of the GDPR remain fundamentally incompatible, in the absence of a transatlantic executive agreement or new legal frameworks. This persistent conflict places multinational service providers and their customers at significant legal risk, heightens digital sovereignty anxieties, and underscores the urgency of negotiating a comprehensive, rights-respecting transatlantic data-sharing regime.

6.2.2. The e-Evidence Regulation v SCA

As examined in chapter five, a central objective of the e-Evidence Regulation is to address the legal and practical challenges faced by Member States' law enforcement authorities in obtaining electronic evidence held by US-based service providers operating within the Union.[24] This new framework introduces a unilateral regime enabling direct production orders to compel service providers to disclose electronic evidence regardless of where the data is physically stored. Although this enhances legal certainty and expediency for EU authorities, it creates new jurisdictional tensions by potentially conflicting with the US's legal regime governing access to electronic communications.

Specifically, the US SCA prohibits the voluntary or compelled disclosure of content data to foreign governments outside the frameworks of the MLAT system, except in narrowly defined emergency circumstances. While the SCA permits disclosure of non-content subscriber information to foreign governments on a voluntary basis, the prohibitive restrictions on content data have been widely identified as one of the principal sources of conflicts of law in transatlantic data access.[25] Critically, the SCA's restrictions apply irrespective of whether the foreign government's request concerns only its own citizens' data and complies with its own domestic legal processes or international human rights standards; the mere fact that the data sought is physically stored on US soil suffices to trigger these restrictions. This strict territorial linkage effectively insulates data held by US service providers from foreign law enforcement access unless channelled through MLAT processes, in which case disclosure would need to meet the probable cause standard and would require US court authorisation.

The collision course between the e-Evidence Regulation and the SCA arises from this fundamental legal divergence. The EU requires compliance with its Regulations, empowering its authorities to directly compel data production from service providers operating in the Union. This creates a situation in which EU law enforcement can issue a production order to compel disclosure of content data

[24] S Carrera, M Stefan, and V Mitsilegas, 'Cross-Border Data Access in Criminal Proceedings and the Future of Digital Justice: Navigating the Current Legal Framework, and Exploring Ways Forward within the EU and across the Atlantic' (Report of CEPS and QMUL Task Force, October 2020) iii.

[25] AK Woods, 'Against Data Exceptionalism: Jurisdictions in the Cloud' (2016) 68 *Sandford Law Review* 748.

situated in the US, in conflict with the SCA prohibitions. The tension is rendered more acute by the predominance of US companies within Europe's cloud infrastructure. Approximately two-thirds of EU criminal investigations that require access to digital evidence involve cross-border requests, underscoring the critical reliance on transatlantic co-operation.

The mechanism that the e-Evidence Regulation introduces to mitigate conflicting obligations is somewhat analogous to that found in the CLOUD Act. The Regulation allows service providers to raise objections when faced with conflicting third-country legal obligations, triggering judicial review in the issuing Member State. The reviewing court then assesses a set of balancing factors. This mirrors the CLOUD Act's comity provisions, whereby US courts evaluate competing jurisdictional claims and may quash warrants if compliance would violate foreign privacy laws – although, crucially, the CLOUD Act's applicability is limited to countries with which the US has entered executive agreements, a status the EU does not yet enjoy.

Consequently, this legal divergence creates an enduring layer of uncertainty for service providers, who must navigate conflicting enforcement demands without clear, harmonised legal frameworks. The resulting tensions emphasise the need for a comprehensive transatlantic agreement on electronic evidence-sharing that reconciles the divergent regulatory priorities of the EU and the US. This imperative motivated the initiation of negotiations in 2019, wherein both jurisdictions seek to avoid overlapping and contradictory legal obligations while safeguarding individual rights and law enforcement interests.

6.3. Towards an EU–US Agreement on Electronic Evidence

At least three primary forces for convergence have shaped the transatlantic approach to cross-border data access, collectively laying the foundation for negotiation efforts towards an EU–US agreement.[26] First, there is a shared technological context in which the major global service providers whose co-operation is indispensable are predominantly headquartered in the US. Scholars such as Schwartz and Peifer observe that these technology companies increasingly act as agents of convergence, seeking accommodations with the EU on government access to data, and thus serving as a critical bridge between the two regulatory regimes.[27]

[26] For a broader discussion on EU–US convergence in the area of data privacy, see CJ Bennett, *Regulating Privacy: Data Protection and Public Policy in Europe and the United States* (Cornell University Press, 1992); P Schwartz and KN Peifer, 'Transatlantic Data Privacy Law' (2017) 106 *The Georgetown Law Journal* 115.

[27] P Schwartz and KN Peifer, 'Data Localization Under the CLOUD Act and the GDPR: A Quest for an Efficient Path to Legal Certainty' (2019) 20 *Computer Law Review International* 1.

Second, there exist shared security and law enforcement objectives.[28] Both the US and the EU confront a common landscape of criminal threats ranging from transnational organised crime and terrorism to cybercrime, necessitating effective mechanisms of co-operation and data-sharing. This alignment has fostered a political agreement recognising the need for streamlined frameworks to facilitate cross-border data access while respecting privacy and fundamental rights.

Third, this convergence of interests has translated into concerted political will to negotiate a comprehensive transatlantic agreement. Both sides acknowledge that such an agreement would address pervasive legal uncertainties and avoid conflicting obligations faced by service providers that are subject to overlapping but divergent laws.[29] This shared understanding has catalysed multiple rounds of negotiations aimed at establishing mutually acceptable norms and procedures.[30] Key legislative instruments – the CLOUD Act and the e-Evidence Regulation – serve as foundational pillars in this process.[31] Both instruments are designed to facilitate expedited access to electronic evidence held by service providers, reducing reliance on the slow and cumbersome MLAT processes.

The importance of reaching an agreement is underscored by official statements from both sides. The US government emphasises that an EU–US agreement on cross-border data access would enhance public safety and national security by enabling more rapid identification of, and response to, criminal threats, while upholding the rule of law, privacy, and civil liberties.[32] The EU Commission similarly highlights that such an agreement would deliver legal clarity for judicial and law enforcement authorities on both sides and avert conflicting legal obligations.[33]

Nonetheless, the negotiation process is inherently complex and delicately poised. It requires grappling with politically sensitive issues rooted in longstanding philosophical and legal divergences, particularly concerning privacy and surveillance law. These challenges can be broadly categorised into three dimensions: statutory design of the CLOUD Act, substantive requirements in both jurisdictions, and the lingering impact of the Court of Justice of the European Union (CJEU)'s *Schrems II* decision.

[28] ibid.

[29] S Ülgen, 'Governing Cyberspace: A Road Map for Transatlantic Leadership' (*Carnegie Europe*, 2016) 73, available at https://carnegieendowment.org/research/2016/01/governing-cyberspace-a-road-map-for-transatlantic-leadership?lang=en.

[30] See 'CLOUD Act Resources', available at www.justice.gov/criminal/cloud-act-resources.

[31] H Farrell and AL Newman, *Of Privacy and Power: The Transatlantic Struggle over Freedom and Security* (Princeton University Press, 2019) 168.

[32] US Department of Justice, 'Joint US-EU Statement on Electronic Evidence Sharing Negotiations', 26 September 2019, available at www.justice.gov/opa/pr/joint-us-eu-statement-electronic-evidence-sharing-negotiations.

[33] 'Recommendation for a Council Decision authorising the opening of negotiations in view of an agreement between the European Union and the United States of America on cross-border access to electronic evidence for judicial cooperation in criminal matters' COM/2019/70 final 8.

6.3.1. Challenges Arising from the CLOUD Act's Statutory Design

As discussed in chapter four, one of the key objectives of the CLOUD Act is to address conflicts of law created by the blocking provisions of the SCA. It envisions reciprocal data-sharing agreements with eligible foreign governments, which would remove the blocking statutes and enable these governments to access US-held data without going through the MLAT process. However, the CLOUD Act has a design problem – perhaps unintended – especially concerning the EU–US negotiations.[34]

The CLOUD Act explicitly contemplates the establishment of bilateral executive agreements negotiated on a country-by-country basis, requiring the US Attorney General, with the concurrence of the Secretary of State, to certify each 'foreign government' as affording sufficiently robust substantive and procedural protections for privacy and civil liberties in light of the data collection. This stringent certification prerequisite raises considerable complexity when applied to the EU, a multinational organisation composed of 27 Member States with diverse legal traditions and law enforcement practices.

A pressing legal question arises: can the EU as an entity be considered a 'foreign government' under the CLOUD Act for the purpose of negotiating a single overarching executive agreement? Or must the Attorney General instead undertake a Member State-by-Member State certification exercise, evaluating the individual domestic laws and practices for each EU Member State as a precondition to approving discrete bilateral agreements? Moreover, what are the implications if one or more Member State fails to meet the CLOUD Act's certification criteria?

Legal scholars with experience in this domain argue that the statutory term 'foreign government' is best interpreted narrowly, meaning either the government of a foreign country or its political subdivisions.[35] Since the EU is neither a sovereign state nor a political subdivision but, rather, a supranational organisation with limited sovereign attributes, it does not qualify as a 'foreign government' under the CLOUD Act. Consequently, the Attorney General is unlikely to issue a blanket certification covering all Member States via the EU as a single entity. This interpretation implies that, for a CLOUD Act agreement to encompass the entire EU, each Member State's legal regime must be individually certified. In light of this predicament, Jennifer Daskal and Peter Swire propose a pragmatic two-part approach to reconciling US statutory requirements with EU political realities. First, they recommend negotiating a general 'framework agreement' between the EU and the

[34] T Christakis and F Terpan, 'EU–US Negotiations on Law Enforcement Access to Data: Divergences, Challenges and EU Law Procedures and Options' (2021) 11 *International Data Privacy Law* 81.

[35] J Daskal and P Swire, 'A Possible EU–US Agreement on Law Enforcement Access to Data?' (*Lawfare*, 21 May 2018), available at www.lawfareblog.com/possible-EU–US-agreement-law-enforcement-access-data.

US that articulates shared standards and resolves core issues of concern across the EU collectively.[36] This approach is neither prohibited nor prescribed under the CLOUD Act. While not itself an executive agreement under the CLOUD Act, such a framework would set out fundamental principles and create a common baseline. Second, they advocate for individual implementing agreements with each of the 27 Member States, each conforming to both the CLOUD Act's certification mandates and the overarching framework provisions.[37]

This approach aligns with official US negotiating positions. US authorities have emphasised their intent to pursue a framework agreement supplemented by bilateral agreement with individual Member States rather than a single pan-EU executive agreement.[38] Deputy Assistant Attorney General Richard Downing has echoed this uncertainty, acknowledging that a single agreement covering all EU Member States seems improbable, given the statutory requirements.[39] Emerging from these positions is a near consensus in Washington that a comprehensive stand-alone CLOUD Act agreement exclusively with the EU as a bloc is unlikely. Rather, the negotiations are expected to unfold as a layered set of agreements, whereby some Member States gain certification while others may fall short. This inevitably harbours the prospect of 'winners and losers' within the EU: certain Member States whose domestic laws meet the stringent CLOUD Act requirements will be certified and included; others may be excluded due to perceived deficiencies.[40]

Even if all Member States ultimately satisfy the requirements of the CLOUD Act, the negotiation and ratification of dozens of separate agreements will be a complex, lengthy, and potentially fragmented process, undermining the EU's political objectives of unified digital sovereignty and legal coherence. Accordingly, the EU advocates a single comprehensive agreement covering all Member States. The European Commission has underscored that fragmented, uncoordinated bilateral arrangements are untenable: 'A satisfactory improvement of cross-border access to electronic evidence in criminal investigations cannot be sufficiently achieved by the Member States acting alone or in an uncoordinated way.'[41]

[36] ibid.

[37] ibid.

[38] Report from the Commission on the opening of negotiations in view of an agreement between the European Union and the United States of America on cross-border access to electronic evidence for judicial cooperation in criminal matters, 12524/19 (25 September 2019) 3.

[39] Quoted in Christakis and Terpan, 'EU–US Negotiations on Law Enforcement Access to Data' (n 34).

[40] T Christakis, 'Lost in the Cloud? Law Enforcement Cross-Border Access to Data After the "Clarifying Lawful Overseas Use of Data" (CLOUD) Act and E-Evidence' (*Cross-Border Data Forum*, 26 June 2018), available at www.crossborderdataforum.org/observatoire-fic-lost-in-the-cloud/; Report of the Commission services on the second round of negotiations in view of an agreement between the European Union and the United States of America on cross-border access to electronic evidence for judicial cooperation in criminal matters (6 November 2019).

[41] European Commission, 'Impact Assessment Accompanying the document Proposal for a Regulation of the European Parliament and of the Council on European Production and Preservation Orders for electronic evidence in criminal matters and Proposal for a Directive of the European Parliament and of the Council laying down harmonised rules on the appointment of legal representatives for the purpose of gathering evidence in criminal proceedings SWD (2018) 118 Final' 38.

In pursuit of this goal, the EU has explicitly committed to negotiating *en bloc*, striving to preserve legal and operational unity among all Member States. Following the CLOUD Act's enactment in 2018, then Commissioner Věra Jourová emphasised the EU's intent to adopt a co-ordinated approach, to avoid a proliferation of separate bilateral agreements, warning that the CLOUD Act's statutory design 'narrows the room for the potential compatible solution between EU–US'.[42] Moreover, EU officials have formally urged US counterparts to refrain from negotiating separate bilateral agreements with individual Member States, highlighting the political and legal sensitivities involved.[43]

Faced with this complicated impasse, the EU can explore two architectural pathways for the envisaged agreement.[44] The preferred option would be a comprehensive, self-executing agreement within the CLOUD Act framework. If the CLOUD Act requirements preclude such an arrangement, the EU can propose negotiating a similarly comprehensive but independent agreement outside the formal scope of the CLOUD Act (a non-CLOUD Act agreement).[45] Notably, the European Parliament's Committee on Civil Liberties, Justice and Home Affairs has called on the Commission to clarify whether and how an EU–US agreement might be realised outside the CLOUD Act's framework, recognising the EU's preference for avoiding fragmentation and preserving a high level of data protection.[46] This alternative could harmonise cross-border data-access standards and protections while circumventing the statutory constraints limiting the Attorney General's certification authority. It could provide a more streamlined, uniform mechanism compatible with the EU data protection framework, strengthening consistency in rights safeguards and judicial oversight across the Union.[47] For its part, the US would retain the CLOUD Act's enforcement requirements domestically but accept this external agreement as a parallel or supplementary mechanism. The major caveat is the potentially lengthy negotiation timeline and complex political balancing required to achieve consensus. Fundamentally, the EU's preference for a comprehensive unified agreement

[42] Quoted in C Stupp, 'Leaked EU Overhaul Gives Tech Companies 10 Days to Share "e-Evidence" Data with Police' (*Euractiv*, 30 March 2018), available at www.euractiv.com/section/data-protection/news/leaked-eu-overhaul-gives-tech-companies-10-days-to-share-e-evidence-data-with-police/.

[43] Christakis and Terpan, 'EU–US Negotiations on Law Enforcement Access to Data' (n 34).

[44] For other possible alternatives and accompanying institutional and structural complexities, see P Swire, 'EU and U.S. Negotiations on Cross-Border Data, Within and Outside of the Cloud Act Framework' (*Cross-Border Data Forum*, 13 April 2019), available at www.crossborderdataforum.org/eu-and-u-s-negotiations-on-cross-border-data-within-and-outside-of-the-cloud-act-framework/; Christakis and Terpan, 'EU–US Negotiations on Law Enforcement Access to Data' (n 34).

[45] Swire, 'EU and U.S. Negotiations on Cross-Border Data' (n 44); Christakis and Terpan, 'EU–US Negotiations on Law Enforcement Access to Data' (n 34).

[46] 4th Working Document (B) on the Proposal for a Regulation on European Production and Preservation Orders for electronic evidence in criminal matters (2018/0108 (COD)) – Relation with third country law, Committee on Civil Liberties, Justice and Home Affairs (11 March 2019) 5.

[47] EDPS Opinion 2/2019 on the negotiating mandate of an EU–US agreement on cross-border access to electronic evidence (2 April 2019) 7.

reflects concerns for both fundamental rights protection and security interests. The Commission has asserted that:

> The European Union has an interest in a comprehensive agreement with the United States of America, both from the perspective of protecting European rights and values such as privacy and personal data protection and from the perspective of our own security interests.[48]

This underscores that resolving the statutory design uncertainties is both a legal and political challenge critical to the feasibility and ultimate success of the envisaged EU–US agreement on cross-border data access.

6.3.2. Substantive Challenges

A second and even more profound source of uncertainty surrounding the envisaged EU–US agreement on cross-border data access concerns substantive matters, particularly whether, and to what extent, the US legal system provides protections for privacy and fundamental rights that are equivalent to those guaranteed by EU law, and vice versa. Unlike the more technical and procedural architectural uncertainties associated with the CLOUD Act's bilateral executive agreements, substantive challenges strike at the core legal and constitutional values of both jurisdictions.

From the outset, the CLOUD Act establishes a threshold of substantive requirements that a 'qualifying foreign government' must meet to enter into an executive agreement with the US. Similarly, the European Council's negotiating directives instruct the Commission to seek strong fundamental rights protections as an explicit precondition for the agreement's conclusion.[49]

Despite this overarching consensus on the importance of privacy and procedural safeguards, the two sides hold deep and enduring divergent views on the precise content, scope, and enforcement of these safeguards, particularly regarding judicial oversight, data protection, necessity and proportionality standards, and remedies for affected data subjects.[50] At the heart of this substantive divide is a mutual conviction that each jurisdiction's standards for law enforcement access to personal data are notably stricter that the other's.[51] The EU maintains that its privacy and data protection regime, solidified by the GDPR and the Charter of Fundamental Rights (Charter), establishes safeguards absent from the US framework – most notably, regarding comprehensive data subject rights, judicial redress, and procedural checks on government surveillance. This view underpinned the

[48] COM/2019/70 final 4.

[49] Explanatory Memorandum, COM (2019) 70 final 5.

[50] Carrera, Stefan, and Mitsilegas, 'Cross-Border Data Access in Criminal Proceedings' (n 24) 63.

[51] For a detailed analysis on this, see P Swire and D Kennedy-Mayo, 'How Both the EU and the U.S. Are "Stricter" than Each Other for the Privacy of Government Requests for Information' (2017) 66 *Emory Law Journal* 617.

judgments of the CJEU in the landmark *Schrems II* decision, which concluded that the US's privacy standards, particularly those related to intelligence surveillance, do not afford an adequate level of protection as required by EU law.

Conversely, the US asserts that it provides robust privacy and civil liberties protections which in many respects meet or exceed those found in the EU.[52] In its response to *Schrems II*, the US administration contended that 'data transferred to the United States enjoys comparable or greater privacy protections relating to intelligence surveillance than data held within the EU'.[53] The US stresses its legal mechanisms for judicial oversight of surveillance, limitations on the bulk collection of data, transparency, and avenues for redress, asserting that these elements collectively ensure a high level of protection for data subjects.

This 'relative strictness'[54] perceived on both sides, regarding law enforcement access, thus necessitates reciprocal assessments. The US must certify that particular EU Member States 'afford robust substantive and procedural protections for privacy and civil liberties in light of the data collection', under the CLOUD Act. It is only after such certification by the US administration that an EU Member State will obtain the status of 'qualifying foreign government' and benefit from streamlined access to data held by US service providers. Whether the EU will accept such a unilateral certification process, effectively subjecting its Member States' sovereign legal systems to US executive scrutiny, remains an open question.[55] In parallel, the EU will determine whether US law can be deemed adequate under EU law to justify cross-border transfers of personal data pursuant to the envisaged agreement, consistent with the CJEU's jurisprudence demanding 'essential equivalence' in data protection standards.[56] As discussed below, this aspect is particularly interesting as the CJEU has repeatedly found that US law does not afford an adequate level of protection of personal data transferred from the Union.

Substantive controversies that are likely to dominate negotiations include, but are not limited to, the following:

1. *Standards for international data transfers*: once concluded, the envisaged agreement will serve as a legal basis for the transfer of personal data from the EU to the US. However, since the US law has historically been judged 'inadequate' from an EU perspective, negotiators must devise novel mechanisms

[52] US Embassy in Luxembourg, 'U.S. Secretary of Commerce Wilbur Ross Statement on Schrems II Ruling and the Importance of EU-U.S. Data Flows' (16 July 2020); see also Written Legal Submission on Behalf of the United States of America as Amicus Curiae, in *Data Protection Commissioner v Facebook Ireland Ltd and Maximilian Schrems* (23 Dec 2016) (High Court) (Ireland).

[53] US Department of Commerce, Department of Justice, and the Office of the Director of National Intelligence, 'Information on U.S. Privacy Safeguards Relevant to SCCs and Other EU Legal Bases for EU-U.S. Data Transfers after *Schrems II*' (White Paper, September 2020) 16.

[54] Swire and Kennedy-Mayo, 'How Both the EU and the U.S. Are "Stricter" than Each Other' (n 51) 617.

[55] Christakis and Terpan, 'EU–US Negotiations on Law Enforcement Access to Data' (n 34).

[56] Opinion 1/15, *EU–Canada PNR Agreement*, ECLI:EU:C:2017:592, para 214; *Schrems II* (n 8).

or assurances to bridge this gap, whether by enhancing protections or incorporating independent oversight and remedy provisions.

2. *Conditions for issuing production orders*: the Commission proposes that the agreement should explicitly outline conditions under which judicial authorities can issue production orders, including procedural modalities.[57] Central among these conditions is that production orders be 'necessary and proportionate' within the criminal proceedings context, aligning with Article 5 of the e-Evidence Regulation. This principled test deeply embedded in EU privacy law is, however, largely unfamiliar in the US legal framework, raising questions about how the agreement might incorporate or mutually recognise such standards.
3. *Effective judicial remedy for data subjects*: Article 52(1) of the Charter of Fundamental Rights of the European Union requires that any limitation on privacy rights and data protection must respect the 'essence of the rights'. The CJEU has held that the absence of an effective judicial redress mechanism is one of the circumstances in which the 'essence of the rights' could be adversely affected: 'legislation not providing for any possibility for an individual to pursue legal remedies … does not respect the essence of the fundamental right to effective judicial protection, as enshrined in Article 47 of the Charter'.[58] Thus, the agreement must include provisions enabling data subjects to seek judicial review or remedy if their data is accessed in criminal proceedings; absence of such clauses would likely render the agreement incompatible with EU primary and secondary law, as well as CJEU jurisprudence.
4. *The circumstances in which service providers may object to production orders*: Under the CLOUD Act, service providers may challenge data production orders only if: (i) the data subject is not a US person and does not reside in the US; and (ii) compliance with the order would cause a conflict of law with a qualifying foreign government. These conditions are narrowly defined and generally more restrictive than objections authorised under the EU's e-Evidence Regulation, which provides for broader safeguards including fundamental rights considerations.[59] Negotiations must clarify whether and how such expanded objections will be incorporated.
5. *Data protection safeguards*: The EU intends for the agreement to complement and enhance the protections enshrined in the EU–US Umbrella Agreement, which governs data-sharing between law enforcement agencies (not between

[57] Annex to the Recommendation for a Council Decision authorising the opening of negotiations in view of an agreement between the European Union and the United States of America on cross-border access to electronic evidence for judicial cooperation in criminal matters, COM (2019) 70 final (Negotiating Directives), para 17.

[58] *Schrems II* (n 8), para 187.

[59] Art 17, Regulation (EU) 2023/1543 of the European Parliament and of the Council of 12 July 2023 on European Production Orders and European Preservation Orders for electronic evidence in criminal proceedings and for the execution of custodial sentences following criminal proceedings, OJ L191/118.

law enforcement and service providers).[60] The Commission's negotiating directives require that the envisaged agreement explicitly applies the Umbrella Agreement by reference while also introducing additional safeguards tailored for cross-border data access.[61]

6. *Categories of data subjects covered*: The negotiating texts emphasise that the agreement must be reciprocal in terms of the categories of data subjects protected from being targeted under cross-border production orders. This provision responds to concerns that the CLOUD Act's protections for US persons may not be reciprocated for EU nationals.[62] For example, US authorities can compel the production of data irrespective of the nationality or residence of the data subject if the provider falls under US jurisdiction, whereas US persons enjoy protections limiting qualifying foreign governments' access.

These substantive uncertainties are further complicated by the lingering impact (the *Schrems* effect) of the CJEU's *Schrems II* decision, which invalidated the EU–US Privacy Shield framework and its predecessor the Safe Harbor arrangement, partly on the grounds that US law failed to provide adequate judicial remedies and safeguards relating to necessity and proportionality – the very issue at the core of the ongoing negotiation on cross-border data access.

6.3.3. The *Schrems* Effect

Data flows between the US and the EU represent the single largest economic conduit in the world, underwriting a relationship valued at an estimated $7.1 trillion in 2021.[63] Indeed, American technology giants not only dominate Europe's cloud industry, with estimates placing their market share at 80 per cent,[64] but also hold almost 92 per cent of the Western world's data.[65] The legal underpinnings for these data flows began with the 2000 EU–US Safe Harbor Framework, which allowed US companies to transfer personal data from the EU to the US.

However, the Safe Harbor quickly become a source of controversy. The agreement's central weakness was its reliance on US companies' self-certification, coupled with minimal oversight and persistent fears about government access to

[60] Agreement between the United States of America and the European Union on the protection of personal information relating to the prevention, investigation, detection, and prosecution of criminal offences, OJ L336, 10.12.2016.

[61] Negotiating Directives (n 57), paras 14–15.

[62] EDPS Opinion 2/2019 on the negotiating mandate of an EU–US agreement on cross-border access to electronic evidence (2 April 2019), paras 48–50.

[63] US Chamber of Commerce, 'Transatlantic Data Flows: Moving Data with Confidence', 20 September 2021.

[64] A Wirth, M Giovanni, and T Maricarmen, 'Clouds on the Horizon: Europe's Cloud Policy Threatens Transatlantic Digital Harmony' (*Center for European Policy Analysis*, 10 May 2022), available at www.cepa.org/article/clouds-on-the-horizon-europes-cloud-policy-threatens-transatlantic-digital-harmony/.

[65] F Burwell and K Propp, 'The European Union and the Search for Digital Sovereignty: Building "Fortress Europe" or Preparing for a New World?', Atlantic Council, Issue Brief 2020.

transferred data. These anxieties grew into outright opposition in the wake of the Snowden revelations in 2013, which exposed the depth of surveillance by the US National Security Agency, including bulk access to foreign citizens' data. European trust in the US approach to privacy eroded, and the legal validity of Safe Harbor was put to the test. On 6 October 2015, the CJEU handed down its landmark decision in *Schrems I*, declaring the Safe Harbor arrangement incompatible with EU fundamental rights.[66] The court held that US law lacked the necessary limitations and redress mechanisms to prevent US government access to EU citizens' data. Critically, the *Schrems I* decision articulated that the heart of the data transfer problem was not merely about commercial practices but the potential for government access and lack of effective remedies.

The invalidation of Safe Harbor did not resolve these concerns but triggered a cycle of legal and diplomatic wrangling that has defined transatlantic relations ever since. The end of Safe Harbor set off a scramble to avoid a catastrophic economic disruption. Within months, European and US negotiators devised a successor, the EU–US Privacy Shield, agreed upon in February 2016.[67] The Privacy Shield purported to tighten controls on corporate self-certification, enhance government oversight, and establish an ombudsperson within the US Department of State to investigate and adjudicate EU citizens' complaints. It also introduced annual joint review and tried to impose some limited transparency on US surveillance activities. Yet, these measures failed to meaningfully address the structural problems identified in *Schrems I*, especially regarding government surveillance. Critics swiftly pointed to the lack of binding safeguards and the inherent limitations of relying on an executive arrangement subject to US executive decision.

In 2020, the *Schrems II* decision once more up-ended the framework. The CJEU invalidated the Privacy Shield on similar grounds as those given in *Schrems I*. The court rejected the Commission's conclusion that US law ensured an adequate level of protection of personal data transferred from the EU. It concluded that the personal data of EU citizens, when transferred to the US, was not afforded the level of fundamental rights protection guaranteed under EU law.

Although *Schrems II* formally concerned the Commission's adequacy decision underpinning the Privacy Shield, the CJEU's reasoning was rooted in structural and legal features of the broader US surveillance regime. In particular, the court scrutinised three central legal instruments on US surveillance operations: FISA Section 702, Executive Order 12-333, and Presidential Policy Directive 28. It found that these authorities failed to meet the EU standards of necessity and proportionality. FISA Section 702 was deemed deficient because it lacked limitations on the surveillance powers it conferred for the purpose

[66] *Maximillian Schrems v Data Protection Commissioner* C-362/14, ECLI:EU:C:2015:650 [2015].

[67] Commission Implementing Decision (EU) 2016/1250 pursuant to Directive 95/46/EC of the European Parliament and of the Council on the adequacy of the protection provided by the EU-U.S. Privacy Shield [2016] OJ L 207/1.

of foreign intelligence-gathering and did not provide explicit safeguards for non-US persons.[68] Further, the Foreign Intelligence Surveillance Court (FISC), while nominally an oversight body, was found not to authorise targeted surveillance or provide sufficient individualised scrutiny.[69] Executive Order 12-333 and Presidential Policy Directive 28, in turn, allow bulk collection of data flowing into the US, including data transmitted in real time, without any judicial oversight.[70]

Of particular concern was the accountability mechanism created by the Privacy Shield – the Ombudsperson – which was created to address the lack of legal remedies for EU persons whose data had been transferred to the US. The court concluded that the Ombudsperson mechanism did not constitute a tribunal within the meaning of Article 47 of the Charter.[71] The Ombudsperson was not an independent authority, being appointed by, and reporting to, the US Secretary of State, and did not possess binding power vis-à-vis US intelligence agencies. Consequently, the framework failed to offer an effective and impartial remedy.

These legal battles had immediate and profound practical impacts for some of the world's largest service providers. The stakes were perhaps never clearer than in 2023, when Meta (the parent company of Facebook) was fined 1.2 billion euros by the Irish Data Protection Commission, on instruction from the EDPB – the largest penalty ever under the GDPR.[72] Meta's violation lay in the systematic transfer of European user data to the US in the absence of adequate legal safeguards, in direct breach of the *Schrems II* logic. The Irish regulator not only applied the fine but also mandated Meta to cease unlawfully processing, including storing, EU user data in the US, and to return or delete data transferred in violation of the GDPR, all within six months. The implication was stark: without some new legal arrangement, Meta and similar companies could be forced to erase a decade's worth of user data, potentially rendering business continuity for many US technology companies nearly impossible.

With time running out and data transfer continuing around the clock, policy-makers pursued a third attempt to regularise transatlantic data flows. The EU–US Data Privacy Framework (DPF) was adopted with an adequacy decision by the European Commission in July 2023.[73] This new arrangement was informed by the lessons of *Schrems II* and featured a concerted effort to

[68] *Schrems II* (n 8), para 180.

[69] ibid, paras 109 and 179.

[70] ibid, para 49.

[71] ibid, paras 65 and 168. Art 47 of the Charter: everyone is entitled to a hearing by an independent and impartial tribunal.

[72] Binding Decision 1/2023 on the dispute submitted by the Irish SA on data transfers by Meta Platforms Ireland Limited for its Facebook service (Art 65 GDPR).

[73] Commission Implementing Decision EU 2023/1795 pursuant to Regulation (EU) 2016/679 of the European Parliament and of the Council on the adequate level of protection of personal data under the EU–US Data Privacy Framework [2023] OJ L231/118.

address the core issues identified by the CJEU. Central to the DPF was an executive order issued by then president Biden, designed to reframe US signal intelligence activities with explicit commitments to principles of necessity and proportionality, and establish a new two-tier redress mechanism for EU citizens whose data might be accessed by intelligence agencies.[74] US intelligence authorities were, in principle, bound to comply with additional restrictions regarding bulk collection, and are now subject to periodic review to verify compliance. European data subjects gained certain new rights, including the ability to seek access, correction, and erasure of their data, as well as access to alternative dispute resolution and oversight by a new Data Protection Review Court (DPRC).

The DPF's adequacy decision explicitly recognises these reforms as bringing the US regime much closer to that of the EU, especially regarding judicial redress and the proportionality of surveillance activity. Meanwhile, the DPF's first assessment, published in late 2024, concluded that, while the DPF constitutes an improvement over previous frameworks, certain caveats remain.[75] While it welcomed certain measures as positive steps, the assessment also highlighted some lingering questions about the application and enforcement of intelligence restrictions in practice, and the overall capacity for effective review and redress for European data subjects.

Despite this, the DPF's fate – like those of its predecessors – remains far from assured. In September 2023, French MP Philippe Latombe initiated a proceeding (Case T-553/23) before the General Court of the European Union, seeking to annul the DPF. Latombe's challenge is built on several legal fronts, most notably the absence of an adequate guarantee of a right to an effective remedy for EU data subjects. He alleges violations of the GDPR's minimisation and proportionality requirements, arguing that US intelligence still entails the bulk collection of personal data. Latombe also objected to the DPF's adequacy decision being published only in English rather than all EU official languages, on grounds of procedural fairness. As of 1 April 2025, the General Court had held its first hearing on the issue, setting in motion a judicial process that could end with the CJEU again overturning an adequacy decision, prolonging the cycle of instability.[76]

[74] European Commission, 'Questions & Answers: EU–US Data Privacy Framework' (*European Commission*, 10 July 2023), available at www.ec.europa.eu/commission/presscorner/detail/en/qanda_23_3752.

[75] EDPB Report on the first review of the European Commission Implementing Decision on the adequate protection of personal data under the EU–US Data Privacy Framework Version 1.1, 4 November 2024.

[76] 'Latombe Case: First Hearing for Annulment of the EU-U.S. Data Privacy Framework' (*Hogan Lovells*, 2 April 2025), available at www.hoganlovells.com/en/publications/latombe-case-first-hearing-for-annulment-of-the-euus-data-privacy-framework.

This legal uncertainty is heightened by mounting controversies on both sides of the Atlantic, particularly amid recent political developments in the US. The new US administration's dismissal of members of the Privacy and Civil Liberties Oversight Board has introduced further doubts over the continued independence and effectiveness of the DPF oversight. Coupled with a more overtly hostile stance towards EU digital sovereignty, and ongoing disputes over cross-border law enforcement access to data, the structural sustainability of the DPF appears fragile.

Each wave of legal and policy turbulence underscores the persistent, intractable tension between differing conceptions of privacy and state power in the EU and the US. More broadly, these developments highlight the US's commitment to maintaining its digital supremacy and the EU's pursuit of digital sovereignty and independence from US technology companies. Each new attempt to fix the fractured system – whether Safe Harbor, Privacy Shield, or the DPF – thus bumps up against the deeper rift between these competing visions.

The '*Schrems* effect' (and the underlying competing visions of digital governance) casts a long shadow over the transatlantic negotiations on cross-border data access under the CLOUD Act framework. The decision affects these negotiations at two critical stages: before and after the conclusion of an agreement. In the negotiation phase, *Schrems II* conditions the scope and substance of what the EU can legally accept in international arrangements. The CJEU has effectively raised the bar for determining what level of rights protection must be guaranteed when personal data is transferred outside the EU. Therefore, when negotiating a cross-border data-access agreement, EU institutions are bound to comply with the constitutional parameters as set out by the court. Even after a CLOUD Act agreement is reached and implemented, its legal status remains fragile. The possible outcome of a future EU–US agreement on cross-border data access, if subjected to scrutiny by the CJEU, remains an open question. Some argue that, without legislative reform from the US side, a post-*Schrems II* agreement covering cross-border data access could potentially be invalidated by the CJEU. According to Schwartz and Karl-Nikolaus, for instance, 'the CJEU will have the ultimate word about the sufficiency of any executive agreements developed under the CLOUD Act'.[77] Others believe it is unlikely that the CJEU would invalidate a future EU–US agreement on cross-border data access. Unlike the decisions in *Schrems I* and *II*, which concerned adequacy decisions rather than binding international agreements, the invalidation of a formal EU–US agreement would carry significant political and international legal consequences.[78] In any case, *Schrems II* continues to cast a long shadow over transatlantic negotiations on cross-border data access.

[77] Schwartz and Peifer, 'Data Localization Under the CLOUD Act and the GDPR' (n 27).
[78] Christakis and Terpan, 'EU–US Negotiations on Law Enforcement Access to Data' (n 34).

6.4. The Cautionary Tale of the US–UK CLOUD Act Agreement

The US–UK Agreement is often portrayed as 'a template', 'a blueprint', or 'a model' for future CLOUD Act executive agreements.[79] For instance, the US Department of Justice stated that the US–UK agreement would establish a framework and standards that could be used to reach similar agreements with other countries.[80] This assessment is problematic in several respects. The US–UK Agreement, while pioneering, as the first bilateral executive agreement under the CLOUD Act framework, must be regarded as a cautionary tale rather than a model for the envisaged EU–US negotiation. Despite its historic significance, the US–UK Agreement embodies several fundamental asymmetries and concerns that fundamentally undermine its suitability as a blueprint for future agreements, particularly those involving the EU, which demands stringent reciprocity and non-discrimination standards.

First, the US–UK Agreement is marked by an inherent lack of equality and reciprocity in its scope of production orders. It imposes stringent requirements targeting restriction that disproportionately constrain UK authorities while granting expansive rights to US authorities. Specifically, UK authorities can compel US service providers only when the data sought concerns non-US persons located in the UK or third countries. UK authorities cannot directly or indirectly target US persons – whether citizens, nationals, or permanent residents – regardless of their geographic location. This means that, if a UK domestic criminal investigation requires access to data of a US national located in the UK, the authorities must still follow the MLAT system and get a US-issued warrant based on probable cause. Even if the UK authorities want to get data of their own national who is located in the US, they must still follow the diplomatic channel. Therefore, a UK production order under the Agreement applies if the only link to the US is the location of the sought-after data. Conversely, US authorities can compel data production concerning anyone, anywhere, except those persons located within the UK. For instance, the Agreement allows US authorities to directly compel the production of personal data of British nationals located in third countries (say, in France). This discrepancy means that, while UK investigations involving US persons require adherence to the slower MLAT procedures, US authorities face no such barriers when targeting UK nationals outside their territory.

[79] See, for instance, J Daskal and P Swire, 'The U.K.-U.S. CLOUD Act Agreement Is Finally Here, Containing New Safeguards' (*Lawfare*, 8 October 2019), available at www.lawfareblog.com/uk-us-cloud-act-agreement-finally-here-containing-new-safeguards; N Swire, 'Applying the CLOUD Act to the U.S.-U.K. Bilateral Data Access Agreement' (*Lawfare*, 28 October 2019), available at www.lawfareblog.com/applying-cloud-act-us-uk-bilateral-data-access-agreement.

[80] 'Legislation to Permit the Secure and Privacy-Protective Exchange of Electronic Data for the Purposes of Combatting Serious Crime Including Terrorism' (*US Department of Justice*, 15 July 2016), available at https://www.aclu.org/sites/default/files/field_document/doj_legislative_proposal.pdf.

Second, related to these targeting restrictions, the US–UK Agreement enforces unequal data minimisation requirements. Both parties agree to adopt and implement procedures to minimise acquisition, retention, and dissemination of data, subject to mutual approval for procedural changes.[81] However, UK authorities face additional procedural burdens not imposed on US authorities. UK authorities must proactively minimise data concerning US persons, segregate or delete unnecessary data, and secure unreviewed data with restricted access. Under Article 7 of the Agreement, UK authorities are required to: (i) adopt and implement appropriate procedures to minimise the acquisition, retention, and dissemination of data concerning US persons; (ii) segregate, seal, or delete, and not disseminate such data that is not necessary for the prevention, detection, investigation, or prosecution of the offence covered by the agreement; and (iii) promptly review data collected pursuant to the order and store any unreviewed data on a secure system accessible only to those persons trained in applicable procedures. Such obligations reflect a heightened level of scrutiny on UK investigative practices for data relating to US persons, a constraint not reciprocated for data about UK persons located outside the UK.

Third, the combination of restrictive targeting and stringent minimisation obligations leads to an uneven protection regime based on nationality and residence.[82] US persons, including those located in the UK, enjoy stronger safeguards, exempting them from UK production orders and triggering enhanced minimisation measures. Meanwhile, British and third-country nationals face fewer protections and greater exposure to cross-border data access. The US–UK Agreement, therefore, is asymmetrical, non-reciprocal, and discriminatory, privileging US privacy protections over those of its UK counterpart and third countries.[83] This is at odds with the core EU negotiating directives, which explicitly require reciprocal rights and obligations, non-discriminatory treatment of persons regardless of nationality, and equal protection for data subjects.[84]

Fourth, a critical and widely criticised feature of the US–UK Agreement is its accommodation for unilateral, exterritorial production orders, whereby domestic laws operate alongside and effectively override the Agreement's safeguards. Article 6(3) states that the Agreement 'does not in any way restrict or eliminate any legal obligation Covered Providers have to produce data in response to Legal Process issued pursuant to the law of the Issuing Party'. In practice, this permits

[81] Art 7, Agreement between the Government of the United States of America and the Government of the United Kingdom of Great Britain and Northern Ireland on Access to Electronic Data for the Purpose of Countering Serious Crime 2019.

[82] Carrera, Stefan, and Mitsilegas, 'Cross-Border Data Access in Criminal Proceedings' (n 24) 34.

[83] ibid 33–35; T Christakis, '21 Thoughts and Questions about the UK/US CLOUD Act Agreement: (And an Explanation of How It Works – with Charts)' (*European Law Blog*, 17 October 2019), available at www.europeanlawblog.eu/pub/21-thoughts-and-questions-about-the-uk-us-cloud-act-agreement-and-an-explanation-of-how-it-works-with-charts/release/1; M Rojszczak, 'CLOUD Act Agreements from an EU Perspective' (2020) 38 *Computer Law & Security Review* 105442; Carrera, Stefan, and Mitsilegas (n 24) 35.

[84] Negotiating Directives (n 57), para 5.

US authorities to continue using the CLOUD Act (Part I) independently to compel US-based service providers to disclose personal data of anyone, irrespective of the target's nationality or location, rendering the Agreement's targeted restrictions and reciprocity provisions largely ineffective.[85] This dual application weakens the Agreement's protective intent and highlights why EU institutions, such as the EDPS and the EDPB, have expressed concerns that any future EU–US agreement must prevail over domestic US law, to avoid undermining EU citizens' data protections.[86]

Finally, the US–UK Agreement insufficiently safeguards the interests of third countries. Both parties are authorised to target nationals residing outside their respective jurisdictions, which can include EU citizens residing in Member States. The only minimal constraint is a notification requirement to the third-country authorities where the data subject is located.[87] However, this obligation is rendered practically optional, as the issuing party may withhold notification if it deems that it would impede investigations. Furthermore, the notified third country has no formal mechanisms to object to or review the production order, nor does the Agreement provide any procedural pathway to resolve conflicts of law with third countries.[88]

Taken together, these five critical limitations demonstrate that the US–UK CLOUD Act Agreement exemplifies a one-sided approach favouring US interests at the expense of genuine reciprocity, equal safeguards, and respect for third-country sovereignty and rights. Its asymmetrical design conflicts fundamentally with the EU's demand for balanced, non-discriminatory agreements ensuring reciprocal obligations and robust privacy protections for all data subjects involved. Therefore, the US–UK Agreement should not be naively adopted as a blueprint, not just for the EU–US negotiations, but also for any executive agreement under the CLOUD Act framework. Rather, it should serve as a cautionary exemplar that highlights the necessity to correct structural inequalities.

6.5. Conclusion

The US and EU share complex, evolving approaches to cross-border data access, balancing territorial sovereignty with extraterritorial enforcement. Both jurisdictions employ flexible regimes that reject a strict territorial/extraterritorial divide, allowing direct law enforcement co-operation with service providers

[85] Christakis, '21 Thoughts and Questions' (n 83).

[86] EDPS Opinion 2/2019 on the negotiating mandate of an EU–US agreement on cross-border access to electronic evidence (2 April 2019), para 30. Letter from EDPB to Members of the European Parliament on the US–UK agreement under the US CLOUD Act (15 June 2020).

[87] Art 5(10), US–UK Agreement.

[88] T Cochrane, 'Digital Privacy Rights and CLOUD Act Agreements' (2021) 47 *Brooklyn Journal of International Law* 1.

worldwide while protecting data within their borders. While both the CLOUD Act and the e-Evidence Regulation authorise extraterritorial production orders that disregard the physical location of data, their respective privacy and data protection regimes impose legal restrictions on disclosing, to foreign authorities, data stored within their territorial boundaries or belonging to their citizens or residents. This flexibility reflects efforts to assert regulatory control over cross-border data flows by redefining jurisdictional boundaries to keep pace with changing technological realities.

These developments have led to persistent conflict between the two systems, especially between the CLOUD Act and the GDPR, where compliance with one often breaches the other. Similarly, the EU's e-Evidence Regulation conflicts with the US SCA. Without a comprehensive transatlantic agreement, these unresolved tensions generate regulatory uncertainty, threaten digital sovereignty, undermine fundamental rights, and expose service providers to significant legal risks. While efforts to conclude an EU–US agreement on cross-border data access are under way, significant challenges persist – notably, the CLOUD Act's bilateral certification requirements clashing with the EU's desire for a unified agreement covering all Member States, as well as substantive divergences over privacy protections and judicial safeguards. The fallout from landmark CJEU rulings (*Schrems I* and *II*) and ongoing challenges to the EU–US Data Privacy Framework continue to influence talks, highlighting EU concerns about the adequacy of US surveillance safeguards and legal remedies. Achieving a comprehensive harmonised agreement that satisfies both US procedural demands and EU fundamental rights standards remains a delicate balance, requiring innovative legal frameworks and political compromise to avoid further fragmentation while securing mutual trust and effective law enforcement access to data across borders. In this respect, the US–UK agreement, while pioneering, as the first bilateral agreement under the CLOUD Act framework, serves more as a cautionary example than a suitable model for future EU–US negotiations.

7

The Left-Outs: Lessons for Africa

As Internet use and digitalisation continue to grow in Africa, cross-border access to electronic evidence (such as emails, files, and text messages) plays an indispensable role in ensuring public safety, security, and the rule of law in the region. Given the fact that a vast majority of the continent's data today is stored, managed, and processed largely by foreign service providers (primarily US and Chinese technology companies), it has become difficult – at times, impossible – for African governments to effectively investigate and prosecute domestic crimes without the assistance of these foreign companies.

Considering this reality, this chapter seeks to address three interrelated questions: how do African law enforcement authorities access data held by foreign service providers for legitimate criminal investigations? How, and to what extent, can African countries benefit from the global cross-border data-access reform initiatives? And how should African stakeholders approach the Internet's increasing cross-border legal challenges? This chapter argues that, despite the intense debates and proliferation of reform initiatives elsewhere, the issue of cross-border data access is yet to draw the attention of African policy-makers, academia, and other stakeholders. It also demonstrates that neither the existing system, such as the MLATs, nor the emerging global initiatives to modernise this system will adequately address African interests and concerns. Addressing these profound challenges require multifaceted measures tailored to Africa's context. This chapter makes the case that it is high time for the African Union (AU), its Member States, and other stakeholders to explore alternative approaches to cross-border data access, and suggests some possible ways forward.

7.1. The Cross-Border Data-Access Problem in the African Context

The cross-border data-access problem is particularly acute for countries that are primarily receivers of foreign-based Internet services, where digital evidence essential for legitimate domestic criminal investigations may be held overseas. This challenge could be particularly pronounced in African countries, as much of the continent's data today is controlled by foreign service providers and housed in data centres in foreign countries.[1] Even routine communications between ordinary people who reside in the same country often involve using these foreign platforms, such as social media networks, webmail, messaging services, and apps. In fact, many African users equate prominent US service providers such as Facebook with the Internet itself.[2] This reality creates a challenge for African governments to obtain digital evidence without the assistance of these service providers.[3] Ultimately, access to data is determined not by African legal frameworks but by the laws applicable in these service providers' home country and the providers' individual policies.

This dependence on foreign service providers is set against the backdrop of Africa's rapidly expanding digital landscape. Recent data from the International Telecommunication Union (ITU) indicates that Internet usage in Africa is expanding at a rate twice the global average, with an average growth rate of 16.7 per cent since 2005, compared with 8 per cent worldwide.[4] This rapid increase reflects significant strides in digital connectivity across the continent, although only 38 per cent of the African population had Internet access in 2024, starkly lower than the global average of 68 per cent.[5] The expansion of Internet connectivity carries transformative potential for Africa's socioeconomic development. Nevertheless, this digital proliferation also engenders considerable risks, prominently the rising incidence of cybercrime. Although comprehensive and reliable data on the prevalence and specific characteristics of cyber threat in Africa remains limited, existing studies suggest that the continent is among the regions experiencing the fastest growth in cybercrime activities globally. Certain reports estimate that cybercrime inflicts substantial economic damage on African economies, amounting to approximately $4 billion annually – about 10 per cent of Africa's total gross domestic product – with some estimates reaching as high as $10 trillion.[6]

The fact that the vast majority of African data is stored overseas could critically exacerbate the challenges of investigating and prosecuting cybercrime. Domestic conventional crimes involving digital evidence also require cross-border data access, which means navigating complex legal and technological hurdles. As

[1] This chapter builds on a previous article by the author: see H Abraha, 'How African Countries Can Benefit from the Emerging Reform Initiatives of Cross-Border Access to Electronic Evidence' (Cross-Border Data Forum, 6 July 2020).

[2] K Mwanza, 'Is Facebook the Internet in Africa? 65% Of Nigerians Think So' (*Moguldom*, 23 April 2015), available a www.moguldom.com/94916/is-facebook-is-the-internet-in-africa-65-of-nigerians-think-so/.

[3] See, for instance, M Thamm, 'David vs Goliath: Anonymously Threatened with Gang Rape and Murder, (South African) Teenager Takes Facebook Inc to Court to Disclose Perpetrator' (*Daily Maverick*, 23 July 2020), www.dailymaverick.co.za/article/2020-07-24-anonymously-threatened-with-gang-rape-and-murder-sa-teenager-takes-facebook-inc-to-court-to-disclose-perpetrator/.

[4] 'State of Digital Development and Trends in the Africa Region: Challenges and Opportunities' (ITU, April 2025).

[5] ibid.

[6] The African Cybercrime Operations Desk, 'Interpol African Cyberthreat Assessment Report' (3rd edn, April 2024); CNBC Africa, 'Cyber Crime Surge Threatens Africa's Economic Growth' (4 November 2024).

digitalisation accelerates in the region, criminal investigations, whether relating to cybercrimes or traditional offences, increasingly require access to user data held by foreign entities. Consequently, cross-border data access becomes a particularly complex and urgent legal challenge for African governments, arguably more acute than in any other region.

The *Internet & Jurisdiction Global Status Report 2019*, a comprehensive study mapping global Internet jurisdiction-related policies and initiatives, analogises these cross-border legal challenges to climate change, emphasising their disproportionate adverse impact on developing countries.[7] Paradoxically, this critical issue has yet to attract adequate attention from African policy-makers, academia, and other stakeholders. Despite vigorous debates and numerous initiatives elsewhere, academic and policy discussions specific to the African context remain scant. Notably, Africa lacks dedicated initiatives addressing these challenges, with only brief mentions in some Internet governance conferences.[8] This inattention hampers a nuanced understanding and articulation of the particular legal and practical obstacles African governments encounter when seeking electronic evidence across borders.

Nonetheless, it is evident that cross-border data access will eventually become a pressing public policy concern for Africa. Law enforcement agencies will increasingly face difficult choices as existing legal and procedural frameworks prove inadequate against the scale and complexity of cyber-enabled crimes. The critical question, therefore, is whether existing cross-border data-access mechanisms and emerging international frameworks, such as the CLOUD Act, the Budapest Convention, and the UN Convention on Cybercrime, offer an adequate legal and institutional pathway for African governments. As will be demonstrated, neither the existing mechanisms nor the nascent international initiatives will sufficiently address the continent's specific needs and concerns unless they are complemented by contextually appropriate African approaches. This gap highlights a vital area of future research and policy development, emphasising the necessity for Africa-focused approaches to international data governance and law enforcement co-operation that align with the continent's sociopolitical realities.

7.1.1. The MLAT System is Less Relevant for African States

Although the MLAT system remains a dominant channel of cross-border legal co-operation in criminal matters around the world, the process is widely regarded

[7] DJB Svantesson, 'Internet & Jurisdiction Global Status Report' (Internet & Jurisdiction Policy Network, 27 November 2019), available at www.internetjurisdiction.net/news/release-of-worlds-first-internet-jurisdiction-global-status-report.

[8] See, for instance, 'African Union Commission and Internet & Jurisdiction Policy Network Regional Conference' (Internet & Jurisdiction Policy Network, 27 May 2020); 'Forum on Internet Freedom in Africa 2019' (CIPESA, 23 September 2019); 'Cyber Security and Cybercrime Policies for African Diplomats' (African Union, 12 April 2018).

as slow, cumbersome, bureaucratic, and ineffective. This inefficiency is so pronounced that any discussion about international digital evidence access almost inevitably calls for MLA reform. International organisations, governments, and industry stakeholders have undertaken various practical and operational steps aimed at streamlining and modernising the MLAT framework, hoping to adapt it to the rapidly evolving digital landscape (see chapter three).

Yet, even if all these efforts were successful, the reality remains that the MLAT system would still be largely irrelevant for the majority of African states seeking electronic evidence from US-based service providers. Currently, only a handful of African countries – namely South Africa, Egypt, Nigeria, Algeria, and Morocco – have formal MLAT agreements with the US.[9] The vast majority of African nations lack any such arrangement with the US, which is home to many of the world's leading technology companies whose co-operation is required. This gap means that, regardless of how much the MLAT system is improved, most African states are effectively excluded from accessing data via this route. For law enforcement authorities in these countries, MLAT reform alone will not alleviate their fundamental challenges.

7.1.2. Voluntary Co-operation Channels are Rarely Utilised

A critical yet under-exploited aspect of cross-border data access in the African context concerns the limited use of voluntary direct co-operation channels with US-based service providers. Although international norms, such as the Budapest Convention and US law, provide mechanisms allowing service providers to respond voluntarily to foreign law enforcement requests for non-content data (notably subscriber information), African governments infrequently leverage these channels. This restrained engagement persists despite the practical importance of subscriber information as a preliminary step to identifying suspects and pursuing further evidence.

A cursory review of transparency reports from major US technology companies concerning government requests for user data illustrates this African reality starkly. While governments worldwide submit hundreds of thousands of data request annually – or millions, in the case of Western jurisdictions – African countries submit surprisingly few. Among the African states that do initiate data requests, the volume is often in single to low double figures, representing a minuscule fraction compared with requests from other regions.[10]

[9] 'Mutual Legal Assistance Treaties of the United States (MLATs)' (Office of International Affairs, Criminal Division, United States Department of Justice, April 2022).

[10] See, eg Meta, 'Government Requests for User Data – Meta Transparency Center', available at www.transparency.meta.com/reports/government-data-requests/; Microsoft, 'Government Requests for Customer Data Report – Microsoft CSR', available at www.microsoft.com/en-us/corporate-responsibility/reports/government-requests/customer-data; Google, 'Requests for User Information – Google Transparency Report', available at www.transparencyreport.google.com/.

This striking discrepancy is compounded by generally low compliance rates for African requests, indicating that even when requests are made, service providers frequently deny them or find them legally deficient, thus hindering access to crucial electronic evidence.

Several interwoven challenges could explain why African governments rarely engage directly with US service providers for user data access. A foundational obstacle is the absence or inadequacy of formal legal frameworks that specifically incorporate or recognise voluntary direct co-operation for cross-border data access. Many African legal systems lack clear procedures or statutory provisions enabling law enforcement authorities to submit data requests directly to foreign providers. Beyond purely legal hurdles, technical compliance requirements mandated by US service providers under US law demand that foreign requests meet robust standards, such as clarity on the legal basis for request, authorised judicial oversight, and adherence to privacy protections. African governments often face difficulties satisfying these criteria due to weak or inconsistent data protection laws, lack of comprehensive procedural safeguards, and limited judicial oversight. These legal and procedural deficiencies are evident in the low number of 'legal process requests' mentioned in transparency reports, as many requests fail to demonstrate a proper legal basis and sufficiency under applicable law and the terms of service of the companies. This mismatch frequently results in rejections of, or incomplete responses to, data requests needed for investigating serious crimes.

From the practical law enforcement side, the transparency reports show that African governments tend to rely heavily on 'emergency requests' and less on formal legal process requests. Emergency requests, typically fast but ad hoc, account for a significant share of African data-access requests, underscoring a reactive investigative posture. This reactive reliance may also reflect broader gaps, including lack of resources and training, exacerbating the legal and administrative obstacles in navigating the complex landscape of transnational data access. Additionally, scepticism about the efficacy of voluntary co-operation, fuelled by reported high rejection rates and perceptions of delay or bias against African governments, further dampens their use. In fact, US service providers are often criticised for treating African governments unfairly regarding data requests for legitimate criminal investigations.[11] Compounding these issues, geopolitical and diplomatic complexities further constrict co-operation with US-based service providers. These service providers operate within a framework shaped by intricate privacy and sovereignty concerns, alongside heightened scrutiny over data-sharing with foreign governments perceived to have poor human rights or governance standards.

These gaps highlight a critical deficiency in African governments' operational capacity, international legal infrastructure, and diplomatic leverage, which are

[11] M Fidler, 'Africans Want Cross-Border Data Access Reform, But They Might Get Left Out' (*Council on Foreign Relations*, 26 October 2016), available at https://on.cfr.org/38w2zVq.

essential for effective cross-border data access. These gaps not only impair routine law enforcement capabilities but also hamper responses to domestic crimes, where digital data housed abroad is required. To bridge this divide, African countries must advance legal reforms, international treaties, and institutional capacity while cultivating trust-based international partnerships.

7.1.3. Extraterritorial Production Orders are Less Viable for Africa

Mandatory unilateral extraterritorial production orders are, for the most part, unenforceable by African governments. Extraterritorial production orders depend on personal jurisdiction over service providers, grounded in specific 'connecting factors' such as physical presence, business operations, or data centre location. As the volume of electronic evidence required for criminal investigations in Africa increasingly resides with foreign service providers, the resulting power imbalance becomes acute. Countries or regions hosting the headquarters or infrastructure of major service providers enjoy disproportionate leverage in compelling the production of data, often enforcing their laws globally.[12] This leaves African countries at a disadvantage, even where their domestic laws mirror those of more powerful jurisdictions. For example, the countries that have cloud servers in their territory can have relatively straightforward access to the data stored in those servers through domestic legal procedures. Some jurisdictions, such as the EU, have the regulatory power to extend their authority even further, compelling data access across borders regardless of a provider's headquarters or infrastructure. As discussed in chapter five, the EU's e-Evidence Directive exemplifies this approach. It requires non-EU service providers to appoint at least one legal representative within the Union, making them directly accountable for the receipt and enforcement of data production orders issued by Member State authorities – even if the provider neither resides in nor has an establishment within the EU. This framework effectively ensures the extraterritorial enforceability of EU law in the context of cross-border data access.

The African situation, by contrast, is defined by jurisdictional and infrastructural disadvantages. Most African governments enjoy neither the jurisdictional leverage to compel US providers nor the regulatory power to enforce their laws in an extraterritorial manner. African governments may pass legislation requiring foreign service providers to disclose data when required for the purpose of legitimate criminal investigations, but mechanisms to enforce such requirements are rare. Therefore, unilateral production orders are less viable options for most African governments.

[12] Svantesson, 'Internet & Jurisdiction Global Status Report' (n 7).

7.1.4. Data Localisation is Unrealistic, Ineffective, and Counter-productive

Data localisation has become a prevalent global response to challenges surrounding cross-border data access. An increasing number of countries impose requirements to store data domestically, motivated by objectives such as protecting personal data, enabling local law enforcement access, ensuring national security, fostering local economic competitiveness, etc. Even traditionally free-data-flow advocates such as the US and the EU are recalibrating their approaches towards greater digital sovereignty and jurisdictional alignment through data localisation policies.[13] This reflects a growing tension between preserving the free flow of data and asserting control over data as a sovereign asset.

Until recently, African policy-makers exhibited considerable ambivalence towards where data was physically stored and who accessed it. Historically, many African data protection laws have included relatively permissive provisions allowing cross-border data flows, reflecting a pragmatic acknowledgement of the continent's limited infrastructure and the benefits of global data connectivity.[14] However, this position is changing rapidly, driven both by global trends and by concerns about the extractive nature of the data economy and the resulting wealth inequalities it exacerbates.[15] African countries now increasingly view data not just as information but as a strategic asset essential to national autonomy and economic development. Consequently, data localisation has gained traction as a purported pathway to digital sovereignty, security, and local economic development, and often as a response to challenges of cross-border data access.

This shift has manifested itself in legislative reforms in Africa that impose data localisation measures.[16] The rationale includes concerns about

[13] F Burwell and K Propp, 'The European Union and the Search for Digital Sovereignty: Building "Fortress Europe" or Preparing for a New World?' (Atlantic Council Issue Brief 1, 2020); C Hobbs (ed), *Europe's Digital Sovereignty: From Rulemaker to Superpower in the Age of US-China Rivalry*' (European Council on Foreign Relations, Essay Collection 2020); A Chander, 'Is Data Localization a Solution for Schrems II?' (2020) 23 *Journal of International Economic Law* 771; S Sacks and P Swire, 'Assessing U.S. Data Policy Toward China: A Proposed Framework' (*Lawfare*, 14 July 2023), available at www.lawfaremedia.org/article/assessing-u.s.-data-policy-toward-china-a-proposed-framework; Preventing Access to US Sensitive Personal Data and Government-Related Data by Countries of Concern or Covered Persons, Executive Order 14117 (2024); S Castic and H Piou, 'New U.S. Regulations Impose Significant Restrictions on Cross-Border Data Flows' (*Hintze Law*, 9 January 2025), available at https://hintzelaw.com/blog/2025/1/9/new-us-regulations-impose-significant-restrictions-on-cross-border-data-flows.

[14] The Digital Transformation Strategy for Africa (2020–2030) 11.

[15] Internet & Jurisdiction Policy Network, 'Framing, Mapping and Addressing Cross-Border Digital Policies in Africa: An Internet & Jurisdiction Policy Network Regional Status Report' (2022).

[16] See, for details, AU Data Policy Framework 2022; M Musoni, P Karkare, and C Teevan, 'Cross-Border Data Flows in Africa: Continental Ambitions and Political Realities' (*ecdom* 2024) Discussion Paper No 379; F Adeleke, 'Exploring Policy Trade-Offs for Data Localisation in South Africa, Kenya and Nigeria' (Mandela Institute, Policy Brief 09, 2021); CIPESA, 'Mapping and Analysis of Privacy Laws in Africa' (November 2021); M Musoni, 'The Role of Data Localisation in Cybercrime Investigations' in R Atuguba Akongburo and others (eds), *African Data Protection Laws: Regulation, Policy, and Practice* (De Gruyter, 2024).

foreign surveillance, unauthorised access, and capturing economic value. Some governments seek to reduce reliance on foreign data centres and cloud providers by encouraging or mandating the development of domestic infrastructure. Certain laws explicitly forbid international transfers of specific data categories without authorisation, reinforcing artificial barriers to data flows.

However, as discussed in chapter three, data localisation policies are not necessarily the right responses to address the challenges associated with the cross-border nature of the Internet. By enforcing data localisation, governments aim to simplify government access and counter unilateral requests from foreign governments. Yet, such localisation measures reflect a fundamental misunderstanding of the nature of the challenges of cross-border data access. The crux of the matter lies not in the physical data storage but in the legal and institutional capacity to enforce legal norms across borders. Restricting data physically within national borders does not guarantee sovereign control or security, especially where technical capabilities to secure data and enforce legal norms are limited. Instead, forced localisation measures can create inefficient, expensive, and vulnerable data ecosystems. For African countries facing significant infrastructure deficits, strict data localisation requirements impose steep costs, including the need to build and maintain high-standard data centres, many of which currently do not exist at the capacity and scale needed.[17]

Furthermore, localisation policies risk undermining broader regional and continental integration efforts, such as those embodied by the African Union's digital strategy and the African Continental Free Trade Area. These frameworks envision seamless cross-border digital commerce and data flow to drive economic growth and innovation. Uncoordinated national data localisation laws erect barriers to these goals by fragmenting digital markets and limiting interoperability.[18] Data localisation also raises the risk of protectionism cloaked in national security and sovereignty rhetoric, which may discourage foreign investment and technological collaboration crucial to Africa's digital future.

Crucially, digital sovereignty, often cited as the justification for data localisation, requires more than controlling the physical location of data. It demands robust legal frameworks that regulate data access, transfer, and use regardless of where data is stored. Many African countries lack the necessary regulatory capacity and infrastructure to exercise real control over data through localisation alone.[19] Moreover, data localisation policies risk unintentionally compromising data security and human rights. Concentrating data within national borders may increase vulnerability to cyberattacks, especially if domestic infrastructure

[17] Internet & Jurisdiction Policy Network 'Framing, Mapping and Addressing Cross-Border Digital Policies in Africa' (n 15).

[18] AU Data Policy Framework 2022.

[19] ibid.

is underdeveloped or poorly secured.[20] It also heightens the risk of authoritarian surveillance, as governments gain easier unmediated access to citizens' data.[21]

Implementation challenges further undermine the viability of localisation policies. Enforcement mechanisms in many African countries remain weak or unclear.[22] For example, data protection authorities often lack adequate mandates or resources to monitor compliance and impose sanctions against violations of data localisation requirements. The notable exception is Uganda's precedent-setting decision by its Personal Data Protection Office that established extraterritorial application of data protection laws and held a global company accountable for compliance.[23] In this case, the regulator ruled that Google's transfer of personal data of Ugandan citizens to jurisdictions outside Uganda, without demonstrating adequate safeguards or accountability, was in breach of the country's data protection law. The regulator maintained that Google's significant commercial activity and legal interactions within Uganda created a sufficient nexus for regulatory jurisdiction, even without a physical presence. The ruling rejected Google's defence that it was neither domiciled nor had a physical presence in Uganda, and required global technology companies to register with the regulator, appoint a local data protection officer, and ensure compliant data transfers. This landmark decision demonstrates Africa's increasing regulatory maturity and ability to assert digital sovereignty without resorting to blunt data localisation measures.

The real problem African governments face is the challenge of cross-border data access in a manner that respects fundamental rights and national sovereignty while enabling economic and social development. Data localisation, understood narrowly as a physical containment of data, fails to address the root causes of this problem – insufficient regulatory harmonisation, lack of international co-operation frameworks, weak enforcement capacity, and inadequate infrastructure. Rather than imposing costly and rigid localisation rules, African states should prioritise building trust, and transparent and interoperable data governance regimes that facilitate legitimate and rights-respecting government access to digital evidence while ensuring cross-border data flows.

In today's interconnected digital environment, sovereignty is less about erecting physical barriers and more about exercising effective jurisdiction, co-operation, and governance mechanisms. Data localisation policies in Africa, while motivated by legitimate concerns, risk being inadequate and counter-productive. As the African Union aptly observes in its Data Policy Framework (2022), data localisation policies cannot succeed without essential structural and institutional foundations. The AU Framework underscores that genuine control over data – and thus digital sovereignty – demands not just legal instruments but also robust

[20] ibid.
[21] CIPESA, 'Mapping and Analysis of Privacy Laws in Africa' (n 16).
[22] ibid.
[23] *Ssekamwa Frank and Others v Google LLC*, Complaint No 08/11/24/6683.

infrastructure, technical expertise, and institutional trust. Recognising the risks inherent in restrictive localisation measures, the AU's Data Policy Framework advocates for a balanced approach. It discourages blanket data localisation laws and instead encourages policies that promote the benefits of data-sharing over data-hoarding. The Framework calls upon Member States to evaluate the potential costs and benefits of data localisation, carefully weighing human rights considerations and prioritising wider economic development goals. Ultimately, it encourages moving beyond localisation, and towards policies that facilitate free and secure flows of data, while simultaneously safeguarding human rights, maintaining security, and ensuring equitable access and sharing of digital benefits.

However, despite the clarity of this guidance, a notable contradiction appears within the AU's digital policy landscape: while the Data Policy Framework discourages data localisation, the Digital Transformation Strategy for Africa (2020–2030) positions 'data sovereignty' as a core objective and signals that full localisation of personal data may soon become necessary, with the AU stating that, 'even though Africa is at the moment less restrictive, soon it will be necessary to ensure localization of all personal data of Africa's citizens'.[24] Whether this apparent inconsistency marks an actual reversal of the AU's position on data localisation or merely reflects ongoing tensions and ambiguities in the regional policy-making remains unclear.

7.1.5. The CLOUD Act Framework is Less Relevant for African Governments

The CLOUD Act was introduced as an innovative mechanism to facilitate access to electronic evidence for legitimate law enforcement purposes. However, the executive agreement framework envisioned by the Act is fundamentally ill-suited for African governments and, in practice, is likely to increase rather than reduce the disparities and frustrations in cross-border data access. As discussed in chapter four, the CLOUD Act's executive agreement model is not designed to be broadly inclusive; rather, it was tailored for a highly selective group of countries. As the US Department of Justice (DOJ) describes, the framework is intended for 'trusted foreign partners' whose legal systems and political values closely align with those of the US.[25] This built-in exclusivity means that only a limited number of countries ever stand to benefit from the CLOUD Act, while the rest of the world, especially African countries, is left out.

The statute's requirements are exacting, and the authority to determine eligibility is vested in the US Attorney General (and Secretary of State), which could be influenced by political and foreign policy interests. It is unlikely for African governments to be able to meet these requirements and participate in the CLOUD

[24] The Digital Transformation Strategy for Africa (2020–2030) 11.
[25] See CLOUD Act Resources, available at www.justice.gov/criminal/cloud-act-resources.

Act framework. As Fidler observes, the US government did not really consider Africa when it designed the CLOUD Act as an international instrument for cross-border data requests.[26] In effect, African governments are excluded three times over: first, because of the blanket prohibition of the SCA; second, because they lack existing co-operation agreements, such as MLATs, with the US; and third, because the executive agreements created under the CLOUD Act are off-limits to them.[27] This exclusion does not mean that African governments will stop seeking data necessary for legitimate law enforcement purposes. Instead, it forces them to take matters into their own hands and pursue alternative options. The problem is that, with no workable path to obtain data, even rights-respecting governments may resort to unilateral and aggressive measures such as data localisation. Others may resort to mass surveillance, blocking or restricting access to online services, or even Internet shutdowns, as desperate means of gaining some leverage over digital activity.

Therefore, the CLOUD Act, far from representing a viable option for African law enforcement authorities, could deepen digital inequality, institutionalise exclusion, and exacerbate law enforcement frustrations. Its framework is neither scalable nor intended for general global use. For African countries, it offers no real solution, only further frustration, and is more likely to foster conflict than genuine international co-operation.

7.2. Confronting Cross-Border Data-Access Challenges in Africa

African governments presently face severely limited options for accessing data held by foreign technology companies, particularly US-based service providers. Neither the traditional system of cross-border legal co-operation (MLAT) nor the new frameworks adequately address their unique challenges in cross-border data access. To illustrate, consider a case: Ethiopian authorities are investigating a homicide committed by an Ethiopian suspect against another Ethiopian citizen. They reasonably suspect that the crime was planned via email exchanges between the suspect and co-conspirators. Accessing those email exchanges is critical for the investigation and prosecution of the crime. However, the emails are stored with a US cloud service provider, physically located on US soil. This scenario exposes the problem of cross-border data access and highlights deficiencies in the current international co-operation framework. Ethiopian authorities have little to no means to access the content of the emails held by the US service provider. Although the crime occurred in Ethiopia, in violation of Ethiopian law, and involves only Ethiopian citizens, access to electronic evidence remains blocked

[26] Fidler, 'Africans Want Cross-Border Data Access Reform' (n 11).
[27] ibid.

solely because the data happens to be stored in the US. Neither the service provider nor the US government has a direct interest (or at least a significant interest) in the matter. Yet, even if the Ethiopian authorities follow a legitimate legal process, they cannot compel disclosure of the required data; doing so would contravene US law. Ethiopian authorities would be denied access to such data not because of concerns regarding human rights or sovereignty but due to the arbitrary and blanket nature of prohibitions by US law.

The lack of timely access to electronic evidence held by foreign service providers undermines legitimate law enforcement efforts and allows serious offenders to avoid prosecution. This frustration is shared by law enforcement authorities around the world, who increasingly find themselves unable to investigate even purely domestic crimes, as more digital evidence is controlled by global service providers. While such cases may have seemed rare in the past, they are rapidly becoming standard practice. Stakeholders in African digital policies have also begun to recognise this dilemma, expressing concern over US service providers' handling of African data requests.[28]

These realities prompt a crucial inquiry: how should African stakeholders confront the persistent challenge of cross-border data access? Before addressing this question, three foundational considerations merit emphasis. First, there is no single, universal solution to the intricate and multi-layered problems inherent in cross-border data access. Second, the challenge at hand is not merely a legal technicality that can be addressed through national legislation; rather, it encompasses complex diplomatic protocols, evolving international policy-making, and significant political considerations. Third, and relatedly, it must be recognised that the cross-border data-access problem represents an inherently global challenge – one that cannot be addressed by any lone actor or jurisdiction. The only plausible remedies require comprehensive cross-border co-operation, regardless of whether such collaboration takes bilateral, multilateral, regional, or fully international forms. In light of these factors, the following sections offer possible pathways and solutions for African policy-makers to consider.

7.2.1. Strengthening International Engagement Through AU Leadership

Effectively addressing the cross-border data-access challenges confronting Africa requires both robust regional co-ordination and deep engagement in international co-operation. One immediate strategy could be for the AU to expand the mandate of the Cybersecurity Expert Group (AU-CSEG).[29] This Expert Group already

[28] ibid; 'African Union Commission and Internet & Jurisdiction Policy Network Regional Conference' (n 8).

[29] See 'African Union Cybersecurity Expert Group Holds Its First Inaugural Meeting' (African Union, 12 December 2019), available at https://au.int/en/pressreleases/20191212/african-union-cybersecurity-expert-group-holds-its-first-inaugural-meeting.

supports both the AU and Member States on international co-operation related to cybersecurity, personal data protection, and combatting cybercrime.[30] To leverage the new legal architecture introduced by the United Nations Convention on Cybercrime, the AU-CSEG should be further empowered and formally mandated not only to co-ordinate and provide continuous technical capacity-building but also to serve as a focal point for treaty implementation and regional harmonisation. Alternatively, the AU could establish a dedicated entity, such as an AU Cross-border Data Expert Group, tasked with developing an African approach that could guide law enforcement access to electronic evidence across borders. Such an approach should combine legislative, institutional, diplomatic, and capacity-building components.

At the global level, active and informed participation by the AU and its Member States in the ongoing work of the UN Cybercrime Convention – particularly within the Conference of States Parties and related working groups – will be critical. This engagement would ensure that Africa's challenges and priorities concerning cross-border data access, technical assistance, and human rights safeguards are systematically embedded in the Convention's operational practices. Strengthened collaboration with other international institutions and stakeholders will also be essential. In this regard, the AU's existing partnerships with the Council of Europe and the Internet & Jurisdiction Policy Network represent valuable platforms for advancing African perspectives with broader global governance processes.[31]

7.2.2. Establishing Institutions for Review and Validation of Cross-Border Data Access

As discussed earlier, one of the key reasons why US service providers often reject law enforcement requests from African countries is the absence of reliable mechanisms to verify the legitimacy of such requests and their compliance with privacy protections and due process standards. In many cases, service providers lack the means to authenticate whether a request originates from a competent law enforcement authority duly authorised to make it, or to determine whether such a request is subject to judicial oversight.[32] To address this gap, the AU should explore institutional frameworks vested with the authority to receive, review, and authenticate cross-border data requests from Member States and internationally, while also co-ordinating national points of contact on cross-border data access. Such a framework could enhance and facilitate co-operation between African authorities and foreign service providers.

[30] ibid.

[31] 'Cyber Security and Cybercrime Policies for African Diplomats' (n 8).

[32] P Swire and D Kennedy-Mayo, 'Two Ways That Smaller Countries Could Participate in Emerging Global Systems for Transfer of Electronic Evidence' (*Cross-Border Data Forum*, 30 May 2019), available at www.crossborderdataforum.org/two-ways-that-smaller-countries-could-participate-in-emerging-global-systems-for-transfer-of-electronic-evidence/.

Swire and Kennedy-Mayo propose two institutional designs that merit consideration.[33] The first approach is the so called Interpol Model, which builds on internationally recognised organisations such as Interpol, offering an authentication process for countries unable to participate in the emerging global systems for transfer of electronic evidence.[34] This approach envisions expanding the mandate of Interpol National Central Bureaus (NCBs), which currently exist in all the 194 member countries. Consistent with Interpol's mission of facilitating global law-enforcement information exchange, vetted persons within each NCB could be authorised to use official Interpol email accounts for making requests for data that does not require mutual legal assistance, such as subscriber information.[35] Such an 'intermediary authenticator' system could provide a promising option for African countries that are unable to engage effectively with voluntary co-operation systems offered by foreign service providers. Beyond authentication, NCBs could support law enforcement authorities by identifying relevant domestic legislation and providing specialised training.[36] This would, in turn, allow service providers to make more informed decisions about whether and to what extent they should comply with law enforcement requests from African authorities. Interpol is already working to develop a secure international platform for the electronic exchange of law enforcement requests.[37]

The second institutional alternative draws on the concept of 'correspondent banking' in the global banking system. In this system, a smaller bank operates through a larger bank, which executes payments on behalf of the smaller bank and its clients. Swire and Kennedy-Mayo argue that applying this 'correspondent banking model' to cross-border data access could similarly help address authentication challenges, particularly for countries that lack the capacity to participate in existing or emerging mechanisms for electronic evidence transfer.[38] Under this framework, regional entities such as the AU would function as 'correspondent' authenticators. As the authors explain:

> The regional platform would enter into a bilateral agreement with the smaller country. The relationship would allow the regional platform to authenticate requests from the requesting country. The regional platform would authenticate the identity of one point of contact or multiple points of contact (POCs) within the requesting country. Requests would thus go from the requesting country … to the regional platform … The regional platform … would then provide the request to the receiving country.[39]

[33] ibid.

[34] ibid.

[35] G Kent, 'Sharing Investigation Specific Data with Law Enforcement: An International Approach' (2014) *Stanford Public Law Working Paper* 12.

[36] ibid.

[37] 'INTERPOL E-MLA Initiative', available at www.interpol.int/en/News-and-Events/News/2018/INTERPOL-s-e-MLA-initiative-focus-of-EU-expert-meeting.

[38] Swire and Kennedy-Mayo, 'Two Ways That Smaller Countries Could Participate' (n 32).

[39] ibid.

As an interim measure, the Interpol model appears particularly viable for at least three reasons. First, because NCBs are already established in all African countries, this model requires no new arrangement or institutional architecture. Second, Interpol is actively engaged in reforming cross-border data access, aligning its ongoing work with these needs. Third, implementation would not require negotiation of a new treaty or agreement but merely an expansion of NCBs' mandate.

7.2.3. Reviewing National and Regional Legal Frameworks on Cross-Border Data Access

A comprehensive review conducted by the AU, in partnership with regional and international key stakeholders, of national and regional frameworks and practices relating to cross-border data access is imperative for achieving effective digital governance in Africa. Such an initiative is essential to systematically mapping best practices, identifying enduring challenges, and framing reform pathways that genuinely reflect African interests and priorities. Through this process, the continent can work towards the development of a robust regional framework that encapsulates Africa's preferred approach to cross-border data access and, more broadly, to data governance.

Currently, the African Union Convention on Cyber Security and Personal Data Protection, known as the Malabo Convention, stands as the principal legal instrument at the AU level addressing the spectrum of cyber governance issues. The Convention aspires to harmonise cyber legislation, enhance regional co-operation, and affirm the autonomy of African states in managing cyberspace affairs. Nearly a decade after its adoption, the Malabo Convention finally entered into force on 8 June 2023, following ratification by its fifteenth Member State – a noteworthy milestone for African cyber governance.[40]

Nevertheless, despite the Convention's entry into force, a significant majority of African states have not exhibited the political will needed to ratify and implement its provisions comprehensively. This lack of widespread commitment undermines the prospects for harmonisation and weakens the Convention's utility as a foundational framework for facilitating cross-border data governance.

A further challenge arises from the Convention's expansive ambition: it attempts to consolidate three distinct legal regimes – cybercrime, data protection, and electronic transactions – within a single treaty. Each of these regimes is complex and rapidly evolving, often requiring specialised legal responses.

[40] N Ifeanyi-Ajufo, 'Africa's Cybersecurity Treaty Enters into Force' (*Directions Cyber Digital Europe*, 21 September 2023), available at https://eucyberdirect.eu/blog/africa-s-cybersecurity-treaty-enters-into-force.

The decision to amalgamate them into one instrument has likely restricted the Convention's ability to address specific thematic challenges with sufficient specificity, contributing to scepticism and limited enthusiasm among Member States regarding its implementation.

Most critically, the Malabo Convention does not contain explicit and detailed provisions addressing the cross-border data-access problem. In comparison with relevant international instruments, such as the Council of Europe's Convention on Cybercrime, the Malabo Convention lacks clear legal mechanisms for Member States to obtain data across borders, such as preservation orders, production orders, or other tools for timely disclosure of electronic evidence.[41] Instead, it continues to encourage reliance on the traditional MLAT system, governed by the principle of dual criminality; that is, a requirement that co-operation on law enforcement matters such as evidence-sharing will be granted if the conduct underlying the request constitutes a criminal offence both in the requesting and the requested states.

In light of these persisting challenges, there is a need for the AU to lead a comprehensive and inclusive review process evaluating the practical realities and legal landscapes of cross-border data access in Africa. Such efforts should focus not only on documenting current obstacles and best practices but also on designing new regional instruments or protocols that provide clarity, flexibility, and expanded capabilities for law enforcement authorities. This institutional and legislative advancement would empower African governments to more effectively interact with global data-governance structures and negotiate future international frameworks tailored to the unique cybersecurity and law enforcement needs of Africa.

7.2.4. Acceding to the Budapest Convention

Considering the lack of an effective regional co-operation framework, and given that most African data is stored outside the continent, African countries should prioritise acceding to the Budapest Convention. Until the recent adoption of the UN Convention on Cybercrime, the Budapest Convention remained the only comprehensive and binding international treaty on cybercrime, open for accession by any country meeting its requirements. Moreover, there has been a global effort for the universalisation of the Budapest Convention instead of relying on a whole new treaty under the auspices of the UN.[42] Consequently, the Budapest Convention has served as a de facto model for cybercrime legislation worldwide,

[41] Z Jamil, 'Comparative analysis of the Malabo Convention of the African Union and the Budapest Convention on Cybercrime' (Council of Europe, 20 November 2016).

[42] See European Parliament Resolution on the Fight Against Cybercrime (2017/2068(INI)) (3 October 2017).

as many countries have used it as the foundation for their national cybercrime legislation.

Among other requirements, the Budapest Cybercrime Convention mandates contracting parties to empower their competent authorities to order service providers offering services in their territory to disclose subscriber information, regardless of where the data or the service provider is located. Furthermore, the adoption of the Second Additional Protocol, which exclusively focuses on enhanced co-operation and disclosure of electronic evidence, clarifies and strengthens the Convention. Crucially, the Protocol provides a legal basis for disclosure of domain name registration information, and for direct co-operation with service providers for subscriber information, effective means to obtain subscriber information and traffic data, immediate co-operation in emergencies, and mutual assistance tools, as well as personal data protection safeguards.[43]

As of 2025, 81 countries (41 per cent of UN Member States) are either parties or signatories to the Budapest Convention or have been invited to accede.[44] Twelve African countries (Benin, Cabo Verde, Cameroon, Côte d'Ivoire, Ghana, Mauritius, Morocco, Nigeria, Rwanda, Senegal, Tunisia, and Sierra Leone) have acceded to, and five (Kenya, Malawi, Mozambique, Seychelles, and South Africa) are in the process of joining, the Budapest Convention.[45]

This fact shows that the Budapest Convention is more appealing for African governments than the AU's own Convention on Cyber Security and Personal Data Protection. This preference stems from the Budapest Convention's practical utility, maturity, and proven track record over the last 20 years. If a greater number of African states were to accede to it, the Budapest Convention could contribute significantly to addressing the core challenges African states currently face with respect to cross-border data access and cybercrime enforcement.

First, African states can benefit from streamlined mutual assistance procedures. The Budapest Convention offers an expedited and flexible regime for international co-operation between authorities, tailored to the unique challenges posed by cybercrime, particularly when no applicable international agreements, such as MLATs, exist. The purpose of these provisions is to facilitate co-operation among states that do not have any specific international co-operation agreements between them. Specifically, Chapter III of the Convention provides the legal and practical framework enabling participating countries to co-operate effectively in cybercrime investigation and data-sharing.

[43] For a detailed discussion of the Second Additional Protocol, see J Daskal and D Kennedy-Mayo, 'Budapest Convention: What Is It and How Is It Being Updated?' (*Cross-Border Data Forum*, 2 July 2020), available at www.crossborderdataforum.org/budapest-convention-what-is-it-and-how-is-it-being-updated/.

[44] See 'Chart of signatures and ratifications of Treaty 185', available at www.coe.int/en/web/conventions.

[45] 'Parties/Observers to the Budapest Convention and Observer Organisations to the T-CY', available at www.coe.int/en/web/cybercrime/parties-observers.

This framework addresses the jurisdictional and procedural hurdles commonly faced in cross-border data access. Article 27 specifically addresses mutual assistance requests in the absence of an applicable MLAT system. It obliges parties to apply the Convention's procedures and conditions as an autonomous legal basis for co-operation. This means that, upon accession, African countries can request mutual assistance directly under the Budapest Convention, from the 80 (and increasing) States Parties, including the US, bypassing the need for formal MLATs, which are often unavailable or dysfunctional. The Convention covers a broad range of mutual assistance actions between parties that are essential for cross-border data access. For instance, Article 29 allows a party to request the expedited preservation of stored computer data located in another party's territory. This enables data to be secured promptly for subsequent access or seizure. Article 31 governs mutual assistance in disclosing data, including data preserved under Article 29. Under Articles 33 and 34, the Convention requires parties to provide assistance to each other in real-time collection of traffic data and interception of content data, subject to relevant domestic laws and treaties. These powers and co-operation measures are further expanded and strengthened by the Second Additional Protocol, which is applicable not only to cybercrime but also to any criminal offence involving digital evidence. Furthermore, these procedural powers apply subject to strict conditions and safeguards to protect privacy and other human rights. African states can significantly benefit from these tailored and streamlined procedures, none of which are present in the Malabo Convention.

Second, African states can benefit from enhanced direct co-operation with foreign service providers, as established under the Second Additional Protocol to the Budapest Convention. Beyond expanding mutual assistance procedures between authorities, this Protocol introduces new frameworks empowering law enforcement authorities in one State Party to issue orders or requests directly to service providers in another party. This addresses the insufficiency of authority-to-authority mutual assistance procedures for accessing volatile electronic evidence. For instance, the Protocol empowers competent authorities to request domain name registration information directly from service providers located in another party's territory. Most importantly, the Protocol enables authorities to issue orders directly to service providers in another party's territory to disclose specified subscriber information necessary for criminal investigations or proceedings. Furthermore, the Protocol requires each of the parties to adopt such legislative and other measures as may be necessary to permit service providers within its territory to disclose the required data in response to requests by other parties. This means each State Party must remove any blocking statutes that prohibit service providers from directly disclosing subscriber information to foreign authorities participating in the Convention, thereby resolving potential conflicting obligations. As a result, African states acceding to the Budapest Convention and its Additional Protocol can issue orders to American service providers (and service providers located in the 80+ Parties to the Convention) to disclose certain types of data covered by these frameworks, bypassing MLAT procedures, overcoming US law's blocking provisions, and avoiding the necessity of entering into executive agreements under the CLOUD Act. Acceding to the Budapest Convention would provide African states with a more direct and efficient pathway to access US-based service providers for digital evidence.

Third, African countries stand to gain from the extensive capacity-building programmes led by the Council of Europe and its partners. The Global Action on Cybercrime (GLACY+) initiative is designed to strengthen states' abilities to implement the Convention and enhance international co-operation. The programme supports countries worldwide in implementing the Convention, providing training, legislative guidance, and institutional support to improve criminal justice capacities related to cybercrime and digital evidence. These programmes could help African states develop effective legal frameworks, law enforcement capabilities, and judicial skills to combat cybercrime and facilitate cross-border data access.

Fourth, participating in the Budapest Convention would place African countries in a stronger position to negotiate future international agreements on cross-border data access. In fact, the adequacy of substantive and procedural laws on cybercrime and electronic evidence required under the CLOUD Act can be demonstrated by being a party to the Budapest Convention.[46]

Lastly, the Budapest Convention and its Protocol can play a central role in modernising and standardising human rights safeguards in cross-border data access. Despite the limitations highlighted in chapter three, both instruments require that their provisions be implemented subject to conditions and safeguards ensuring adequate protection of human rights and fundamental freedoms, including the right to privacy, as enshrined in constitutional and international human rights frameworks. Notably, the Protocol explicitly references the 1981 African Charter on Human and People's Rights, among other regional and international human rights instruments, underscoring the growing interest of African states in accession. The Protocol acknowledges the necessity of ensuring that effective criminal justice measures against cybercrime and the collection of evidence in electronic form are implemented under conditions and safeguards that protect human rights and fundamental freedoms, consistent with obligations arising from international human rights instruments such as the African Charter. Beyond these general safeguards, the Protocol embeds principles of lawfulness, fairness, transparency, and proportionality, permitting cross-border data access only for legitimate criminal justice purposes. It further reinforces accountability and privacy protection by establishing requirements for judicial or independent oversight, effective remedies for data subjects, and safeguards

[46] See Clarifying Lawful Overseas Use of Data (CLOUD) Act 1625, 115th Cong div V (2018), s 102(1)-(6), s 105(a) (codified at 18 USC, s 2523[b][1][B][i]).

against excessive or unauthorised use. Collectively, these requirements are essential for harmonising domestic legal frameworks in line with the Convention and its Protocol.

7.2.5. Leveraging the UN Cybercrime Convention

The UN Convention on Cybercrime (UNCC) can offer African countries a valuable framework to strengthen their fights against cybercrime while addressing key challenges related to cross-border data access. One of its stated objectives is to promote technical assistance and capacity-building for developing countries. Through voluntary technology transfer and knowledge exchange, the UNCC can help African countries modernise their national legislation and improve the operational capacity of law enforcement bodies. By aligning with the UNCC's standards, African countries can better harmonise their cybercrime governance norms, including frameworks for cross-border data access.

Crucially, the UNCC underscores its goal of enhancing international co-operation in matters involving electronic evidence and serving as a substitute mutual legal assistance framework for states that lack existing agreements in this area. Article 47 explicitly allows States Parties to use the Convention as a legal basis for law enforcement co-operation where no bilateral or multilateral MLAT exists. This mechanism effectively positions the UNCC as a fall-back MLAT, offering African countries a clear legal avenue for obtaining or sharing digital evidence with foreign authorities. However, it is important to note that, as discussed in chapter four, a notable limitation of the UNCC is its failure to establish a legal basis for direct co-operation between law enforcement authorities and foreign service providers – an essential element for effectively addressing the cross-border data-access problem. Finally, African countries should make fuller use of the Conference of States Parties established under the UNCC. This forum serves to strengthen co-operation and capacity among States Parties, achieve the Convention's objectives, and oversee its implementation.

7.3. Conclusion

The challenges of cross-border data access are particularly acute for African countries, as most African data is controlled by foreign service providers. Moreover, many African countries lack the regulatory and operational capacity to enforce their laws against these multinational companies. This chapter analyses these challenges and explores possible avenues for African countries to pursue. The analysis shows that several initiatives adopted elsewhere – such as reforming the traditional MLAT mechanism, engaging directly with foreign service providers on a voluntary basis, issuing unilateral mandatory extraterritorial production orders, adopting data localisation policies, or relying on the executive agreements envisaged under the US CLOUD – are less viable options for African governments. Instead, African countries should focus on strengthening international engagement through co-ordinated participation in international policy discussions; establishing regional and national institutions dedicated to the review and validation of cross-border data-access requests; reviewing and harmonising national and regional legal frameworks to better address cross-border data-access issues; acceding to the Budapest Convention to benefit from established and updated international co-operation mechanisms; and leveraging the UN Convention on Cybercrime.

8

Ways Forward: Advancing a Data-Subject-Centric Framework for Cross-Border Cloud Data Access

The central question animating contemporary debates on criminal justice and the cloud is deceptively simple yet complex: which state's legal rules govern when law enforcement authorities seek to obtain electronic data stored across global cloud infrastructure? In other words, when is it legitimate for a state to rely on its domestic law to compel the production of data stored on foreign soil without the consent of the state where the data is located? This question lies at the heart of landmark cases – *Microsoft Ireland*, *Yahoo! Belgium*, and *Skype Belgium* – and recent legal instruments, including the CLOUD Act and the EU e-Evidence Regulation. The question has gained unprecedented urgency as criminal investigations increasingly cross borders, data routinely transits multiple jurisdictions, and cloud service providers operate globally while processing the personal data of billions of individuals worldwide.

As discussed throughout this book, a number of states have been exploring under what conditions authorities may request access to data, using their own domestic tools. Jurisdictional responses to the challenges have been fragmented and often contradictory, reflecting a deeper struggle over which organising principles should determine legitimate reach to cloud data. This chapter contends that, with limited exceptions, existing frameworks share a fundamental structural omission: they systematically disregard or minimise the significance of the data subject – whether a suspect, victim, or any other individual whose data is sought – particularly that person's nationality and habitual residence, in their jurisdictional analysis, thereby undermining human rights protections and the legitimate interests of other states. While much attention has been paid to facilitating investigative co-operation and expediting access to electronic evidence, the perspectives and interests of the individuals whose data is at stake – the data subjects – have often remained peripheral. Whether through data controllership-based regimes (CLOUD Act and e-Evidence Regulation) or data localisation measures, contemporary approaches have oriented themselves towards the data itself or its custodians, treating the individual whose data is sought as a secondary consideration. This presents a profound inversion of human rights priorities and an obstacle to coherent international legal development.

To address this gap, this chapter advances a data-subject-centric framework that positions the individual at the centre of jurisdictional analysis. Rather than relying on service provider location or formal controllership status as a primary hook, the proposed framework refocuses jurisdictional locus on the nationality and habitual residence of the individual whose data is being sought. As cross-border legal frameworks continue to evolve, there is an urgent need to reorient thinking and processes towards approaches that place data subjects at the heart of legal decision-making, ensuring that their rights and interests are fully respected and protected in a rapidly digitalising world. This approach recognises that states possess legitimate sovereign interests in protecting their own citizens' and residents' data, and that individuals retain justified expectations of privacy rooted in their domicile. As will be outlined below, a data-subject-centric approach would better serve competing interests, ultimately advancing both law enforcement effectiveness and robust human rights protection in digital investigations, whilst substantially alleviating potential conflicts of law.

8.1. The Limits of Data Controllership as a Determining Factor

Recognising the inadequacy of the MLAT process, recent legal instruments have pivoted to data controllership- or provider-based jurisdiction. This approach focuses not on where the data is stored but on who controls it – specifically on the service providers that exercise technical (and legal) control over data. The CLOUD Act exemplifies this paradigm. It authorises American law enforcement to compel US-based service providers to disclose data in their possession, custody, or control, regardless of where that data is physically stored. The EU's e-Evidence Regulation adopts a structurally similar approach by authorising competent authorities to issue binding production orders to providers offering services in the Union, regardless of where the data is located. Provided that the provider offers its services in at least one Member State and the requested data relates to that service, neither the nationality, residence, or location of the data subject nor the place of establishment of the service provider is determinative. The architecture of both instruments reveals a striking structural parallel: neither the nationality, residence, nor physical location of the data subject, is, in principle, determinative of jurisdictional reach.

Both instruments explicitly authorise extraterritorial production orders that operate independently of the data subject's nationality and habitual residence. At the same time, the respective privacy and data protection laws in both jurisdictions impose strict constraints on the transfer, to foreign authorities, of data stored within their territories or relating to their citizens and residents. This dual posture reveals asymmetry in the exercise of sovereignty: while both jurisdictions vigorously shield their nationals' data from external access, they exhibit far less regard for the sovereign and regulatory interests of other states. In effect, these frameworks expand their own law enforcement reach while circumscribing reciprocal access by foreign governments (chapter six).

International legal instruments address the cross-border data-access problem more cautiously while ultimately embracing a data controllership-based conception of jurisdiction. The Budapest Convention requires parties to empower their authorities to compel service providers offering services in their territory to disclose subscriber information, irrespective of where the data or the provider are located. The United Nations Cybercrime Convention (UNCC) reproduces this model for production orders concerning subscriber information. Notably, the Second Additional Protocol to the Budapest Convention further expands this toolbox by enabling production orders for subscriber information to be addressed to service providers in another party's territory, no longer tying such orders solely to the condition that the provider offers services in the issuing party's territory. Critically, these instruments confine such production orders to subscriber information, reflecting a deliberate incremental approach to extraterritorial data acquisition. Nevertheless, they crystallise an emerging international norm that the presence of a provider or its services within a jurisdiction suffices to ground authority to compel data disclosure, without regard to the nationality or residence of the data subject. Neither the Budapest Convention nor the UNCC specify the role, if any, that the data subject's nationality or residence plays in determining jurisdiction. The Budapest Convention and the UNCC differ from the CLOUD Act and the e-Evidence Regulation in that, under the former instruments, extraterritorial production orders are limited to subscriber information and are premised on prior consent of the affected state expressed through the respective treaties; by contrast, the extraterritorial powers under the CLOUD Act (except where qualified foreign government arrangements apply) and under the e-Evidence Regulation (in relation to third countries) are essentially unilateral. Although the production orders established under the Budapest Convention and the UNCC are treaty-based, the fact that they do not take account of the nationality and residence of the data subject nevertheless entails significant privacy and other fundamental rights risks, as will be highlighted below.

What, then, unites these frameworks is that they systematically disregard both the physical location of data and the location, residence, or nationality of the data subject. Instead, they consistently follow the cloud provider, grounding jurisdiction in service provision and controllership over data. Across these new regimes, jurisdiction turns less on the data's place of storage or the identity of the data subject and more on who, in practice, exercises control over the data.

However, it is important to note that, despite the rise of provider-based jurisdiction, certain instruments do acknowledge data subject nationality and residence, albeit in structurally marginal ways. The CLOUD Act, while fundamentally provider-based, explicitly recognises potential conflicts when data belongs to 'non-US persons' or when disclosure would violate the law of a 'qualifying foreign government'. Unfortunately, these considerations function only as defences to be raised post hoc through comity analysis rather than as a threshold limitation on jurisdiction. The service provider may raise such a defence only where the data relates to a person who is both a national and resident of a foreign country with which the US has an executive agreement. In deciding whether the defence is acceptable, a US court must consider, among other factors, the location and nationality of the target and whether 'the interests of justice dictate that the legal process should be modified or quashed'. Furthermore, the statute permits qualifying foreign governments to access non-US-person data according to their own law, so long as the data subject is not located in the US. To obtain data relating to US citizens and other persons residing in the US, foreign governments – including those that have executive agreements under the CLOUD Act – must still use the MLAT process.

This model partially shifts the jurisdictional focus from who controls the relevant data to the location and nationality of the target. As Daskal summarises, this shift

> reflects the normative view that states have a legitimate interest in controlling access to their own citizens' and residents' data, but have much less of a justification in controlling access to the data of other extraterritorially located targets simply because of the fact that the sought-after data happens to be held locally.[1]

It is intended to accommodate states' legitimate interests in investigating and prosecuting crime whilst simultaneously respecting their interests in controlling access to citizens' and residents' data, a logic embodied in the US–UK executive agreement implementing the CLOUD Act. Yet, both the CLOUD Act and the executive agreements it enables incorporate nationality and residence through separate reciprocity clauses, leaving them peripheral to the core jurisdictional analysis. In particular, the executive agreement sidelines the nationality and residence of third-country data subjects located outside the US and the UK, thereby undermining the legitimate interests of other states in controlling access to their citizens' data. Similarly, the e-Evidence Regulation recognises data subject nationality and residence only in exceptional circumstances.[2] The nationality and place of residence of a non-EU person may only play a role when the competent court of the issuing EU Member State establishes that the law of the third country prohibits disclosure of the data concerned and determines whether to uphold or lift the production order.

Apart from these limited and non-determinative exceptions, the nationality and residence of the data subject play no constitutive role in the jurisdictional analysis of these new legal frameworks, particularly with respect to outbound demands for data. As demonstrated throughout this book, disregarding the location of data generally makes sense, given the un-territoriality of cloud data storage and processing. However, tying jurisdiction exclusively to the service provider or to

[1] J Daskal, 'Borders and Bits' (2018) 71 *Vanderbilt Law Review* 179.
[2] See chapter five.

service offerings, while ignoring the normative interests linked to the nationality and residence of the target, carries serious systemic and human rights risks.

First, sidelining the nationality and residence of the target renders conflicts of law all but inevitable and places service providers in untenable positions. While the CLOUD Act and the e-Evidence Regulation represent significant steps towards addressing the cross-border data-access problem, they may also produce unintended consequences by incentivising data localisation measures and blocking statutes in other jurisdictions (see chapters four to six). They may likewise inspire other states to adopt analogous models, compelling providers to disclose data relating to US and EU nationals even when these data subjects reside in their own territories, thereby exacerbating conflicts of law. Second, and relatedly, the extraterritorial reach of these instruments risks being perceived as an intrusion upon other states' sovereign interests, particularly where the requested data concerns sensitive matters or involves citizens of the third country. In doing so, they marginalise the legitimate interests of those states in regulating access to their own citizens' and residents' data. Third, and most importantly, reliance on the controller doctrine can significantly weaken the protection of privacy and other fundamental rights.[3] The CLOUD Act is particularly problematic: US-based service providers control a substantial share of global data flows, and virtually all this data is, in principle, accessible from the US. As a result, any individual's data worldwide can become a potential target of the CLOUD Act. For instance, this statute may apply to EU citizens' data produced and stored in the EU, so long as that data is processed by US-based service providers. In such circumstances, EU citizens whose data is requested would be highly vulnerable: EU authorities are not involved in the process, EU safeguards are effectively circumvented, domestic judicial remedies are unavailable, and US Fourth Amendment protections do not extend to them. A mirror-image problem arises for US persons whose data may be obtained under the e-Evidence Regulation without adequate involvement of US authorities or effective avenues of redress in their home jurisdiction. Ultimately, these dynamics risk undermining both the perceived legitimacy and practical effectiveness of the new frameworks introduced by the CLOUD Act and the e-Evidence Regulation.

8.2. Towards a Data-Subject-Centric Approach

A data-subject-centric framework reorients jurisdictional analysis to prioritise the nationality and residence of the individual whose data is sought. It shifts the focus from provider control to data subject nationality and residence, effectively allowing states to claim jurisdiction over their citizens' data even when

[3] T Christakis, 'Lawful Access to Data: the US v. Microsoft Case, Sovereignty in the Cyberspace and European Data Protection' (CEIS, The Chertoff Group, December 2017).

held abroad by foreign companies. In other words, the legitimacy of law enforcement access to cloud data should be generally determined not by who controls that data but by who the user is and which state has the more compelling interest in that data. By asserting jurisdiction wherever their citizens' data resides, states could demand direct access from foreign providers, subject to minimum privacy and other fundamental rights protections, due process standards, and consideration of other affected interests. Under this framework, service providers would be permitted to respond to foreign governments' data-access requests when the data belongs to the requesting state's citizens or residents and when the request concerns exclusively domestic matters (ie local crime, local suspect, local victim, and local account holder) of the requesting country. This book is not the first to call for refocusing the jurisdictional analysis of cross-border data access on the individual whose data is sought, alongside other legitimate interests. Although not yet widely translated into legislative instruments, the data-subject-centric approach has been advanced in policy proposals, legislative initiatives, judicial opinions, and academic commentary.

In the landmark case of *Microsoft Ireland*, the nationality and residence of the customer whose data was sought was not communicated to the court, and it was, therefore, unclear whether the customer was a US citizen or resident. Had the nationality and residence of the target been known to the court, it might well have influenced both the legal debate and the legislative response that followed. This possibility was explicitly articulated by Judge Gerard E. Lynch in his concurring opinion, where he observed that the case would look very different depending on whether the target was an Irish customer in Ireland or an American customer in the United States:

> If [the customer] … is Irish … the case might present a troubling prospect from an international perspective: the Irish government and the European Union would have a considerable grievance if the United States sought to obtain the emails of an Irish national, stored in Ireland, from an American company which had marketed its services to Irish customers in Ireland. The case looks rather different, however … if the American government is demanding from an American company emails of an American citizen resident in the U.S. … which are stored on a server in Ireland only as a result of the American customer's misrepresenting his or her residence, for the purpose of facilitating domestic violations of American law, by exploiting a policy of the American company that exists solely for reasons of convenience and that could be changed … at the whim of the American company.[4]

In this concurring opinion, Judge Lynch constructed two hypotheticals: one where the customer is genuinely Irish and targeted by US authorities, and one where the customer is in reality American in the US but uses an Irish server only because of Microsoft's data storage and routing policy. By doing so, Judge Lynch isolated

[4] US Court of Appeals for the Second Circuit, *Microsoft v United States*, No 14-2985 (2d Cir 2016), 14 July 2016 15.

the factors that raise international law and comity concerns (foreign nationality, foreign territory, foreign regulatory interests) from cases where the foreign element is largely artificial or accidental. In the first scenario, Judge Lynch noted that compelling Microsoft to disclose data implicates Irish sovereignty and EU data protection interests. The simple fact that the US-based company offers its services worldwide should not justify the US government's demand to unilaterally access data across borders, including the personal data of non-US persons residing outside the territorial jurisdiction of the US.[5] Such a broad extraterritorial reach for data of non-US persons could be seen by the foreign country whose citizens or residents are targeted as a significant infringement of sovereignty. The scenario also illustrates the reciprocity problem: if the US asserts such power over data abroad, irrespective of the nationality or residence of the target, other states could also claim comparable authority over data about US persons stored in the US. Such uncoordinated extraterritorial enforcement would erode mutual respect for territorial limits, undermine users' privacy, and generate new conflicting obligations. By contrast, in the second scenario, there is little to no impact on Ireland's or the EU's sovereignty, privacy, or regulatory interests. In this scenario, the foreign territorial link is thin and the risk that the US is encroaching on another state's legitimate regulatory interest appears weaker. It also aligns with the users' reasonable expectation of privacy, as US protections apply.

In the debates leading up to the adoption of the CLOUD Act, legislative initiatives in the US explicitly engaged with the question of how to align jurisdictional rules with data subject nationality or location. For example, the unsuccessful Law Enforcement Access to Data Stored Abroad (LEADS) Act sought to amend the Electronic Communications Privacy Act so that warrants would require disclosure of communications regardless of storage location, but only where the account holder was a 'United States person' (US citizens and other persons living in the US).[6] The LEADS Act tried to balance law enforcement's legitimate needs to obtain data stored overseas and the legitimate rights and interests of the individuals whose data is sought. It would have prohibited warrants seeking content of foreign account holders and confined the SCA's jurisdiction to US citizens or persons otherwise subject to US courts' jurisdiction. The LEADS Act would also have required a US court issuing a warrant on a motion made promptly by the service provider to modify or vacate such warrant if the court finds that the warrant would require the provider of an electronic communications or remote computing service to violate the laws of a foreign country. This requirement recognises the legitimate interests of foreign countries over the data, particularly when the data belongs to their own citizens and residents. Unfortunately, these requirements did not make it into the CLOUD Act. Instead, the CLOUD Act adopts a broader, provider-based jurisdictional model,

[5] Christakis, 'Lawful Access to Data (n 3); Daskal, 'Borders and Bits' (n 1).
[6] The Law Enforcement Access to Data Stored Abroad Act (LEADS Act) 114th Congress S 512.

although it incorporates a motion-to-quash procedure that partially reintroduces data-subject-linked factors. Under the CLOUD Act, the nationality and location of the data subject have been folded into a comity-based balancing test rather than being used as primary jurisdictional anchors, thereby reflecting – but also diluting – the data-subject-centric impulse.

The latest and most explicit policy articulation of a data-subject-centric jurisdictional model appears in the Indian contribution to the UN Ad Hoc Committee on the Cybercrime Convention, which proposes a move from territorial to 'data-oriented jurisdiction'.[7] Under this model, the state whose citizens' data is stored anywhere in the world would hold primary and 'broader' jurisdiction over such data, irrespective of its physical location or the infrastructure through which it is routed. India grounded this claim in two interrelated premises: first, that data ownership is closely tied to privacy and other fundamental rights; and second, provider- or data-location-based frameworks are ill-suited to cloud computing.[8] On this view, the state's protective and access authority should follow the citizens' data, not the servers on which the data resides. This approach recognises that individuals retain rights and interests in their data even when the data leaves their home jurisdiction, and states therefore have a legitimate basis to assert jurisdiction to safeguard those rights and interests wherever the data is located. This approach is also consistent with the GDPR, which focuses on whether the data subject is an EU citizen or resident instead of on the location of data or its custodian.

Industry perspectives have also embraced variations of a data-subject-centred paradigm. Google's White Paper on 'Modernizing Government Access' explicitly proposes that privacy protections should turn on 'who the user is, not where the data is stored'.[9] It argues for a framework in which users' privacy rights are determined by their legal and national affiliations, and under which citizens of particular countries would have a tangible stake in the outcome of legislative debates addressing government access to data. The proposal observes that, under current arrangements, US law often governs the disclosure of non-US persons' data to their own governments: a German law enforcement agency, for example, must frequently satisfy US legal standards to obtain communications content concerning a German Gmail user. A user-centric approach would invert this configuration by allowing, or even requiring, alignment between the laws that protect individuals domestically and the regimes that govern access to their data held abroad, thus empowering data subjects themselves. Practically, some service providers apply nationality-based criteria when deciding whether to comply with law enforcement requests. They comply with foreign governments' requests only if the requested data concerns nationals of the requesting state, and otherwise refuse such requests

[7] Indian Contribution to UN Cybercrime Treaty (12 May 2022) DOC9_3AC.

[8] ibid.

[9] Google, 'Digital Security and Due Process: Modernizing Cross-Border Government Access Standards for the Cloud Era' (2017).

on the ground that the data subject falls outside the requesting state's territorial jurisdiction.[10]

Several academic commentators have also advocated for a data-subject-centric approach. In this regard, Christakis provides a more nuanced strand of the argument, reflecting on the criteria that should structure the legal regime governing access to data in cross-border criminal investigations, particularly in the aftermath of the *Microsoft Ireland* case.[11] He argues that the legal framework should place the 'individual at centre stage', and that, as a consequence, the nationality of the data owner and the place where that person resides or is located ought to become central factors in determining which state may assert jurisdiction. This position implicitly rejects the sufficiency of data location or controller doctrine as organising criteria and insists that the legal framework governing cross-border data access must reflect the lived connections between individuals and the states that plausibly claim both regulatory authority and protective obligations towards them.

Arguing along similar lines, Daskal suggests that jurisdictional analysis should incorporate 'a multi-factored assessment', but still focusing on the location and nationality of the target rather than where data is.[12] In Daskal's view, the rules that govern cross-border data access should be premised on respect of the 'key sovereign interests at stake'.[13] In this regard, legal regimes governing access to data should protect, among others, states' interests in protecting their nationals and residents against foreign government surveillance and, relatedly, data subjects' interests in protecting their privacy and 'having some knowledge and control (via democratic processes or otherwise) over the rules that apply'.[14] These interests are often delinked from the mere physical location of data or the location of the service provider. A data-subject-centric framework protects not only sovereign regulatory interests but also the subjective and normative expectations of affected individuals who reasonably anticipate that the jurisdiction in which they are physically present may access their data for legitimate law enforcement reasons but do not generally expect foreign governments to subject their data to surveillance simply because that data is stored or routed abroad. Daskal describes as 'intuitively creepy' a regime that would permit states to surreptitiously access data in other countries' jurisdictions, insisting that law and policy should track user expectations about which states may legitimately intrude on their informational sphere. A French national residing in France rightfully expects that his

[10] 'UNODC and Partners Release Practical Guide for Requesting Electronic Evidence Across Borders' (*UNODC*, 1 February 2019), available at www.unodc.org/unodc/en/frontpage/2019/January/unodc-and-partners-release-practical-guide-for-requesting-electronic-evidence-across-boarders.html.

[11] Christakis, 'Lawful Access to Data' (n 3).

[12] J Daskal, 'Transnational Government Hacking' (2020) 10 *Journal of National Security Law & Policy* 677.

[13] ibid.

[14] Daskal, 'Borders and Bits' (n 1).

government, not the American or Hungarian government, will be the primary actor regulating government access to his data.

In his proposal for a 'Next Generation' Communications Privacy Act, Kerr endorses the user-focused solution to cross-border data access from a privacy protection perspective, arguing that 'privacy protections should follow the user'.[15] Drawing on existing technologies, he argues that providers typically have at least a rough sense of user location through language settings and IP addresses, even if these can be manipulated. He therefore proposes a two-part regime in the US for both inbound and outbound data requests that hinges on perceived user location. For users based in the US, providers doing business there would be obliged to comply with US privacy law for all access requests, regardless of where data is stored, ensuring that all state and federal government access to information about US-based users meets US legal standards. For users based outside the US, by contrast, providers would be permitted, but not required, to disclose data in response to foreign legal processes issued by the state associated with the user. Kerr stresses that disclosure to foreign processes should remain permissive rather than mandatory, to guard against abuses by authoritarian regimes, while allowing co-operation with democratic states that offer robust privacy protections.

8.3. The Merits of Re-orienting Jurisdiction Around Data Subjects

As discussed in chapter three, any sustainable regime for cross-border data access must mediate between at least four sets of interests: effective access to evidence across borders, protection of fundamental rights, respect for sovereign interests and comity, and mitigation of conflicts of law. A data-subject-centric framework can advance these four objectives by tying governmental authority to the concrete relationship between individuals and states – nationality, residence, and territorially anchored activities – rather than to the contingent location of servers or the corporate seat of service providers or service offerings. This model treats the state's relationship to the individual whose data is sought as the decisive jurisdictional hook and then calibrates cross-border access rules and safeguards by reference to that relationship. It reflects the normative insight, articulated by Daskal and others, that states have a stronger claim to control access to their own citizens' and residents' data than to data concerning foreign individuals whose only connection to the state lies in the happenstance of server location or corporate structure.[16] The aim is not to deny that other states may assert

[15] OS Kerr, 'The Next Generation Communications Privacy Act' [2013] *University of Pennsylvania Law Review* 373, 417.

[16] Daskal, 'Borders and Bits' (n 1).

concurrent jurisdiction in particular cases, but to ensure that the primary locus of regulatory authority – and of responsibility for rights protection – tracks the individual whose data is at stake rather than the infrastructure through which that data transits. This section elaborates how a data-subject-centric approach can mediate the key objectives.

8.3.1. Effective Access to Cross-Border Electronic Evidence

A first rationale for a data-subject-centric framework lies in its potential to enhance the effectiveness and timeliness of cross-border access to electronic evidence in routine criminal investigations. Under provider-centric regimes, authorities often depend on the law of the provider's home state, or on slow mutual legal assistance (MLA) channels, even when the crime, the suspect, and the victim are all located in a single jurisdiction, but the relevant data is stored abroad. For example, where Belgian authorities investigate a serious offence involving both a victim and a suspect residing in Belgium, access to data held by a US-headquartered cloud provider may ultimately be governed by US law simply because the provider falls under US jurisdiction. This creates delays, legal uncertainty, and potential conflicts with domestic criminal procedure, even though the case is substantively 'domestic' from the Belgians' perspective. By contrast, a data-subject-centric rule would permit Belgian authorities, acting through their own judicial mechanisms, to compel production of data concerning Belgian residents from any provider offering services in Belgium, irrespective of where that data is stored or where the provider's legal headquarters are located. In such a scenario, the investigating state and the state entitled to regulate access to the data subject's information coincide, thereby eliminating the need to route requests through foreign procedures or to rely on unilateral foreign legislation as the ultimate arbiter of access. In practice, this would mean that providers operating in Belgium would be under a clear obligation to comply with Belgian production orders relating to Belgian data subjects, while conflicts arising from competing assertions of provider-based authority would be substantially reduced.

This design also offers a more coherent way of categorising 'domestic' and 'cross-border' cases from the standpoint of criminal procedure. Cases in which both the suspect and the victim are nationals or residents of the requesting state, and in which the core criminal conduct is territorially anchored there, would be treated as domestic even if the data traverse multiple jurisdictions or is fragmented across distributed cloud infrastructures. Cross-border co-ordination and comity mechanisms would still be essential for genuinely transnational cases –such as when victims, suspects, or constitutive elements of the offence are spread across multiple states – but the baseline presumption would no longer be that every cross-border data flow converts a domestic investigation into an international one. In this way, a data-subject-centric approach promises more targeted use of MLA and treaty-based instruments and a reduction in the systemic overload currently experienced by MLA channels in high-volume electronic evidence cases.

8.3.2. Protecting Fundamental Rights and Procedural Safeguards

A second rationale for a data-subject-centric framework is its capacity to provide greater certainty and robustness in the protection of privacy, data protection, and related procedural safeguards. In the absence of harmonised, globally applicable rules on law enforcement access to data, individuals using cloud services face a pervasive uncertainty about which country's laws govern access to their data at any given time, as this data flows across borders. A data-subject-centric rule would ensure that the core privacy and due process protections applicable to a person's data follow that person, rather than the data or the provider, thereby offering a more intelligible and predictable framework from the standpoint of user expectations.[17] In this respect, the proposed model resonates with the logic of the GDPR's extraterritorial scope, which seeks to guarantee that EU data subjects enjoy a consistent level of protection regardless of where their personal data is stored or which entity processes that data. A data-subject-centric law enforcement access regime would mirror this structure on the access side: foreign governments could not circumvent domestic privacy and data protection rules applicable to a given person simply by compelling production from a provider in a more permissive jurisdiction that happens to control the relevant data.

This alignment between regulatory scope and user expectations is normatively significant. When users access services from within a particular jurisdiction, they can reasonably anticipate that that jurisdiction's authorities may lawfully access their data, subject to domestic legal safeguards; what they do not ordinarily expect is that foreign authorities, operating under unfamiliar standards, and with limited avenues of redress for the user, may secretly compel access simply because data transit or rest on foreign infrastructure.[18] A data-subject-centric regime tracks these intuitive expectations by tying the baseline legal protections to the user's community of membership and physical environment, while at the same time clarifying when and how foreign authorities may, exceptionally, obtain access through interoperable or treaty-based mechanisms. As Kerr argues, a user-focused solution better accommodates the global nature of the Internet: while data can be replicated and stored worldwide, users remain anchored in particular jurisdictions and subject to particular sovereign interests.[19] Hinging protections on user location would ensure that individuals receive the same localised protections in the cloud as they do in their homes, and would enable providers to tailor compliance practices to the laws of states with genuine claims of protective authority.[20]

[17] Kerr, 'The Next Generation Communications Privacy Act' (n 15).
[18] Daskal, 'Borders and Bits' (n 1).
[19] Kerr, 'The Next Generation Communications Privacy Act' (n 15).
[20] ibid.

8.3.3. Sovereign Interests and International Comity

A third advantage of the data-subject-centric approach lies in how it reconceptualises sovereignty and comity in the cloud environment. Sovereignty is typically understood to encompass, among other things, a state's responsibility to protect the fundamental rights of persons within its territory and under its jurisdiction, including citizens and residents who entrust their data to private intermediaries. From this perspective, the primary sovereign interest in regulating access to a given person's data rests with that person's home or host state, not with the state in which a provider happens to store data or incorporate subsidiaries. A user-centric definition of cross-border law enforcement jurisdiction thus 'reflects the normative view that states have a legitimate interest in controlling access to their own citizens'.[21]

This reorientation does not eliminate the possibility of concurrent jurisdictional claims, particularly where data subjects maintain multiple nationalities or where their activities are materially connected to several states. In such situations, however, a data-subject-centric framework would give priority, for both jurisdiction and applicable standards, to the state or states that bear the closest personal and territorial connection to the individual, thereby acknowledging that these states have a qualitatively stronger interest in the rights and welfare of their own citizens.[22] At the same time, by preventing states from unilaterally compelling providers within their jurisdiction to disclose data about foreign nationals and residents whose only connection is data storage or provider presence, the framework would help 'strengthen the norms of international sovereignty and comity' by encouraging states to respect each other's authority over their own citizens.[23]

This logic has important implications for current debates on data sovereignty and localisation. Some data localisation measures are driven by fears that foreign governments might otherwise access citizens' data unilaterally through provider-based mechanisms, leading states to require that such data be stored domestically, as a defensive measure (chapter three). A user-centric access regime, under which foreign authorities cannot compel disclosure of a state's citizens' data solely on the basis of server or provider location, directly addresses that concern and thereby reduces the perceived need to localise data for law enforcement reasons. Conversely, if law enforcement authorities can reliably compel production of data concerning persons located in their country, regardless of storage location, they have less reason to insist that data be stored domestically solely to ensure

[21] Daskal, 'Borders and Bits' (n 1).

[22] R Shah, 'Law Enforcement and Data Privacy: A Forward-Looking Approach' (2015) 125 *The Yale Law Journal* 545; M McKenna, 'Up in the Cloud: Finding Common Ground in Providing for Law Enforcement Access to Data Held by Cloud Computing Service Providers' (2016) 49 *Vanderbilt Journal of Transnational Law* 1417.

[23] Shah, 'Law Enforcement and Data Privacy' (n 22).

investigative access. It also gives citizens a tangible stake in their own state's legislative processes around government access to data, because the standards adopted by their home or host jurisdiction will govern access wherever their data travels rather than being superseded by foreign rules whenever data crosses a border.

8.3.4. Legal Certainty and Reduced Conflicts for Service Providers

A fourth key objective of the data-subject-centric framework is to mitigate conflicts of law and enhance legal certainty for providers operating global cloud infrastructures. Under current provider-based regimes, service providers frequently confront inconsistent or mutually incompatible demands: one state may require disclosure of certain data while another prohibits such disclosure under its own privacy or data localisation rules. In the absence of clear, accepted jurisdictional hierarchies, providers resort to ad hoc decision-making, balancing legal risks against reputational concerns and commercial interests, and sometimes refusing co-operation, even in serious cases, to avoid liability under other states' laws. This not only undermines effective law enforcement but also imposes significant compliance costs and legal uncertainty on providers. By establishing that providers may comply with foreign law enforcement requests only when the data subject is a national or resident of, or is otherwise territorially connected to, the requesting state, a data-subject-centric rule would significantly clarify the conditions under which providers can lawfully disclose data. Providers would no longer be forced to navigate a patchwork of competing provider-based claims whenever they store data in multiple jurisdictions; instead, they could use relatively stable criteria – nationality and residence of the data subject, combined with the location of the relevant activities – to determine whether a foreign request falls within the legitimate sphere of the requesting state. This would 'decrease any potential costs arising from the current murky legal environment' and reduce the leverage of states seeking to use provider presence or infrastructure as a jurisdictional hook to reach foreign citizens.[24]

8.4. Challenges and Possible Responses

Despite its normative and functional attractions, a data-subject-centric approach is not without difficulties, some of which are highlighted in the existing literature.[25] One central challenge is that it may be hard for law enforcement

[24] McKenna, 'Up in the Cloud' (n 22).

[25] Kerr, 'The Next Generation Communications Privacy Act' (n 15); Christakis, 'Lawful Access to Data (n 3).

or providers to ascertain a data subject's nationality or location, especially where suspects deliberately conceal their identity, use anonymisation tools, or operate across multiple jurisdictions. Many online services do not systematically collect or verify nationality, and while providers routinely log IP addresses and other technical indicators, these can be manipulated or may not accurately reflect a user's citizenship or enduring residence. In practice, the information necessary to apply a data-subject-centric rule may therefore be incomplete or contested, particularly at early stages of an investigation. Several authors suggest that this challenge, while real, is not insurmountable. First, providers typically have at least a 'rough sense' of users' locations, based on IP addresses, billing information, language settings, and historical usage patterns, and cloud service analytics have become increasingly sophisticated in inferring geographic clusters of users.[26] Second, uncertainties can be managed through legal presumptions and standards of proof, such as presuming that a user is located within a given jurisdiction absent clear and convincing evidence to the contrary, or requiring authorities to demonstrate reasonable efforts to ascertain a data subject's location and nationality before invoking compulsory powers.[27] Such presumptions would not eliminate ambiguity, but they would provide a structured way of allocating risks and responsibilities while leaving room for post hoc contestation and remedy where misclassification occurs.

A second challenge concerns the risk that empowering states to compel disclosure of their citizens' and residents' data, wherever stored, may facilitate abusive practices by governments that do not respect baseline human rights standards.[28] Authoritarian regimes might invoke data-subject-centric principles to demand access to dissidents' data stored abroad, thereby extending surveillance and repression into foreign-hosted spaces. Moreover, if jurisdiction is tied too rigidly to nationality or residence, law enforcement in democratic states could face undue restrictions in accessing data concerning foreign suspects whose activities significantly affect their territory, especially where the home state is unwilling or unable to co-operate. Critics also warn that, where a data subject has multiple nationalities or moves frequently, competing claims could generate new layers of conflict rather than resolving existing ones.

Addressing these concerns requires embedding the data-subject-centric rule within a broader framework of substantive and procedural safeguards. One component would be to condition cross-border access based on minimum human rights standards, allowing or requiring providers and partner states to refuse co-operation where requests originate from jurisdictions that lack independent oversight, meaningful due process, or effective remedies. Another would be to distinguish between mandatory and permissive disclosure: for foreign data subjects, providers could be permitted, but not obliged, to comply with requests

[26] ibid.
[27] ibid.
[28] Shah, 'Law Enforcement and Data Privacy' (n 22).

from states that meet agreed criteria, while being barred from co-operation with manifestly abusive regimes, thus combining flexibility with rights protection.[29] Finally, existing treaty-based frameworks and MLA channels would remain essential for genuinely transnational cases where multiple states have compelling interests, and where structured co-operation rather than unilateral compulsion is the appropriate mode for reconciling those interests.

Taken together, the responses to the challenges identified above suggest that the difficulties associated with a data-subject-centric approach – uncertainty about user location or nationality, risks of authoritarian abuse, and complex multi-nationality scenarios – do not defeat the model, but rather indicate areas where additional institutional design and safeguards are required. A carefully crafted framework that re-anchors jurisdiction in the relationship between states and individuals while deploying technological tools, evidentiary presumptions, and human-rights-based limits to manage its edge cases offers a promising pathway for reconciling effective cross-border data access with privacy, due process, and respect for sovereignty in the era of cloud computing. At the normative level, a genuinely data-subject-centric approach – as distilled from the scholarly and policy literature – converges on the view that states have a stronger claim to regulate access to data concerning their own citizens, residents, and territorially anchored activities, and that these connections should take precedence over purely territorial or provider-centric hooks in determining jurisdiction and applicable standards. By re-anchoring jurisdictional and protective frameworks in the concrete relationship between individuals and states, rather than in the contingent geography of servers or corporate headquarters, such an approach can better serve the overlapping interests of effective law enforcement, human rights protection, legal certainty for providers, and respect for international sovereignty and comity.

8.5. Policy Implications

The data-subject-centric approach to cross-border data access carries policy and legislative implications, particularly for the reforms of the US CLOUD Act and the EU's e-Evidence Regulation, as well as for other jurisdictions with similar legislation. It suggests that both the EU and the US would need to amend their rules on inbound and outbound data requests so that the nationality and residence of the data subject becomes a key factor in determining jurisdictional criteria, rather than the mere location of data or the provider.

For the EU, this would require modifying the e-Evidence Regulation so that the production orders it enables are limited to obtaining data relating to EU nationals and individuals located in the Union, regardless of where the relevant data

[29] Kerr, 'The Next Generation Communications Privacy Act' (n 15).

is stored. Such a reform would enable EU law enforcement authorities to secure cross-border access to the data of EU citizens and residences, while precluding them from unilaterally accessing the data of foreign citizens and residents solely on the basis that a provider offers services in the Union. In parallel, the EU should recognise that third countries enjoy a correspondingly stronger claim to protect and regulate access to data relating to their own citizens and residents, mirroring the protective and access authority that the GDPR and the e-Evidence Regulation already afford the EU in relation to EU data. The same logic also applies to inbound requests: the EU should not automatically block foreign government requests simply because the requested data happens to be stored in the Union. Where the request does not concern EU citizens or residents, there is no compelling policy rationale to prohibit service providers from co-operating with foreign law enforcement authorities.

For the US, the shift in focus from the service provider to the nationality and residence of the targeted individual as a determinative factor would require reform of the legislative framework regulating cross-border data access in two main aspects. First, the CLOUD Act would need to be aligned with a user-centric model. While Part II of the CLOUD Act represents an important step in this direction by affording protection based on the location and nationality of the targeted person, its effects are currently limited to situations in which a 'qualified foreign government' has negotiated an executive agreement that restricts US authorities from targeting the partner state's nationals. Absent such an executive agreement, US authorities may rely on the CLOUD Act to compel disclosure of data concerning any person in the world, regardless of nationality or residence, provided that the sought-after data is in the possession, custody, or control of a service provider headquartered or doing business in the US. To mitigate the consequences of this far-reaching extraterritorial scope, Congress should reconsider the statute's reach and limit cross-border compulsion to situations in which the targeted data concerns a US person or an individual located (or reasonably presumed to be located) in the US. Just as the US resists foreign governments unilaterally targeting the data of US nationals and residents, it should refrain from unilaterally accessing the data of foreign citizens and residents merely because the data happens to be controlled by a US-based service provider. In addition, service providers should be permitted to challenge warrants and production orders that conflict with foreign law regardless of whether the relevant foreign state has concluded an executive agreement under the CLOUD Act, rather than conditioning the operation of a conflict-of-laws clause on the existence of such an executive agreement.

Second, making nationality and residence determinative for cross-border data access would require the US to reconsider the mechanisms by which foreign governments may obtain data held by US-based service providers without a CLOUD Act executive agreement. As discussed throughout this book, the current prohibition on direct disclosure of content data to foreign authorities fails to acknowledge the legitimate investigative needs of other states. The mere fact that, for example, an EU national has chosen to use US-based cloud services cannot plausibly justify a blanket prohibition on EU law enforcement access to that person's data for the purpose of a legitimate domestic investigation. Under a user-centric model, US-based service providers should be permitted to respond directly to foreign government requests where the only connection to the US is the location of the provider or data. This permissive regime could be qualified by baseline conditions designed to prevent potential abuse by non-democratic regimes, such as requiring that: (i) the requesting state honours international standards of privacy, human rights, and due process; (ii) the request seeks data only about the nationals and residents of the requesting state, and does not target a US person; (iii) the requested data is necessary to investigate a serious domestic offence – where the crime, suspect, victim, and account holder are locally anchored; and (iv) the request complies with domestic legal procedures of the requesting state.

Allowing US-based service providers to respond directly to foreign governments that respect privacy and human rights, even in the absence of a CLOUD Act agreement, would be particularly significant for developing countries that are effectively excluded from current cross-border data-access reform processes. For many small and developing states, cross-border data access is especially challenging because the vast majority of data generated by their citizens is controlled by foreign service providers. If ongoing efforts to modernise international rules on access to electronic evidence do not incorporate the legitimate interests and capacities of these countries, they risk being left without viable and timely avenues for obtaining data necessary to investigate and prosecute crime (chapter seven).

8.6. Conclusion

The analysis in this chapter has shown that contemporary frameworks for cross-border access to electronic evidence are structurally misaligned with the realities of cloud computing, and with the normative commitments of human rights and public international law. By privileging provider controllership, instruments such as the CLOUD Act and the e-Evidence Regulation expand states' investigative reach while sidelining the nationality, residence, and reasonable expectations of the individuals whose data is sought, and while marginalising the sovereign protective and regulatory interests of other states over their own citizens' data. This provider-centric paradigm generates systemic risk: it incentivises data localisation and blocking statutes, entrenches conflicts of law, places service providers in untenable positions, and exposes foreign data subjects to intrusive surveillance with limited safeguards or avenues of redress.

In response, this chapter has developed a data-subject-centric framework that re-anchors jurisdictional claims and applicable standards in the concrete relationship between individuals and states, rather than in the contingent geography of servers, corporate headquarters, or service offerings. Grounded in case law, legislative proposals, state practice, industry initiatives, and scholarly commentary, this framework seeks to ensure that states' protective and access authority follow their citizens and residents, subject to baseline human rights guarantees, while constraining unilateral access to the data of foreign nationals and residents. Properly designed, a data-subject-centric model can simultaneously improve the effectiveness and timeliness of access to electronic evidence, strengthen privacy and due process protections, reinforce sovereignty and comity, and provide greater legal certainty for service providers. Although it is not a panacea, and must be complemented by robust safeguards and co-operative mechanisms, reorienting jurisdiction around data subjects offers a more principled and practical way forward for governing law enforcement access to data in the cloud era.

9

Conclusion

This book has examined the question of which state's legal frameworks legitimately govern when law enforcement authorities seek to obtain electronic data stored across global cloud infrastructure. Throughout the preceding chapters, this inquiry has unfolded across multiple themes – from the practical crises confronting courts and law enforcement in landmark cases, to the proliferation of unilateral, bilateral, and multilateral policy responses, to the normative underpinnings of sovereignty, human rights, and international comity in the digital age. The central contention advanced throughout this book is that existing frameworks for cross-border data access are structurally misaligned with both the technological realities of cloud computing and the normative commitments of international human rights and public law. More significantly, they have systematically marginalised the individual – the data subject – whose fundamental rights and expectations lie at the heart of the cross-border data-access problem.

The book's core claim is that a sustainable, legitimate, and effective regime for cross-border access to electronic evidence must reorient jurisdictional analysis away from the contingent location of servers, the corporate seat of service providers, or service offerings and instead anchor it in the concrete relationship between individuals and states. This data-subject-centric reorientation offers a more coherent normative foundation than existing approaches while simultaneously advancing the practical objectives that motivate cross-border data-access regimes: effective law enforcement, robust protection of fundamental rights, respect for state sovereignty and international comity, and legal certainty for service providers operating in globally distributed ecosystems.

Chapters two to seven documented the emergence of a fragmented, incoherent landscape of cross-border data-access regimes. The traditional system of mutual legal assistance (MLAT), premised on state-to-state co-operation and formal judicial proceedings, has proven increasingly inadequate to meet the demands of modern criminal investigation. As chapter two established, four landmark judicial disputes (*Microsoft Ireland*, *Google Pennsylvania*, *Yahoo! Belgium*, and *Skype Belgium*), adjudicated in courts on either side of the Atlantic, revealed the fundamental tensions and contradictions lurking beneath the surface of contemporary law enforcement practice. All these cases grappled with the overarching question of how states can use their domestic legal procedures to legitimately compel the production of data stored overseas. They distilled five critical factors that are reshaping how states approach cross-border data access: the distinctive role and global reach of service providers; the de-territorialisation of data in cloud architectures; the globalisation of criminal evidence; the proliferation of conflicting legal norms across jurisdictions; and the systemic failure of MLAT mechanisms to process the volume and velocity of modern electronic evidence requests.

In response to these pressures, states have adopted multiple and divergent strategies. Chapter three identified four broad policy approaches: the treaty-based models exemplified by the Budapest Convention and UN Convention on Cybercrime; unilateral cross-border data-access regimes; bilateral executive agreements; and regional frameworks, such as the EU's e-Evidence Regulation. While these initiatives reflect genuine attempts to modernise law enforcement capabilities in the digital age, they have collectively produced a fragmented ecosystem characterised by overlapping jurisdictions, competing claims, and unresolved conflicts.

The US CLOUD Act exemplifies this trend. By anchoring jurisdiction in the service provider's location and status – specifically, whether the provider is subject to US jurisdiction – the Act authorises US law enforcement to compel disclosure of any data within the provider's possession, custody, or control, regardless of the data's physical location or the data subject's nationality and residence. While the Act incorporates certain safeguards, including a motion-to-quash procedure that invokes data-subject factors through a comity-based balancing test, these protections remain peripheral to the core jurisdictional analysis rather than constitutive of it. As a result, US-based service providers effectively become surrogates through which the US projects its investigative authority globally, with the consequence that individuals and states with no traditional connection to the US nonetheless fall within the Act's reach. The EU's e-Evidence Regulation is not structurally different in this respect either. By empowering EU authorities to issue binding production orders to service providers that offer services in the Union, it effectively sidelines the nationality and residence of the data subject – and the normative significance of these connections – in the jurisdictional analysis. While the Regulation incorporates review procedures and due process safeguards, these mechanisms operate largely within the EU's own institutional framework, affording limited voice or protection to affected individuals in third countries, or to the sovereign interests of non-EU states.

The tension between the US and EU approaches has generated persistent conflicts. The CLOUD Act's unilateral extraterritorial reach collides with GDPR restrictions on transferring personal data of EU residents to US authorities absent 'adequacy' findings that remain contested following landmark European Court of Justice rulings. Similarly, the e-Evidence Regulation's expansive reach conflicts with US statutory protections under the Stored Communications Act. Absent a comprehensive transatlantic agreement, these tensions generate regulatory uncertainty, expose service providers to legal risk, threaten the fundamental rights of data subjects caught between incompatible regimes, and incentivise defensive measures – most notably, data localisation policies that fragment the global digital economy.

For developing countries and regions, particularly Africa, the situation is even more acute. Most data generated by African citizens is controlled by foreign service providers headquartered in the Global North. The CLOUD Act, e-Evidence Regulation, and bilateral agreements negotiated between Western states effectively leave African governments without viable channels for accessing their own citizens' data stored abroad. Traditional MLATs remain slow and cumbersome, unilateral extraterritorial measures would likely provoke international objections and lack practical enforceability, and data localisation, while a potential defensive response, imposes enormous costs on developing economies while fragmenting global infrastructure. Across all these variations, a common structural deficiency emerges: the marginalisation or near-complete absence of the data subject from the jurisdictional calculus. Whether jurisdiction is anchored in data location, provider controllership, or service offerings, the nationality, residence, and fundamental rights of the individual whose data is sought play, at most, a secondary or peripheral role in determining when and how cross-border access may occur. This represents a profound inversion of human rights priorities. The individual – the holder of privacy rights and due process interests – is treated as incidental to questions of technological control and corporate location. Sovereignty, understood through a human-rights-protective lens, encompasses a state's responsibility to safeguard the fundamental rights and dignitary interests of persons within its territory and under its jurisdiction, including citizens and residents who entrust their data to private intermediaries. When an individual creates, stores, or accesses data from within a particular jurisdiction, that person reasonably expects that the jurisdiction's authorities may seek to access the data, subject to domestic legal safeguards, procedural protections, and judicial oversight. Conversely, the individual does not ordinarily anticipate that distant foreign authorities, operating under unfamiliar legal standards and offering limited avenues of effective redress, may unilaterally compel access to their information simply because the data happened to transit or rest on foreign infrastructure beyond their control or knowledge.

More fundamentally, law and policy should track user expectations about which states may legitimately intrude on their informational sphere. Data subjects rightfully expect that their government – subject to their domestic constitutional constraints, and bearing direct protective responsibility for their welfare – will be the primary actor regulating government access to their data. Those same data subjects have no comparable basis for expecting that a distant government will unilaterally compel access to their most intimate communications simply because those communications were routed through or stored on servers in that state's territory. The data-subject-centric reorientation advanced in this book reflects this normative intuition. It rests on several foundational premises: (1) that data ownership – in the sense of ongoing control, protective authority, and dignitary interest – is intimately linked to fundamental rights, particularly privacy, autonomy, and dignity; (2) that individuals retain justified expectations of legal protection rooted in their domicile and the community of political membership to which they belong; (3) that states have a qualitatively stronger claim to regulate access to data concerning their own citizens and residents than to data concerning foreign individuals whose only connection to the state lies in the happenstance of technological infrastructure; and (4) that the location of servers and the corporate headquarters of service providers represent contingent, easily manipulated proxies for meaningful jurisdictional connections, whereas nationality and residence reflect enduring, legally recognised ties between individuals and states.

Against this normative backdrop, the book developed a coherent data-subject-centric framework for cross-border data access (chapter eight). The framework treats the state's relationship to the individual whose data is sought – specifically, the data subject's nationality, habitual residence, and territorial anchorage of their activities – as the decisive jurisdictional hook. Rather than asking 'who controls the data?' or 'where is the data located?', the framework asks 'who is the person whose data are sought, and which state bears the closest political and protective relationship to that person?' Under this model, a state may issue compulsory production orders for data concerning its own citizens and residents, regardless of where such data is stored or where the service provider is headquartered, provided that the provider offers services in the state's territory and is thus subject to its regulatory authority. Conversely, states are constrained from unilaterally compelling disclosure of data concerning foreign nationals and residents whose only connection to the issuing state lies in data location or provider presence. This reorientation does not eliminate the possibility of concurrent jurisdictional claims, particularly where data subjects maintain multiple nationalities or where their activities are materially connected to several states. In such situations, the framework gives priority to the state or states bearing the closest personal and territorial connection to the individual, acknowledging that these states have a qualitatively stronger interest in the rights and welfare of their own populations.

A data-subject-centric framework simultaneously advances four critical objectives that motivated the creation of cross-border data-access regimes in the first place. First, it enhances the effectiveness and timeliness of access to electronic evidence. Under provider-centric regimes, authorities investigating crimes that are substantively domestic – where suspect, victim, and investigative authority all coincide within a single jurisdiction – nonetheless become entangled in complex cross-border procedures simply because data happens to transit foreign infrastructure. A data-subject-centric rule eliminates this artificial barrier. When authorities investigate a serious offence involving both suspect and victim residing in their jurisdiction, those authorities may compel production of data from any provider offering services there, regardless of data location. The investigating state and the state entitled to regulate the data subject's information coincide, eliminating unnecessary reliance on slow MLAT channels or unilateral foreign legislation as the ultimate arbiter of access. More broadly, cases would be categorised as 'domestic' or 'cross-border', based on whether the crime, suspect, and victim are anchored in a single jurisdiction, rather than based on the happenstance of data location. This would enable more targeted use of treaty-based instruments and reduce the systemic overload currently plaguing MLAT channels.

Second, it provides greater certainty and robustness in protecting privacy, in data protection, and in procedural safeguards. In the absence of globally harmonised rules, individuals using cloud services face pervasive uncertainty about which country's laws govern access to their data as that data flows across borders. A data-subject-centric rule ensures that the core privacy and due process protections applicable to a person's data follow that person rather than the data or the provider. This resonates with the GDPR's logic: EU data subjects enjoy consistent protection regardless of data location or processor identity because the EU's protective jurisdiction is anchored in the data subject's status as an EU resident, not in the location of servers. By ensuring that the state with the strongest protective relationship to an individual governs law enforcement access to that person's data, the framework provides users with intelligible, predictable protections rooted in their physical location and community of membership.

Third, it reconceptualises sovereignty and comity in alignment with normative international law. Sovereignty encompasses a state's responsibility to protect the fundamental rights of persons within its territory and jurisdiction, including citizens and residents whose data is entrusted to private intermediaries. A state has a stronger claim to control access to its own citizens' and residents' data than to data concerning foreign individuals whose only connection is server location. By preventing states from unilaterally compelling providers to disclose data about foreign nationals and residents whose sole link to the state is data storage or provider presence, the framework strengthens norms of international sovereignty and comity. It encourages states to respect each other's authority over their own populations rather than competing to project investigative reach across borders. Lastly, it mitigates conflicts of law and enhances legal certainty for service providers. Under provider-centric regimes, providers frequently confront mutually incompatible demands: one state requires disclosure while another prohibits it. In the absence of clear jurisdictional hierarchies, providers resort to ad hoc decision-making or refuse co-operation, even in serious cases. By establishing that providers may comply with foreign requests only when data subjects are nationals or residents of the requesting state, a data-subject-centric rule provides providers with stable, intelligible criteria for compliance decisions. Providers could use nationality and residence of the data subject, combined with location of relevant activities, to determine whether a foreign request falls within the legitimate sphere of the requesting state.

Ultimately, the core claim of this book is that a state should not be permitted to unilaterally access the data of foreign nationals and residents around the world merely because it has the technical and legal capacity to do so through global cloud providers. At the same time, the simple fact that data is stored abroad should not, in itself, prevent a state from accessing its own citizens' and residents' data in accordance with its domestic rules and subject to appropriate safeguards. While acknowledging that there is no single 'silver bullet' for the cross-border data-access problem, this book has argued that redefining the jurisdictional reach over data around the nationality and residence of the target offers a more normatively defensible and practically workable way of balancing the competing interests at stake and alleviating some of the systemic challenges of cross-border data access.

BIBLIOGRAPHY

Books and Chapters

Bennett, CJ, *Regulating Privacy: Data Protection and Public Policy in Europe and the United States* (Cornell University Press, 1992).

Bradford, A, *The Brussels Effect: How the European Union Rules the World* (Oxford University Press, 2020).

Chander, A, and Sun, H, *Data Sovereignty: From the Digital Silk Road to the Return of the State* (Oxford University Press, 2023).

Farrell, H and Newman, AL, *Of Privacy and Power: The Transatlantic Struggle over Freedom and Security* (Princeton University Press, 2019).

Goldsmith, JL and Wu, T, *Who Controls the Internet? Illusions of a Borderless World* (Oxford University Press, 2006).

Hobbs, C (ed), *Europe's Digital Sovereignty: From Rulemaker to Superpower in the Age of US-China Rivalry* (European Council on Foreign Relations, Essay Collection 2020).

Hon, WK and Millard, C, 'Cloud Technologies and Service' in Christopher Millard (ed), *Cloud Computing Law* (Oxford University Press, 2014).

Koops, B-J and Goodwin, M, *Cyberspace, the Cloud, and Cross-Border Criminal Investigation: The Limits and Possibilities of International Law*' (Tilburg University, 2014).

Kuijer, M and Werner, W, 'The Paradoxical Place of Territory in International Law' in M Kuijer and W Werner (eds), *Netherlands Yearbook of International Law 2016: The Changing Nature of Territoriality in International Law* vol 47 (TMC Asser Press, 2017).

Lessig, L, *Code: Version 2.0* (Basic Books, 2006).

Mueller, M, *Will the Internet Fragment? Sovereignty, Globalization and Cyberspace* (Polity, 2017).

Musoni, M, 'The Role of Data Localisation in Cybercrime Investigations' in R Atuguba Akongburo and others (eds), *African Data Protection Laws: Regulation, Policy, and Practice* (De Gruyter, 2024).

Rubinstein, IS, Nojeim, GT and Lee, RD, 'Systematic Government Access to Private-Sector Data: A Comparative Analysis' in FH Cate and JX Dempsey (eds), *Bulk Collection: Systematic Government Access to Private-Sector Data* (Oxford University Press, 2017).

Smith, B and Browne, CA, *Tools and Weapons: The Promise and the Peril of the Digital Age* (Hodder & Stoughton, 2019).

Soghoian, C, 'The Spies We Trust: Third Party Service Providers and Law Enforcement Surveillance' (PhD, Indiana University 2012).

Swire, P and Hemmings, J, 'Stakeholders in Reform of the Global System for Mutual Legal Assistance' in FH Cate and JX Dempsey (eds), *Bulk Collection: Systematic Government Access to Private-Sector Data* (Oxford University Press, 2017).

Walden, I, 'Law Enforcement Access to Data in Clouds' in C Millard (ed), *Cloud Computing Law* (Oxford University Press, 2013).

Journal Articles

Abraha, H, 'How African Countries Can Benefit from the Emerging Reform Initiatives of Cross-Border Access to Electronic Evidence' (*Cross-Border Data Forum*, 6 July 2020).

Abraha, H, 'Law enforcement access to electronic evidence across borders: mapping policy approaches and emerging reform initiatives' (2021) 29 International Journal of Law and Information Technology 118.

Austin, LM, 'Technological Tattletales and Constitutional Black Holes: Communications Intermediaries and Constitutional Constraints' (2016) 17 *Theoretical Inquiries in Law* 451.

Bagu, S and Nguyen, LT, 'Database Sharding: To Provide Fault Tolerance and Scalability of Big Data on the Cloud' (2015) 5 *International Journal of Cloud Applications and Computing* 36–52.

Bilgic, S, 'Something Old, Something New, And Something Moot: The Privacy Crisis Under the CLOUD Act' (2018) 32 *Harvard Journal of Law & Technology* 321.

Brier, TF, 'Defining the Limits of Governmental Access to Personal Data Stored in the Cloud: An Analysis and Critique of Microsoft Ireland' (2017) 7 *Journal of Information Policy* 327.

Burger, C, 'Domesticating Comity: Territorial U.S. Discovery in Violation of Foreign Privacy Laws' (2020) 105 *Cornell Law Review* 549.

Chander, A, 'Is Data Localization a Solution for Schrems II?' (2020) 23 *Journal of International Economic Law* 771.

Chander, A and Lê, UP, 'Data Nationalism' (2015) 64 *Emory Law Journal* 677.

Christakis, T and Terpan, F, 'EU–US Negotiations on Law Enforcement Access to Data: Divergences, Challenges and EU Law Procedures and Options' (2021) 11 *International Data Privacy Law* 81.

Cochrane, T, 'Digital Privacy Rights and CLOUD Act Agreements' (2021) 47 *Brooklyn Journal of International Law* 1.

Daskal, J, 'Borders and Bits' (2018) 71 *Vanderbilt Law Review* 179.

Daskal, J, 'Law Enforcement Access to Data Across Borders: The Evolving Security and Rights Issues' (2016) 8 *Journal of National Security Law & Policy* 473.

Daskal, J, 'Privacy and Security Across Borders' (2019) 128 *The Yale Law Journal Forum* 1029.

Daskal, J, 'The Un-Territoriality of Data' (2015) 125 *Yale Law Journal* 326.

Daskal, J, 'Transnational Government Hacking' (2020) 10 *Journal of National Security Law & Policy* 677.

Daskal, J, 'Unpacking the CLOUD Act' [2019] *eucrim* 220.

Desai, DR, 'Beyond Location: Data Security in the 21st Century' (2013) 56 *Communications of the ACM*.

'Developments in the Law – More Data, More Problems' (2018) 131 *Harvard Law Review* 1714.

Eichensehr, KE, 'Data Exterritoriality' (2017) 95 *Texas Law Review* 145.

Esayas, SY, 'A Walk in to the Cloud and Cloudy It Remains: The Challenges and Prospects of "Processing" and "Transferring" Personal Data' (2012) 28 *Computer Law & Security Review* 662.

Franssen, V, 'The Belgian Internet Investigatory Powers Act – A Model to Pursue at European Level?' (2017) 3 *European Data Protection Law Review* 534.

Fraser, E, 'Data Localisation and the Balkanisation of the Internet' (2016) 13 *SCRIPTed: A Journal of Law, Technology & Society* 359.

Gimelstein, S, 'A Location-Based Test for Jurisdiction Over Data: The Consequences for Global Online Privacy' (2018) *Journal of Law, Technology & Policy.*

Gimsai, A, Jr, 'Companies Caught in the Middle' (2007) 41 *University of San Francisco Law Review* 535.

Goldsmith, JL, 'Against Cyberanarchy' (1998) 65 *The University of Chicago Law Review* 1199.

Greenleaf, G, 'Global Data Privacy Laws 2023: 162 National Laws and 20 Bills' [2023] *SSRN Electronic Journal.*

Hathaway, OA, Bradley, CA, and Goldsmith, JL, 'The Failed Transparency Regime for Executive Agreements: An Empirical and Normative Analysis' (2020) 134 *Harvard Law Review* 632.

Hemmings, J, Srinivasan, S, and Swire, P, 'Defining the Scope of "Possession, Custody, or Control" for Privacy Issues and the CLOUD Act' (2020) 10 *Journal of National Security Law & Policy* 631.

Hert, P de, Parlar, C, and Thumfart, J, 'Legal Arguments Used in Courts Regarding Territoriality and Cross-Border Production Orders: From Yahoo Belgium to Microsoft Ireland' (2018) 9 *New Journal of European Criminal Law* 326.

Johnson, DR and Post, D, 'Law and Borders – The Rise of Law in Cyberspace' (1996) 48 *Stanford Law Review* 1367.

Jordan, JD, 'Out of "Control" Federal Subpoenas: When Does a Nonparty Subsidiary Have Control of Documents Possessed by a Foreign Parent?' (2016) 68 *Baylor Law Review*.

Kattan, LR, 'Cloudy Privacy Protections: Why the Stored Communications Act Fails to Protect the Privacy of Communications Stored in the Cloud' (2011) 13 *Vanderbilt Journal of Entertainment and Technology Law* 617.

Kerr, OS, 'The Next Generation Communications Privacy Act' [2014]162 *University of Pennsylvania Law Review* 373.

Kilovaty, I, 'Privatized Cybersecurity Law' (2020) 10 *UC Irvine Law Review* 1181.

McKenna, M, 'Up in the Cloud: Finding Common Ground in Providing for Law Enforcement Access to Data Held by Cloud Computing Service Providers' (2016) 49 *Vanderbilt Journal of Transnational Law* 1417.

Milanovic, M, 'Human Rights Treaties and Foreign Surveillance: Privacy in the Digital Age' (2015) 56 *Harvard International Law Journal* 81.

Morris, SA, 'Rethinking the Extraterritorial Scope of the United States' Access to Data Stored by a Third Party' (2018) 42 *Fordham International Law Journal* 183.

Narayanan, V, 'Harnessing the Cloud: International Law Implications of Cloud-Computing' (2012) 12 *Chicago Journal of International Law* 783.

Rojszczak, M, 'CLOUD Act Agreements from an EU Perspective' (2020) 38 *Computer Law & Security Review* 105442.

Rozenshtein, AZ, 'Surveillance Intermediaries' (2018) 70 *Stanford Law Review* 99.

Rutherford, M, 'The CLOUD Act: Creating Executive Branch Monopoly Over Cross-Border Data Access' (2019) 34 *Berkeley Technology Law Journal* 1177.

Ryngaert, C, 'Extraterritorial Enforcement Jurisdiction in Cyberspace: Normative Shifts' (2023) 24 *German Law Journal* 537.

Schwartz, P and Peifer, KN, 'Data Localization Under the CLOUD Act and the GDPR: A Quest for an Efficient Path to Legal Certainty' (2019) 20 *Computer Law Review International* 1.

Schwartz, P and Peifer, KN, 'Transatlantic Data Privacy Law' (2017) 106 *The Georgetown Law Journal* 115.

Schwartz, PM, 'Legal Access to the Global Cloud' (2018) 118 *Columbia Law Review* 1681.

Scott, J, 'The New EU "Extraterritoriality"' (2014) 51 *Common Market Law Review* 1343.

Selby, J, 'Data Localization Laws: Trade Barriers or Legitimate Responses to Cybersecurity Risks, or Both?' (2017) 25 *International Journal of Law and Information Technology* 213.

Shah, R, 'Law Enforcement and Data Privacy: A Forward-Looking Approach' (2015) 125 *The Yale Law Journal* 545.

Shurso, J, 'Data protection and law enforcement access to digital evidence: resolving the reciprocal conflicts between EU and US law' (2020) 28 *International Journal of Law and Information Technology* 1.

Siddiqui, S, 'International Comity and the Non-State Actor, Microsoft: Why Law Enforcement Access to Data Stored Abroad Act (LEADS Act) Promotes International Comity' (2018) 26 *Catholic University Journal of Law and Technology* 171.

Soghoian, C, 'Caught in the Cloud: Privacy, Encryption, and Government Back Doors in the Web 2.0 Era' (2018) 8 *Journal on Telecommunications & High Technology Law* 359.

Svantesson, D, 'European Union Claims of Jurisdiction over the Internet: An Analysis of Three Recent Key Developments' (2018) 9 *Journal of Intellectual Property, Information Technology and Electronic Commerce Law* 113.

Swire, P, 'From Real-Time Intercepts to Stored Records: Why Encryption Drives the Government to Seek Access to the Cloud' (2012) 2 *International Data Privacy Law* 200.

Swire, P, and Hemmings, JD, 'Mutual Legal Assistance in an Era of Globalized Communications: The Analogy to the Visa Waiver Program' (2017) 71 *NYU Annual Survey of American Law* 687.

Swire, P, and Kennedy-Mayo, D, 'How Both the EU and the U.S. Are "Stricter" than Each Other for the Privacy of Government Requests for Information' (2017) 66 *Emory Law Journal* 617.
Tuinenga, B, 'Log in to Danger Zone: Data Privacy Under the SCA and Microsoft' (2016) 51 *Valparaiso University Law Review*.
Vatanparast, R, 'Data Governance and the Elasticity of Sovereignty' (2020) 46 *Brooklyn Journal of International Law* 1.
Vergnolle, S Swire, P and Hemmings, JD, 'A Mutual Legal Assistance Case Study: The United States And France' (2017) 34 *Wisconsin International Law Journal* 102.
Wells, RB, 'The Fog of Cloud Computing: Fourth Amendment Issues Raised by The Blurring of Online and Offline Content' (2009) 12 *Journal of Constitutional Law* 223.
Westmoreland, K and Kent, G, 'International Law Enforcement Access to User Data: A Survival Guide and Call for Action' (2015) 13 *Canadian Journal of Law and Technology* 226.
Woods, AK, 'Against Data Exceptionalism: Jurisdictions in the Cloud' (2016) 68 *Sandford Law Review* 729.
Woods, AK, 'Litigating Data Sovereignty' (2018) 128 *Yale Law Journal* 328.

Working Papers and Reports

Ad Hoc Committee to Elaborate a Comprehensive International Convention on Countering the Use of Information and Communications Technologies for Criminal Purposes (Second session Vienna, 30 May–10 June 2022) A/AC.291/9/Add.3.
Adeleke, F, 'Exploring Policy Trade-Offs for Data Localisation in South Africa, Kenya and Nigeria' (Mandela Institute, Policy Brief 09, 2021).
African Union, 'Cyber Security and Cybercrime Policies for African Diplomats' (12 April 2018).
Article 29 Working Party, 'Data Protection and Privacy Aspects of Cross-Border Access to Electronic Evidence' (29 November 2017).
AU Data Policy Framework 2022.
Barnett, B and others, 'Forecasting the Impact of the New US CLOUD Act' (Dechert LLP, 2018).
Bauer, M and others, 'The Costs of Data Localization: Friendly Fire on Economic Recovery' (2014) ECIPE Occasional Paper No 3/2014.
Böse, M, 'An Assessment of the Commission's Proposals on Electronic Evidence' (European Parliament, Policy Department for Citizens' Rights and Constitutional Affairs, 2018).
Brown, I and others, 'Towards Multilateral Standards for Surveillance Reform' (Oxford Internet Institute Discussion Paper, January 2015).
Burwell, F and Propp, K, 'The European Union and the Search for Digital Sovereignty: Building "Fortress Europe" or Preparing for a New World?' (Atlantic Council Issue Brief 1, 2020).
Cannataci, J, 'Report of the Special Rapporteur on the Right to Privacy' (2017) A/HRC/34/60.
Carrera, S and others, 'Access to Electronic Data by Third-Country Law Enforcement Authorities: Challenges to EU Rule of Law and Fundamental Rights' (Centre for European Policy Studies, 2015).
Carrera, S, Stefan, M and Mitsilegas, V, 'Cross-Border Data Access in Criminal Proceedings and the Future of Digital Justice: Navigating the Current Legal Framework, and Exploring Ways Forward within the EU and across the Atlantic' (Report of CEPS and QMUL Task Force, October 2020).
Center for Strategic & International Studies (CSIS), 'Cybercrime Symposium International Electronic Evidence Gathering 2025' (21 June 2016).
Christakis, T, '"European Digital Sovereignty": Successfully Navigating Between the "Brussels Effect" and Europe's Quest for Strategic Autonomy' (Multidisciplinary Institute on Artificial Intelligence/ Grenoble Alpes Data Institute, December 2020).
Christakis, T, 'Lawful Access to Data: the US v. Microsoft Case, Sovereignty in the Cyberspace and European Data Protection' (CEIS, The Chertoff Group, December 2017).
CIPESA, 'Forum on Internet Freedom in Africa 2019' (23 September 2019).

CIPESA, 'Mapping and Analysis of Privacy Laws in Africa' (November 2021).
CISPE, 'Response to the Public Consultation on Improving Cross-Border Access to Electronic Evidence in Criminal Matters' (CISPE Cloud, 2017).
Clarke, RA and others, 'Liberty and Security in a Changing World: Report and Recommendations of The President's Review Group on Intelligence and Communications Technologies' (2013).
CNBC Africa, 'Cyber Crime Surge Threatens Africa's Economic Growth' (4 November 2024).
Commission d'enquête sur la souveraineté numérique, Rapport de Gérard Longuet sur la souveraineté numérique, fait au nom de la commission d'enquête, Rapport n° 7 (2019–2020) (1 October 2019).
Committee of Experts under the Chairmanship of Justice BN Srikrishna, 'A Free and Fair Digital Economy Protecting Privacy, Empowering Indians' (July 2018).
Committee on Civil Liberties, Justice and Home Affairs, '4th Working Document (B) on the Proposal for a Regulation on European Production and Preservation Orders for electronic evidence in criminal matters (2018/0108 (COD)) – Relation with third country law' (11 March 2019).
Cory, N and Dascoli, L, 'How Barriers to Cross-Border Data Flows Are Spreading Globally, What They Cost, and How to Address Them' (ITIF, 19 July 2021).
Cory, N, Dick, E, and Castro, D, 'The Role and Value of Standard Contractual Clauses in the EU-U.S. Digital Trade' (ITIF, 17 December 2020).
Council of the European Union, 'Explanatory Memorandum Relating to the Initiative by a Group of Member States for a Directive of the European Parliament and of the Council Regarding the European Investigation Order in Criminal Matters' (2010).
Cybercrime Convention Committee (T-CY), 'Assessment Report on Mutual Legal Assistance' (2017).
Cybercrime Convention Committee (T-CY), 'Transborder Access to Data and Jurisdiction: Options for Further Action' T-CY (2014).
EDPB, 'Report on the first review of the European Commission Implementing Decision on the adequate protection of personal data under the EU-US Data Privacy Framework' (Version 1.1, 4 November 2024).
EDPB and EDPS, 'Initial Legal Assessment of the Impact of the US CLOUD Act on the EU Legal Framework for the Protection of Personal Data and the Negotiations of an EU-US Agreement on Cross-Border Access to Electronic Evidence' (10 July 2019).
European Commission Cloud Strategy (16 May 2019).
European Commission, 'Impact Assessment Accompanying the document Proposal for a Regulation of the European Parliament and of the Council on European Production and Preservation Orders for electronic evidence in criminal matters and Proposal for a Directive of the European Parliament and of the Council laying down harmonised rules on the appointment of legal representatives for the purpose of gathering evidence in criminal proceedings SWD (2018) 118 Final'.
European Commission, 'Non-paper: Progress Report following the Conclusions of the Council of the European Union on Improving Criminal Justice in Cyberspace' (2 December 2016).
EVIDENCE2e-CODEX Project, 'Digital Cross-Border Cooperation in Criminal Justice Conference' (21 January 2020).
Gauvain, R, 'Rétablir la souveraineté de la France et de l'Europe et protéger nos entreprises des lois et mesures à portée extraterritoriale' (Rapport à la demande de Monsieur Édouard Philippe, Premier Ministre, 26 June 2019).
Global Network Initiative, 'New World Borders: How Governments Assert Authority Across Borders in the Internet Age' (18 September 2018).
Google, 'Digital Security and Due Process: Modernizing Cross-Border Government Access Standards for the Cloud Era' (2017).
Hill, JF, 'The Growth of Data Localization Post-Snowden: Analysis and Recommendations for U.S. Policymakers and Industry Leaders' (2014) 2 Lawfare Research Paper Series.
Hill, JF and Noyes, M, 'Thinking Data, Geography, and Jurisdiction: Towards A Common Framework for Harmonizing Global Data Flow Controls' (New America and Cybersecurity Initiative, 2018).
Hobbs, C (ed), 'Europe's Digital Sovereignty: From Rulemaker to Superpower in the Age of US-China Rivalry' (European Council on Foreign Relations, Essay Collection 2020) ECFR/336.

Hohmann, M and Barnett, S, 'Improving Cross-Border Access to Electronic Evidence' (Global Public Policy Institute, Policy Brief, January 2019).

House Judiciary Hearing on Law Enforcement Access to Data Stored Across Borders: Facilitating Cooperation and Protecting Rights (24 May 2017).

Improving Cross-Border Access to Electronic Evidence: Findings from the Expert Process and Suggested Way Forward (Non-paper from the Commission services, 8 June 2017).

Indian Contribution to UN Cybercrime Treaty (12 May 2022).

International Bar Association, 'Report of the Task Force on Extraterritorial Jurisdiction' (2009).

International Conflicts of Law and Their Implications for Cross Border Data Requests by Law Enforcement: Hearing before the H Comm on the Judiciary, 114th Cong Serial No 114–84 (2016) 106.

Internet & Jurisdiction Policy Network, 'Framing Access to User Data Across Jurisdictions' (12 May 2017).

Internet & Jurisdiction Policy Network, 'Framing, Mapping and Addressing Cross-Border Digital Policies in Africa: An Internet & Jurisdiction Policy Network Regional Status Report' (2022).

ITU, 'State of Digital Development and Trends in the Africa Region: Challenges and Opportunities' (April 2025).

Jamil, Z, 'Comparative analysis of the Malabo Convention of the African Union and the Budapest Convention on Cybercrime' (Council of Europe, 20 November 2016).

Keller, D (ed), Law, Borders, and Speech: Proceedings and Materials (Center for Internet and Society, 2017).

Kent, G, 'Sharing Investigation Specific Data with Law Enforcement – An International Approach' (2014) Stanford Public Law Working Paper.

Kushwaha, N, Roguski, P and Watson, BW, 'Up in the Air: Ensuring Government Data Sovereignty in the Cloud', *2020 12th International Conference on Cyber Conflict* (NATO CCDCOE Publications 2020) 52.

La Chapelle, B de and Fehlinger, P, 'Jurisdiction on the Internet: From Legal Arms Race to Transnational Cooperation' (Global Commission on Internet Governance, Paper Series: No 28, April 2016).

Lee-Makiyama, H, 'A Multilateral Legal Assistance Protocol: Preventing Fragmentation and Re-Territorialisation of the Internet' (ECIPE Policy Briefs No 09/2013).

Lin, T and Fidler, M, 'Cross-Border Data Access Reform: A Primer on the Proposed U.S.-U.K. Agreement' (A Berklett Cybersecurity publication, Berkman Klein Center for Internet & Society, 2017).

McQuinn, A and Castro, D, 'How Law Enforcement Should Access Data Across Borders' (ITIF, 2017).

MAPPING Project, 'Managing Alternatives for Privacy, Property and Internet Governance' (2019).

Marel, E van der and Ferracane, MF, 'Patterns of Trade Restrictiveness in Online Platforms: A First Look' (2019) European Centre for International Political Economy DTE Working Paper 03.

Maxwell, W, Brennan, MW and Sura, AA, 'Demystifying the U.S. CLOUD Act: Assessing the Law's Compatibility with International Norms and the GDPR' (Hogan Lovells, 2019).

Maxwell, W and Wolf, C, 'A Global Reality: Governmental Access to Data in the Cloud' (A Hogan Lovells White Paper, 2012).

Musoni, M, Karkare, P and Teevan, C, 'Cross-Border Data Flows in Africa: Continental Ambitions and Political Realities' (ecdom 2024) Discussion Paper No 379.

Perault, M and Salgado, R, 'Untapping the Full Potential of CLOUD Act Agreements' (Center for Strategic and International Studies, 2024).

Report from the Commission on the opening of negotiations in view of an agreement between the European Union and the United States of America on cross-border access to electronic evidence for judicial cooperation in criminal matters, 12524/19 (25 September 2019).

Richards, N, 'Secret Government Searches and Digital Civil Liberties' (National Constitution Center, A Twenty-First Century Framework for Digital Privacy White Paper series, 2018).

Rizer, A and Hobson, A, 'Cross-Border Data Requests: Evaluating Reforms to Improve Law Enforcement Access' (R Street Policy Study No 120, November 2017).

Schneier, B and others, 'Don't Panic: Making Progress on the "Going Dark" Debate' (Berkman Center for Internet & Society, Research Publication, 1 February 2016).

Schwerha, JJ, 'Law Enforcement Challenges in Transborder Acquisition of Electronic Evidence from Cloud Computing Providers' (Council of Europe Discussion Paper, 2010).
Stefan, M and Fuster, GG, 'Cross-Border Access to Electronic Data through Judicial Cooperation in Criminal Matters: State of the Art and Latest Developments in the EU and the US' (Centre for European Policy Studies, No 2018-07, November 2018).
Svantesson, D, 'Internet & Jurisdiction Global Status Report' (Internet & Jurisdiction Policy Network, 27 November 2019).
Swire, P, 'When Does GDPR Act as a Blocking Statute: The Relevance of a Lawful Basis for Transfer' (Georgia Tech Scheller College of Business Research Paper No 3473187, 2019).
The African Cybercrime Operations Desk, 'Interpol African Cyberthreat Assessment Report' (3rd edn, April 2024).
The Digital Transformation Strategy for Africa (2020–2030).
The Information Society Project, 'Extraterritorial Enforcement: Developing Norms for the Information Society' (Workshop White Paper, 2018).
Thompson, RM and Cole, JP, 'Stored Communications Act: Reform of the Electronic Communications Privacy Act (ECPA)' (Congressional Research Service, 19 May 2015).
UN Special Rapporteur on the right to privacy, 'Working Draft Legal Instrument on Government-Led Surveillance and Privacy' (2018).
UNODC, 'Comprehensive Study on Cybercrime' (2013) xxv.
UNODC, 'Data Disclosure Framework: General practices developed by international service providers in responding to overseas government requests for data' (2021).
US Chamber of Commerce, 'Transatlantic Data Flows: Moving Data with Confidence' (20 September 2021).
US Department of Commerce, Department of Justice, and the Office of the Director of National Intelligence, 'Information on U.S. Privacy Safeguards Relevant to SCCs and Other EU Legal Bases for EU-U.S. Data Transfers after *Schrems II*' (White Paper, September 2020).
US Department of Justice, 'Promoting Public Safety, Privacy, and the Rule of Law Around the World: The Purpose and Impact of the CLOUD Act' (White Paper, April 2019).
US Department of Justice, 'Seeking Enterprise Customer Data Held by Cloud Service Providers' (December 2017).
US Embassy in Luxembourg, 'U.S. Secretary of Commerce Wilbur Ross Statement on Schrems II Ruling and the Importance of EU-U.S. Data Flows' (16 July 2020).
Wirth, A, Tricco, G and Martinez, M, 'Clouds on the Horizon: Europe's Cloud Policy Threatens Transatlantic Digital Harmony' (CEPA, 10 May 2022).
Woods, AK, 'Data Beyond Borders: Mutual Legal Assistance in the Internet Era' (Global Network Initiative, 2015).
Written Testimony of Paddy McGuiness, United Kingdom Deputy National Security Adviser, before the Judiciary Subcommittee on Crime and Terrorism, US Senate, at a hearing entitled 'Law Enforcement Access to Data Stored Across Borders: Facilitating Cooperation and Protecting Rights' (10 May 2017).
Yanqin, H, '"Game of Laws": Cross-Border Data Access for Law Enforcement Purposes Models in the United States, Europe, and China' (Paul Tsai China Center, Yale Law School 2021).

Webpages

'African Union Cybersecurity Expert Group Holds Its First Inaugural Meeting' (*African Union*, 12 December 2019), https://au.int/en/pressreleases/20191212/african-union-cybersecurity-expert-group-holds-its-first-inaugural-meeting.
Ahmed, M and Waters, R, 'Microsoft Unveils German Data Plan to Tackle US Internet Spying' (*Financial Times*, 11 November 2015), www.ft.com/content/540a296e-87ff-11e5-9f8c-a8d619fa707c.

'Azure Storage Redundancy' (*Microsoft Ignite*, 22 September 2023), www.learn.microsoft.com/en-us/azure/storage/common/storage-redundancy.

Bannelier, K, 'The U.N. Cybercrime Convention Should Not Become a Tool for Political Control or the Watering Down of Human Rights' (*Lawfare*, 31 January 2023), www.lawfaremedia.org/article/the-u.n.-cybercrime-convention-should-not-become-a-tool-for-political-control-or-the-watering-down-of-human-rights.

Barlow, JP, 'A Declaration of the Independence of Cyberspace' (*Electronic Frontier Foundation*, 8 February 1996), www.eff.org/cyberspace-independence.

Castic, S and Piou, H, 'New U.S. Regulations Impose Significant Restrictions on Cross-Border Data Flows' (*Hintze Law*, 9 January 2025), https://hintzelaw.com/blog/2025/1/9/new-us-regulations-impose-significant-restrictions-on-cross-border-data-flows.

Castro, D, 'The False Promise of Data Nationalism' (*The Information Technology & Innovation Foundation*, 9 December 2013), www.itif.org/publications/2013/12/09/false-promise-data-nationalism/.

Cerulus, L, 'France Wants Cyber Rule to Curb US Access to EU Data' (*Politico*, 13 September 2021), www.politico.eu/article/france-wants-cyber-rules-to-stop-us-data-access-in-europe/.

'China's Positions on Global Digital Governance' (*Ministry of Foreign Affairs of the People's Republic of China*, 25 May 2023), www.mfa.gov.cn/eng/wjb/zzjg_663340/jks_665232/kjlc_665236/qtwt_665250/202406/t20240606_11405184.html.

Christakis, T, 'Lost in the Cloud? Law Enforcement Cross-Border Access to Data After the "Clarifying Lawful Overseas Use of Data" (CLOUD) Act and E-Evidence' (*Cross-Border Data Forum*, 26 June 2018), www.crossborderdataforum.org/observatoire-fic-lost-in-the-cloud/.

Christakis, T, '21 Thoughts and Questions about the UK/US CLOUD Act Agreement: (And an Explanation of How It Works – with Charts)' (*European Law Blog*, 17 October 2019), www.europeanlawblog.eu/pub/21-thoughts-and-questions-about-the-uk-us-cloud-act-agreement-and-an-explanation-of-how-it-works-with-charts/release/1.

CLOUD Act Resources, www.justice.gov/criminal/cloud-act-resources.

'Cross-Border Requests for Data Project' (*Georgia Tech, Institute for Information Security & Privacy*), www.peterswire.net/cross-border-requests-data-project/.

Daskal, J and Kennedy-Mayo, J, 'Budapest Convention: What Is It and How Is It Being Updated?' (*Cross-Border Data Forum*, 2 July 2020), www.crossborderdataforum.org/budapest-convention-what-is-it-and-how-is-it-being-updated/.

Daskal, J and Swire, P, 'A Possible EU-US Agreement on Law Enforcement Access to Data?' (*Lawfare*, 21 May 2018), www.lawfareblog.com/possible-eu-us-agreement-law-enforcement-access-data.

Daskal, J and Swire, P, 'The U.K.-U.S. CLOUD Act Agreement Is Finally Here, Containing New Safeguards' (*Lawfare*, 8 October 2019), www.lawfareblog.com/uk-us-cloud-act-agreement-finally-here-containing-new-safeguards.

Daskal, J, Swire, P and Christakis, T, 'The Globalization of Criminal Evidence' (*International Association of Privacy Professionals*, 16 October 2018), www.iapp.org/news/a/the-globalization-of-criminal-evidence.

Daskal, J and Woods, AK, 'Cross-Border Data Requests: A Proposed Framework' (*Lawfare*, 24 November 2015), www.lawfareblog.com/cross-border-data-requests-proposed-framework.

European Commission, 'Questions & Answers: EU-US Data Privacy Framework' (*European Commission*, 10 July 2023), www.ec.europa.eu/commission/presscorner/detail/en/qanda_23_3752.

Fidler, M, 'Africans Want Cross-Border Data Access Reform, But They Might Get Left Out' (*Council on Foreign Relations*, 26 October 2016), www.cfr.org/blog/africans-want-cross-border-data-access-reform-they-might-get-left-out.

Frank, J and Cossette, L, 'E-Evidence: Robust Fundamental Rights Protections Are Needed for European Law Enforcement Authorities' Access to Data' (*Microsoft EU Policy Blog*, 6 November 2019), https://blogs.microsoft.com/eupolicy/2019/11/06/e-evidence-fundamental-rights-protections-needed/.

GIP Digital Watch Observatory for Internet Governance and Digital Policy, 'At a Glance: UN GGE and OEWG', www.dig.watch/processes/un-gge.

Greenberg Traurig LLP, 'Memorandum-Application of the CLOUD Act to EU Entities' (*Dutch Ministry of Justice and Security –NCSC 2022*), https://english.ncsc.nl/latest/weblog/weblog/2022/how-the-cloud-act-works-in-data-storage-in-europe?trk=public_post_comment-text.

J Hemmings and N Swire, 'The Cloud Act Is Not a Tool for Theft of Trade Secrets' (*Lawfare*, 23 April 2019), www.lawfaremedia.org/article/cloud-act-not-tool-theft-trade-secrets.

Hern, A, 'Facebook Moves 1.5bn Users out of Reach of New European Privacy Law' (*The Guardian*, 19 April 2018), www.theguardian.com/technology/2018/apr/19/facebook-moves-15bn-users-out-of-reach-of-new-european-privacy-law.

Hicks, J, 'Digital Colonialism: Why Some Countries Want to Take Control of Their People's Data from Big Tech' (*The Conversation*, 26 September 2019), https://theconversation.com/digital-colonialism-why-some-countries-want-to-take-control-of-their-peoples-data-from-big-tech-123048.

'How the CLOUD-Act works in data storage in Europe' (*National Cyber Security Centre*, 16 August 2022), https://english.ncsc.nl/latest/weblog/weblog/2022/how-the-cloud-act-works-in-data-storage-in-europe.

Ifeanyi-Ajufo, N, 'Africa's Cybersecurity Treaty Enters into Force' (*Directions Cyber Digital Europe*, 21 September 2023), https://eucyberdirect.eu/blog/africa-s-cybersecurity-treaty-enters-into-force.

'INTERPOL E-MLA Initiative', www.interpol.int/en/News-and-Events/News/2018/INTERPOL-s-e-MLA-initiative-focus-of-EU-expert-meeting.

'Joint Statement on the Signing of the UN Convention on Cybercrime' (*Human Rights Watch*, 24 October 2025), www.hrw.org/news/2025/10/24/joint-statement-on-the-signing-of-the-un-convention-on-cybercrime.

Judge, P, 'Microsoft Puts Deutsche Telekom in Charge of German Data' (*Datacenter Dynamics*, 12 November 2015), www.datacenterdynamics.com/en/news/microsoft-puts-deutsche-telekom-in-charge-of-german-data/.

Kris, D, 'Preliminary Thoughts on Cross-Border Data Requests' (*Lawfare*, 28 September 2015), www.lawfareblog.com/preliminary-thoughts-cross-border-data-requests.

'Latombe Case: First Hearing for Annulment of the EU-U.S. Data Privacy Framework' (*Hogan Lovells*, 2 April 2025), www.hoganlovells.com/en/publications/latombe-case-first-hearing-for-annulment-of-the-euus-data-privacy-framework.

'Legislation to Permit the Secure and Privacy-Protective Exchange of Electronic Data for the Purposes of Combatting Serious Crime Including Terrorism' (*US Department of Justice*, 15 July 2016), https://www.aclu.org/sites/default/files/field_document/doj_legislative_proposal.pdf.

Markoff, M, 'Explanation of Position at the Conclusion of the 2016–2017 UN Group of Governmental Experts (GGE) on Developments in the Field of Information and Telecommunications in the Context of International Security' (*United States Mission to the United Nations*, 23 June 2017), https://2017-2021.state.gov/explanation-of-position-at-the-conclusion-of-the-2016-2017-un-group-of-governmental-experts-gge-on-developments-in-the-field-of-information-and-telecommunications-in-the-context-of-international-sec/.

Meyers, Z, 'Can the EU Afford to Drive out American Cloud Services?' (*Centre for European Reform*, 2 March 2023), www.cer.eu/insights/can-eu-afford-drive-out-american-cloud-services.

Microsoft, 'Law Enforcement Requests Report', www.microsoft.com/en-us/corporate-responsibility/law-enforcement-requests-report.

Mignon, E, 'The CLOUD Act: Unveiling European Powerlessness' (*Le Grand Continent*, 5 September 2020), https://legrandcontinent.eu/fr/2020/09/05/the-cloud-act-unveiling-european-powerlessness/.

Mishra, V, 'Sixty-five nations sign first UN treaty to fight cybercrime, in milestone for digital cooperation' (*UN News*, 25 October 2025), news.un.org/en/story/2025/10/1166182.

Mitnick, D, 'The Urgent Need for MLAT Reform' (*Access Now*, 12 September 2014), www.accessnow.org/the-urgent-needs-for-mlat-reform/.

Mwanza, K, 'Is Facebook the Internet in Africa? 65% Of Nigerians Think So' (*Moguldom*, 23 April 2015), www.moguldom.com/94916/is-facebook-is-the-internet-in-africa-65-of-nigerians-think-so/.

Nojeim, G, 'MLAT Reform: A Straw Man Proposal' (*CDT*, 3 September 2015), www.cdt.org/insights/mlat-reform-a-straw-man-proposal/.

Novo, L, 'The UN finally advances a convention on cybercrime … and no one is happy about it' (*Atlantic Council*, 14 August 2024), www.atlanticcouncil.org/blogs/new-atlanticist/the-un-finally-adopts-a-convention-on-cybercrime-and-no-one-is-happy/.

Poireault, K, 'UN Adopts Controversial Cybercrime Treaty' (*Infosecurity Magazine*, 12 August 2024), www.infosecurity-magazine.com/news/un-adopts-controversial-cybercrime/.

Priyandita, G and Hogeveen, B, 'The UN cybercrime convention: a victory for state sovereignty' (*The Strategist*, 16 August 2024), www.aspistrategist.org.au/the-un-cybercrime-convention-a-victory-for-state-sovereignty/.

Propp, K, 'Gentlemen's Rules for Reading Each Other's Mail: The New OECD Principles on Government Access to Personal Data Held by Private Sector Entities' (*Lawfare*, 10 January 2023), www.lawfaremedia.org/article/gentlemens-rules-reading-each-others-mail-new-oecd-principles-government-access-personal-data-held.

Propp, K, 'Waving the Flag of Digital Sovereignty' (*Atlantic Council*, 11 December 2019), www.atlanticcouncil.org/blogs/new-atlanticist/waving-the-flag-of-digital-sovereignty/.

'Reform Government Surveillance (RGS) Coalition', www.reformgovernmentsurveillance.com/.

Reisman, D, 'Where Is Your Data, Really? The Technical Case Against Data Localization' (*Lawfare*, 22 May 2017), www.lawfareblog.com/where-your-data-really-technical-case-against-data-localization.

Remarks of Deputy Assistant Attorney General Richard W Downing at the International Symposium on Cybercrime Response (13 September 2023), www.justice.gov/criminal/cloud-act-resources.

Sacks, S and Swire, P, 'Assessing U.S. Data Policy Toward China: A Proposed Framework' (*Lawfare*, 14 July 2023), www.lawfaremedia.org/article/assessing-u.s.-data-policy-toward-china-a-proposed-framework.

Smith, B, 'A Call for Principle-Based International Agreements to Govern Law Enforcement Access to Data' (*Microsoft on the Issues*, 11 September 2018), https://blogs.microsoft.com/on-the-issues/2018/09/11/a-call-for-principle-based-international-agreements-to-govern-law-enforcement-access-to-data/.

Smith, B, 'The CLOUD Act Is an Important Step Forward, but Now More Steps Need to Follow' (*Microsoft on the Issues*, 3 April 2018), https://blogs.microsoft.com/on-the-issues/2018/04/03/the-cloud-act-is-an-important-step-forward-but-now-more-steps-need-to-follow/.

Smith, B, 'Time for an International Convention on Government Access to Data' (*Microsoft on the Issues*, 20 January 2014), https://blogs.microsoft.com/on-the-issues/2014/01/20/time-for-an-international-convention-on-government-access-to-data/.

Stupp, C, 'Leaked EU Overhaul Gives Tech Companies 10 Days to Share "e-Evidence" Data with Police' (*Euractiv*, 30 March 2018), www.euractiv.com/section/data-protection/news/leaked-eu-overhaul-gives-tech-companies-10-days-to-share-e-evidence-data-with-police/.

Swire, N, 'Applying the CLOUD Act to the U.S.-U.K. Bilateral Data Access Agreement' (*Lawfare*, 28 October 2019), www.lawfareblog.com/applying-cloud-act-us-uk-bilateral-data-access-agreement.

Swire, P, 'EU and U.S. Negotiations on Cross-Border Data, Within and Outside of the Cloud Act Framework' (*Cross-Border Data Forum*, 13 April 2019), www.crossborderdataforum.org/eu-and-u-s-negotiations-on-cross-border-data-within-and-outside-of-the-cloud-act-framework/.

Swire, P and Kennedy-Mayo, D, 'Two Ways That Smaller Countries Could Participate in Emerging Global Systems for Transfer of Electronic Evidence' (*Cross-Border Data Forum*, 30 May 2019), www.crossborderdataforum.org/two-ways-that-smaller-countries-could-participate-in-emerging-global-systems-for-transfer-of-electronic-evidence/.

Tahraoui, M, 'Unilateralism Ahead? Human Rights, Digital Surveillance and the "Extraterritorial Question" in International Law' (*International Law Blog*, 12 December 2016), www.voelkerrechtsblog.org/unilateralism-ahead/.

Thamm, M, 'David vs Goliath: Anonymously Threatened with Gang Rape and Murder, (South African) Teenager Takes Facebook Inc to Court to Disclose Perpetrator' (*Daily Maverick*, 23 July 2020), www.dailymaverick.co.za/article/2020-07-24-anonymously-threatened-with-gang-rape-and-murder-sa-teenager-takes-facebook-inc-to-court-to-disclose-perpetrator/.

'The need for a Digital Geneva Convention' (*Microsoft*, 14 February 2017), blogs.microsoft.com/on-the-issues/2017/02/14/need-digital-geneva-convention/.

UK Parliament, 'UK-US Data Access Agreement: first year of use (Written Statements by Tom Tugendhat' (UK Parliament) (Statement UIN HCWS152), https://questions-statements.parliament.uk/written-statements/detail/2023-12-19/hlws151.

Ülgen, S, 'Governing Cyberspace: A Road Map for Transatlantic Leadership' (*Carnegie Europe*, 2016), https://carnegieendowment.org/research/2016/01/governing-cyberspace-a-road-map-for-transatlantic-leadership?lang=en.

United States and Canada Negotiations of a CLOUD Act Agreement, www.justice.gov/criminal/cloud-act-resources.

United States and European Commission Negotiations of a CLOUD Act Agreement, www.justice.gov/criminal/cloud-act-resources.

'UNODC and Partners Release Practical Guide for Requesting Electronic Evidence Across Borders' (*UNODC*, 1 February 2019), www.unodc.org/unodc/en/frontpage/2019/January/unodc-and-partners-release-practical-guide-for-requesting-electronic-evidence-across-boarders.html.

US Department of Justice, 'Joint US-EU Statement on Electronic Evidence Sharing Negotiations', 26 September 2019, www.justice.gov/opa/pr/joint-us-eu-statement-electronic-evidence-sharing-negotiations.

US Department of Justice Criminal Division, 'Performance Budget FY 2019 Congressional Submission', www.justice.gov/doj/fy-2019-congressional-budget-submission.

Vahdat, A and Koley, B, 'Espresso Makes Google Cloud Faster, More Available and Cost Effective by Extending SDN to the Public Internet' (*Google*, 4 April 2017), https://cloud.google.com/blog/topics/inside-google-cloud/making-google-cloud-faster-more-available-and-cost-effective-extending-sdn-public-internet-espresso.

Woods, AK, 'Why Does Microsoft Want a Global Convention on Government Access to Data?' (*Just Security*, 19 February 2014), www.justsecurity.org/7246/microsoft-global-convention-government-access-data/.

Zittrain, J, 'Lost in the Cloud' (*New York Times*, 20 July 2009), www.nytimes.com/2009/07/20/opinion/20zittrain.html.

INDEX

www.ingramcontent.com/pod-product-compliance
Ingram Content Group UK Ltd.
Pitfield, Milton Keynes, MK11 3LW, UK
UKHW020807290926
15470UKWH00003B/997

9 781509 973279